The Roots of the
Catholic Tradition

The Roots
of the
Catholic Tradition

by

Thomas P. Rausch, S.J.

Wipf and Stock Publishers
EUGENE, OREGON

Wipf and Stock Publishers
199 West 8th Avenue, Suite 3
Eugene, Oregon 97401

The Roots of the Catholic Tradition
By Rausch, Thomas P.
©1986 Rausch, Thomas P.
ISBN: 1-59244-056-8
Publication date: September, 2002
Previously published by The Liturgical Press, 1986.

*Biblical citations unless
otherwise noted are from
the New American Bible*

CONTENTS

Maps

To my parents

INTRODUCTION

Years ago someone asked me why the word "catholic" was not capitalized in the text of the creed in the missalette where it appears in the sentence "We believe in one holy catholic and apostolic Church." He assumed that the church referred to in the creed was the Roman Catholic Church, and therefore, that the word catholic should reflect that proper particularity with the capital "C." It is true that the word catholic has come to stand for a particular church. Indeed, the Roman Catholic Church in its official texts simply refers to itself as "the Catholic Church."

But the word catholic is broader than that. The Orthodox churches as well as the churches of the Anglican Communion can also be said to belong to the catholic tradition. And prior to the split between the Eastern and the Western Church in 1054, the term catholic was used of the undivided church in its original Greek sense of universal, literally, "referring to the whole" (*kath holou*). But the adjective catholic, first used by Ignatius of Antioch around the year 110, took on more than a descriptive meaning early in the history of the church. By the third century it was being used to distinguish the true church from heretical groups or movements separate from it. In this way the word catholic became part of the one church's proper name. Thus Augustine wrote in the fifth century: "We must remain true to the Christian faith and to the community of that Church which is catholic and which is called the Catholic Church as well by its opponents as by all the members of it."[1] In speaking of the Catholic tradition here I use the term in relation to this particular church which since the 16th century Reformation has been known as the Roman Catholic Church, though both the term catholic and the tradition continue to have broader implications.

Our concern is to explore the roots of the Catholic tradition. Where did it come from, how did it develop, what is the relationship between the New Testament Christian communities and the church today, and specifically, how did the Catholic tradition emerge out of the period of Christian origins? These are some of the questions to be considered. In doing so we will have to summarize the story of Israel, for it is from this living tradition that Jesus came and the Christian community evolved. We will consider also the teachings of Jesus and the growth of the community which gathered after him, with its personalities and problems, its developing traditions and structures, and its emerging identity. In the process of this history certain elements appear which came to characterize the Catholic tradition. Today there is less disagreement among Christians as to how they developed as there is on what meaning they might have for the church of tomorrow. But for many Roman Catholics whose Christian identity has been shaped by the church's eucharistic worship and sacramental consciousness, by its Marian piety as well as by a sense for the universality of the church presided over by the bishop of Rome, these dimensions of the Catholic tradition remain an important part of the church's continuing heritage.

Recovering the history of the early church is a difficult task. The only New Testament author who appears to be interested in describing the growth of the early church is the author of the Acts of the Apostles, but even here the principal concern is more theological than historical in our modern sense. For our purposes we need to be able to move

---

[1] *De vera religione*, 7, 12.

through the various levels of the New Testament tradition and get at the roots. Therefore to recover something of the history we will have to rely on the results of modern biblical scholarship.

It is difficult to overestimate the importance of biblical research today. Its practitioners using the historical-critical method have helped the churches to rediscover their common heritage and often freed them to approach old problems in new ways. Yet for some the impact of critical analysis has been unsettling, challenging inherited certainties and cherished beliefs. So analysis by itself is not enough. There is a need also for synthesis. Hopefully this will be our approach here, not an attempt to break new ground but rather an effort to use the results of modern biblical scholarship to reconstruct the history and thus to retell the story of the emergence of the Catholic tradition from its biblical foundations.

But our concern is not only with the past. Part of the genius of the Catholic tradition over the centuries has been its comprehensiveness, its ability to embrace and include within itself diversity. Therefore in examining the roots of the tradition we should try to preserve an openness to the church's ecumenical future. In the concluding chapter we will consider what the Catholic tradition might contribute to that future.

In concluding I would like to mention a number of people who were very helpful in the preparation of this book. The basic idea for the book came from Michael Glazier. Fr. William Fulco, S.J., and Dr. Michael Downey read parts of the manuscript and offered helpful suggestions. Suzanne Marbach did the typing and editing and kept the project organized. To all of them I am very grateful.

Thomas P. Rausch, S.J.

1. THE CONCEPT OF TRADITION

> I handed on to you first of all what I myself received, that
> Christ died for our sins in accordance with the Scriptures;
> that he was buried and, in accordance with the Scrip-
> tures, rose on the third day.

> 1 Corinthians 15:3-4

Tradition and Scripture

As a religious term, "tradition" is used in many different
senses. Within the Bible, different collections of material or
schools of thought are called traditions. We speak of the
oral tradition, the different traditions which constitute the
Pentateuch, and the synoptic tradition. In turn the synoptic
tradition can be broken down into the traditions of Matthew, Mark, and Luke respectively, as well as earlier traditions such as the pre-Markan and the Palestinian collection
of the sayings of Jesus known as Q. Outside the biblical
context, tradition often suggests a collection of propositions, customs, and practices, or an objectified body of
"truths" handed on from generation to generation. Thus,

13

the tradition of a community can easily be confused with the different traditions or practices which accumulate within it, expressing and institutionalizing its life. Wearing black preaching gowns when celebrating the Lord's Supper instead of colored vestments is part of the Reformed tradition. The official Roman Catholic Church feels that it cannot ordain women to the priesthood because it is contrary to the tradition. The Orthodox Church ordains married men, but a bishop must be celibate according to the Orthodox tradition. The confusion between venerable practice, custom, and theological opinion on the one hand and what belongs to the essence of the tradition on the other lies at the heart of much of the Reformation controversy over the proper roles of Scripture and tradition as norms for the faith of the church.

The word tradition (Gk. *paradosis*, Lt. *traditio*) means literally that which has been "handed over" or "passed on." In the New Testament the word tradition is often used in reference to customs, practices, and teachings. Jesus criticizes the scribes and Pharisees for setting aside God's commandment for the sake of their own human traditions (Mk. 7:1-13; Matt. 15:1-5). Acts 6:14 speaks of the customs Moses "handed down" to the Jews. Paul uses the word tradition to refer to his instructions to the community at Thessalonica (2 Thes. 2:15) and in the sense of his rules of conduct, from which no member of the community should deviate (2 Thes. 3:6).

Yet Paul also refers to both the eucharistic institution narrative (1 Cor. 11:23) and to an early summary of the entire Gospel (1 Cor. 15:3-4) as the objects of tradition. Here a far more primary and fundamental meaning of tradition comes into focus. In its most basic sense, tradition refers to the living faith experience of the Christian community. When Paul writes of the institution of the Eucharist he uses formulas or expressions which had already become fixed in a particular liturgical tradition. But at the same time there is an immediacy in his language when he says, "I received from the Lord what I handed on to you" which reflects this primary meaning of tradition: it is the sense of the Lord's presence in the midst of his people, grasped through faith. Paul is not speaking about a memory of the historical Jesus; for him "to receive from the Lord" is often "to receive from the community," for he has a vivid sense of the Lord's dynamic presence through his Spirit. This is the Gospel, the risen Lord present among the disciples sharing his new life.

This same basic sense of tradition as a living faith shared, confessed, and handed on is what constitutes the Old Testament. The process becomes explicit in Psalm 78:

> What we have heard and know,
> and what our fathers have declared to us,
> We will not hide from their sons;
> We will declare to generations to come
> the glorious deeds of the Lord and his strength
> and the wonders he has wrought.

Psalm 78:3-4

Almost the same language, though even more strongly expressed, appears at the beginning of the First Epistle of John: "What we have seen and heard we proclaim in turn to you so that you may share life with us" (1 John 1:3; cf Lk 1:1-4).

Thus the primary theological sense of tradition is the community's shared experience of the Lord through faith. In a second sense, tradition is the handing on—in different ways—of that faith experience. The tradition of the church comes to expression in various forms, official and unofficial. Unofficially, it comes to expression in hymns and Christian art, in theology and catechetical material, in the various spiritualities and devotional traditions, and in the life stories of individual Christians. Officially, the tradition comes to expression in the worship and sacraments of the community, in those written works recognized by the church as inspired or sacred scriptures, and in the formal definitions and creeds formulated by the church's teaching authority. But that living faith experience of the community is always prior to any of the various forms through which it may come to expression. Without it, there would be nothing to express, no faith to proclaim, no life to celebrate, no identity to make the community self-aware. A community without a tradition would be like an individual without memory. And like memory in an individual, tradition helps a community to grow and assimilate new experience in a way which preserves its fundamental integrity and identity.

In the case of both Israel and the early Christian community, the religious tradition of the community eventually appeared in written form. Again, many written expressions of the two different traditions emerged over a period of time, some eight hundred years or more in the case of Israel, sixty or seventy years for the various books of the New Testament.

Not all of the religious works produced were accepted as authentic expressions of the community's faith. Those writings and "books" which did not win acceptance — and they were many — are generally called today "apocryphal" writings. There are apocryphal or pseudo prophetic books, epistles, and gospels. Those works which the community recognized as authentically reflecting its own faith continued to be read; they became part of the official collection or "canon," books in which the community recognized the voice and authority of its Lord. They became the community's sacred scriptures and God himself was claimed as their author. Scripture is God's word.[1]

Sacred Scripture is thus the living tradition of the community or church coming to written expression. Because the church recognizes the inspired nature of the scriptures, they constitute the primary or normative expression of the church's faith, the standard by which all theological expressions of faith are to be measured. The Reformers of the sixteenth century so stressed the ultimate authority of the Bible that the expression "*sola Scriptura,*" Scripture alone, became a kind of theological battle cry for the Protestants,

[1]The conventual masculine usage here by no means implies that God is male.

while Roman Catholics emphasized that both Scripture and tradition witnessed to God's revelation. Today the two approaches are not so polemically defined over and against each other. Protestants recognize that Scripture is an expression of the church's tradition and that the Bible is read and interpreted within a living faith community while Catholics acknowledge that the biblical witness is normative for the church's faith and doctrine.

Biblical Interpretation

Though both Catholics and Protestants acknowledge Scripture as God's word, they also know that it is God's word expressed in words of human beings. The books of the Old and New Testament were written by believers; they are statements of faith which reflect the faith experience of their authors or, more often, the faith experience or tradition of their communities.

At the same time, as expressions of faith, they also represent interpretations on the part of their authors of what God has done or is doing within the community, for the inspiration of the Holy Spirit does not take away the freedom or creativity of the human authors. Because of this, the Bible represents many different interpretations or theologies. In the New Testament, Mark's theology is different from Matthew's and both are different from John's. So also John theologizes in a different way and out of a different context than does Paul, and so on. All are reflecting upon, interpreting, and writing out of the same Christian tradition, but each expresses that tradition in a different way. Each has unique personal gifts, each belongs to a different community, writes at a different moment in the life of the early church, and in the face of different historical circumstances.

When we approach a biblical text, we frequently find that the biblical author uses a kind of language very different from our own. In our quest for understanding and with our Western desire to control our environment, we generally use the abstract, conceptual languages of the sciences which enable us to single out key issues and concepts and to study how they are related. Our theological language is no exception to the rule. We reserve the language of poetry for personal expression or artistic enjoyment.

Our modern technical languages would be totally incomprehensible to the biblical authors. They wrote in a language that is at once cognitive, concrete, and affective; meaning is conveyed through images, symbols, myths, and stories. The difference between the two kinds of discourse can be suggested by comparing the language of a lecture in systematic theology to that of a charismatic prayer meeting. Both are valid, but they convey their meaning differently, presuming their own proper principles of interpretation. And so too Scripture, as the normative expression of the Christian tradition, needs to be interpreted.

Discovering the meaning of a text is the task of exegesis, the critical interpretation and exposition of a passage of Scripture. Good exegesis is important if one is to avoid the extremes of fundamentalism and rationalism in approaching Scripture. The fundamentalist identifies the meaning of a text with a literal reading of the words; the text means exactly what it says, for example, that God created the world in seven days or nearly destroyed it with a great flood. The fundamentalist is not accustomed to distinguishing between religious meaning and historical truth. Truth is understood univocally; if the Bible is "true," it must be true in every sense, religiously, historically and scientifically.

On the other hand, rationalism in its various forms prejudges the possible meaning of a text on the basis of a particular philosophical or scientific criterion of truth. Frequently truth is defined as that which can be empirically demonstrated. From such a perspective, many biblical stories need to be "demythologized" or reinterpreted to make them intelligible for contemporary men and women. The miracle of the loaves becomes an occasion in which Jesus moved the people to share the little they had with one another, the resurrection becomes only a symbol of the disciples' new faith, not a statement about Jesus himself, and the ecclesiological and eschatological dimensions of the Gospel are reduced to ethical considerations. The result is that the Bible becomes a collection of religious symbols and stories that can inspire and move us, but not something that can tell us anything about the actual world in which we live.

The challenge of interpreting a biblical text today is precisely to discover how God can communicate himself to his people through the message of a human author, not only at the time that the text was written, but even more, when it is read or proclaimed today. Biblical interpretation must be concerned not only with the meaning intended by the author, but also with its meaning for the contemporary church.

The first task of biblical interpretation is to discover the meaning intended by the human author, what scripture scholars term the "literal sense" or "historical meaning" of the passage. The literal sense is not to be confused with the literalism of the fundamentalist who fails to distinguish between the meaning of the words and the meaning intended by the author. When the literal sense is not immediately clear, it can be discovered using the tools of the historical-critical method, a historical and literary approach to biblical interpretation developed largely by Protestant scholars, but since the publication of Pope Pius XII's encyclical on biblical interpretation, *Divino Afflante Spiritu* (1943), presumed and used by Catholic biblical scholars as well.

A good rule of thumb for discovering the literal sense of a passage is the following: first, identify the literary form; second, establish the *Sitz im Leben* of the text; and third, discover the perspective of the author.

"Literary form" is a classification of a text according to its literary type or species. Literary forms differ from one another in purpose, structure, and ways in which they are to be understood. The two most general forms of writing are prose and poetry, though there are many species of each. In the Old Testament, particularly in the psalms, one finds a great variety of poetic forms, including epic, lyric, and didactic poetry, songs of praise, and lamentations. In addition, the Old Testament contains various narrative forms such as popular myths, patriarchical legends, romanticized national sagas, and factual court histories, as well as prophetic oracles, law codes, proverbs, fictional tales, love stories, and apocalyptic visions. In the New Testament, besides the distinct forms of epistles and gospels, scholars distinguish miracle stories, sayings, ethical teachings, parables, hymns, liturgical formulas, catechetical material, and doxologies. Just as a parable teaches a lesson without implying that the story itself actually happened, so a biblical author, drawing on the images and stories of his or her culture, can use a popular myth or fictional tale to teach a particular religious truth. The reader who recognizes the literary form as being myth or legend doesn't make the mistake of interpreting it as history or science, just as he or she would not confuse a novel with a historical study. Therefore, it is essential to identify the literary form if one wants to avoid confusing a particular story with the meaning intended by the author. This is the object of form criticism (*Formgeschichte*, literally form history), a literary science developed largely by German scholars which is concerned with distinguishing the various literary forms in the Bible according to their purpose and function. In approaching a text, the form critic seeks to identify its literary form and to trace its history through the various levels of the tradition, from its original place and function in the oral tradition through its various uses and modifications in the different communities to its appearance in the text. Thus form criticism is extremely useful in recovering the history of the various biblical traditions.

Secondly, it is important to identify the *Sitz im Leben* of the text. Literally "situation in life," *Sitz im Leben* refers to the historical context of a text, the time, place, and circumstances affecting the community at the time of composition, all of which are factors influencing what a particular author will say. Paul's counsel against entering into marriage in 1 Corinthians 7 is not because he is against marriage, but because he is writing in a period in which the community was expecting the imminent return of the Lord, as a full reading of the chapter itself makes clear. Similarly, the "anti-Semitic" character of some of the statements against the Pharisees or the Jews in Matthew and John reflect neither the attitude of Jesus nor a mere prejudice on the part of the evangelists, but rather a struggle between the synagogue and the Jewish Christians that led to the actual excommunication of the latter from the synagogues which took place around the time that these gospels were being written (see John 9:22). The *Sitz im Leben* of a text is perhaps the most important clue to an author's meaning. Here the historical and archaeological sciences have an important role to play.

Finally it is important to discover the particular perspective and point of view of the author. This is the task of redaction criticism (*Redaktionsgeschichte*). The New Testament writers were working with already existing material, collections of stories, independent units of tradition, as well as the traditions of their own particular communities. Redaction criticism seeks to determine the theologies and points of view of the different New Testament writers by analyzing the way in which they received, modified, and passed on the tradition in their works. Changes introduced in a particular story, where an event is situated in a work, how the work itself is structured, what themes are stressed or introduced — all these are important clues to an author's concerns and theological viewpoint and thus a help towards recognizing the meaning intended in a particular passage.

One text can serve to illustrate the various approaches we have been considering. In the gospel of Luke, the rather solemn account of the Last Supper is interrupted by an argument which breaks out among the disciples over who should be regarded as the greatest (Lk. 22:24-27). Form criticism identifies this dispute over rank with its parallels (Mk. 10: 35-45; Matt. 20:20-28) as a tradition on ministry and church order.[2] What was originally a saying of Jesus

[2]See John Hall Elliott, "Ministry and Church Order in the NT: A Traditio-Historical Analysis (1 Pt 5, 1-5 & p 1 1s.)," *The Catholic Biblical Quarterly* 32 (1970) 367-91, pp. 374 ff.

about his own ministry of humble service (Mk. 10:45; Lk. 22:27) has been adapted by the later communities to underline the nature of authority and leadership in the church as a ministry or service. A variant tradition appears in 1 Peter 5:1-4, instructing the presbyters to exercise their authority without "lording it over" others. Thus the text has a foundation in the sayings of Jesus, but its *Sitz im Leben* in the early church is to be found in the emerging questions over ministry and authority. Finally the redaction critic would point out that in Luke's gospel this tradition has been inserted rather abruptly into the account of the institution of the Eucharist, admonishing church leaders to serve as Jesus did. Going a step further, John Hall Elliott suggests that Luke's redactional work here might represent the early stages of a later, post-New Testament tradition associating ministry and Eucharist.[3]

The various methods of historical investigation and literary analysis are crucial for discovering the literal sense of the text. Without the historical meaning of the text, theology remains uncritical and runs the risk of being determined by the literalism of the fundamentalist or the dogmatics of a particular confessional tradition. But biblical interpretation cannot be confined to the concerns of historical critical scholarship; that would leave the Bible in the hands of the specialists, confine its meaning to that of a particular historical moment, and deny its character as God's living word. Therefore, discovering the literal sense can only be one moment in the process of interpretation.

Modern biblical scholars are well aware of the inadequacy of limiting biblical meaning to the literal sense. In recent years, they have begun to concern themselves with recovering the living quality of the biblical word, its ability to address the believer and the church as the word of God today. Using terms such as "the fuller sense," the "plus value" or "excess of meaning" of the text, its "meaning now" or "existential reference," they have developed different theories to suggest how a particular text or passage can have

[3]Ibid, p. 385.

revelatory value which extends beyond its original historical meaning and yet remains in continuity with it.[4]

Therefore understanding the biblical text means more than grasping the literal sense. It also involves recognizing the insight or issue behind the text which in its historical meaning represents the word of God become concrete in the historical context of the author, but which must also become concrete in the context of the community today. In this way the gap between "meaning then" and "meaning now" is bridged in a way mediated by the text itself and the text can recover its religious significance. Revelation is not a static collection of propositions, but God freely disclosing his presence in the Judeo-Christian tradition; in a special way revelation is God's gift of himself, especially in the person of Jesus. The Bible mediates that revelation when we are able to encounter the Christ present in the witness and experience of the early Christian community.

Uncovering the literal sense of a passage frequently demands the historical and literary training of the exegete or biblical theologian. Allowing the meaning of the text to become concrete and revelatory in the life experience of the community today demands faith. Only when the text is received and proclaimed in faith does it escape the confines of its own history and become again God's living, creative, life-giving word.

Let us consider two examples. The first comes from Isaiah, chapter 55:

> All you who are thirsty
> Come to the water!
> You who have no money,
> Come, receive grain and eat;
> Come, without paying and
> without cost,
> Drink wine and milk   Isaiah 55:1

---

[4]See for example Sandra M. Schneiders' article, "Faith, Hermeneutics, and the Literal Sense of Scripture" *Theological Studies* 39 (1978) 719-36.

The chapter goes on to develop the covenant made with David (v. 3); it refers to the mysterious ways of God, so far beyond human comprehension (vv. 8-9); and it proclaims "in joy you shall depart, in peace you shall be brought back" (v. 12). An exegete or biblical commentary would interpret this passage in terms of its literal sense. The *Sitz im Leben* is the Babylonian captivity; the Kingdom of Judah has fallen and the Israelites have been led into exile (cf. Ps. 137). The chapter represents a prophetic oracle, addressed to the people by a prophet exercising his ministry during the exile in Babylon, known today as Second Isaiah; it is a call to conversion and a message of consolation and hope, promising a departure from Babylon and return to the land of Israel. This is the historical meaning of the text.

How can it become God's living word today? The text is frequently used by retreat directors as a way of putting a retreatant in touch with the invitation that God constantly addresses to each of us to turn to him and find the nourishment we need, the satisfaction of our hunger for God and our thirst for his healing presence in our lives. A preacher might interpret the passage in a similar way, calling a congregation to a deeper conversion of life and to confidence in God. A pastoral minister might offer the passage to someone struggling with a painful personal problem as an invitation to trust and as a message of hope. In each case, the passage received in faith becomes God's life-giving word, an invitation from the Creator and Lord to seek him in prayer, in scripture, in one's daily life, in surrender to his grace.

For a second example, we turn to Luke's account of Jesus' inaugural sermon in Nazareth where he reads and then interprets as being fulfilled in himself the following passage from Isaiah:

> The Spirit of the Lord is upon me;
> Therefore he has anointed me.
> He has sent me to bring glad
> tidings to the poor,
> to proclaim liberty to captives,
> recovery of sight to the blind

and release to prisoners,
To announce a year of favor
from the Lord.

Luke 4:18-19

Here again an exegete would clarify the literal sense of the passage. He or she would point out that Luke uses an oracle, slightly edited, from the sixty-first chapter of Isaiah (61:1-2; cf. 58:6-8) to concretize for largely non-Jewish Christians Jesus' preaching, his good news of the reign of God (cf. Mk. 1:15). The passage from Isaiah refers to the fulfillment of all the prophetic messianic expectations and outlines the ministry Jesus will exercise. He will free men and women from their bondage to the demonic powers and heal those with physical infirmities. In his ministry God's salvation appears, releasing the people from all the evil forces which oppress them.

What about the contemporary meaning of the passage? Imagine the same text being proclaimed in a North American middle-class suburban parish and in a basic Christian community of campesinos in El Salvador or of the working poor in Brazil. In affluent communities a passage such as this one is often spiritualized. "Captives" and "prisoners" are understood as those in bondage to alcohol, drugs, their instinctual drives, psychological fears, or emotional inhibitions. The blind are those blinded by sin, or lacking in faith. Good news to the poor doesn't of course exclude the poor, but it includes all those who are "poor in spirit," to use Matthew's way of expressing this tradition (Matt. 5:3). How much more literally will the passage be interpreted by the church of the poor in Latin America! Here the good news Jesus proclaims to the poor will be concretized by a daily experience of injustice, oppression, and struggle; his words will be personalized in the faces of hungry children, murdered husbands, struggling women, imprisoned or "missing" sons and daughters.

In both communities, the passage can become God's living word. But here especially, where there is always the danger that one or another group will reinterpret the passage simply in terms of their own concerns and situation, the importance of the exegete or biblical theologian in drawing out the continuity between historical meaning and its contemporary reference becomes apparent.

The Canon of Scripture

Not all written expressions of the religious community's tradition were accepted as authentic expressions of its faith. Those that were became part of its official collection or "canon" of sacred books. The Greek word *kanōn*, meaning "reed," was frequently used to denote an instrument for measuring, hence a standard. In ecclesiastical language canon is used for the decrees of church councils and church laws ("canon laws") and for the collection of those books recognized as divinely inspired, while to "canonize" means to add to the number of sacred books or to the calendar of the saints. We speak of the canon of Scripture, but actually there are separate Catholic and Protestant Old Testament canons, the result of the differences between the Hebrew and Greek canons of the Jewish scriptures.

The Hebrew canon was defined over a long process of time. In 621, during the reign of Josiah, a code of laws was found in the Temple (2 Kings 22-23; 2 Chron. 34). This book, an early version of the book of Deuteronomy, was accepted as "the law of the Lord given through Moses" (2 Chron. 34:14). Some scholars see this as the first of many steps in the development of the Jewish canon.

By the year 400 B.C., the book of Deuteronomy had been expanded by the integration of other historical and legal traditions — the Jahwist, Elohist, and Priestly traditions — into what we refer to as the Pentateuch: Genesis, Exodus, Leviticus, Numbers, and Deuteronomy. These five books, attributed to Moses, were henceforth recognized as the Torah or law. The author of the Book of Sirach (c. 180 B.C.) speaks of "the law, the prophets, and the rest of the books" (Sirach, Preface). But a clearly defined Jewish canon did not exist until the Christian era when the Pharisees drew one up at Jamnia around A.D. 90 in the process of their religious reconstruction of Judaism after the destruction of Jerusalem and the Temple.

At the time of the Jamnian reform, both Jewish and Christian communities were reading from two different collections of the Jewish scriptures. Jewish communities in Palestine read the Scriptures in the original Hebrew while the Hellenistic Jewish communities of the Diaspora, as well as the early Christian communities — with an increasing number of Greek-speaking Jewish Christians as well as Gentile converts — used the Greek translation of the Jewish scriptures known as the Septuagint. This "Greek" or "Alexandrian" canon originated in Alexandria, Egypt somewhere after 250 B.C. Produced for the Greek-speaking Jews of Alexandria and the Diaspora, it was according to an ancient legend the miraculous work of 72 scholars brought from Jerusalem who accomplished the task in 70 days, hence the name Septuagint, from the Latin for "seventy" (LXX).

When the Pharisees drew up what was henceforth to be the Jewish canon, they followed the traditional division of books into the Law, the Prophets, and the Writings. Only books available in Hebrew or Aramaic were included, hence the name Hebrew canon. The result was a collection of twenty-four books, divided into three parts.

THE LAW	THE PROPHETS	THE WRITINGS
Genesis	Joshua	1, 2 Chronicles
Exodus	Judges	Ezra-Nehemiah
Leviticus	1, 2 Samuel	Esther
Numbers	1, 2 Kings	Ruth
Deuteronomy	Isaiah	Psalms
	Jeremiah	Proverbs
	the minor prophets	Job
	(counted as one book:	Lamentations
	Hosea, Joel, Amos,	Ecclesiastes
	Obadiah, Jonah, Micah,	Song of Solomon
	Nahum, Habakkuk,	Daniel
	Zephaniah, Haggai,	
	Zechariah, Malachi)	

The so-called "Greek canon" or Septuagint included all of the above, plus some additional books and parts of books which had been preserved only in Greek.

1, 2 Maccabees	Sirach
Tobit	Wisdom of Solomon
Judith	Baruch
and some additional	
parts in Daniel and	
Esther	

The slightly larger Septuagint collection was used by the apostolic church at least from the time of Paul and remained the Christian Old Testament canon until the Reformation, in spite of some questions raised about the additional books in the fourth century. In the 16th century Luther returned to the Hebrew canon, excluding the additional Greek books as "apocrypha," not to be considered inspired. The Council of Trent reaffirmed their inclusion in the canon for the Roman Catholic Church. The additional books are called by Catholics the "deutero-canonical" books. Hence the slight difference between the Roman Catholic and Protestant Old Testament canons.

The books of the New Testament were written over a period of some sixty years. If that time is extended back to the first days of the Christian community, it divides easily into two periods, the Apostolic Age, from A.D. 33 to 70, the year in which the Roman legions of Titus destroyed Jerusalem and the Temple, and the Sub-Apostolic Age, from 70 to about the year 110 which with the appearance of 1 Peter marks the end of the New Testament period.

The earliest New Testament documents are the authentic letters of Paul, written in the early fifties. Scholars agree that Paul himself wrote 1 Thessalonians, 1 and 2 Corinthians, Galatians, Philippians, Romans, the short Philemon, and possibly Colossians. There is a general agreement that differences in style, vocabulary, and theology as well as a literary dependence on earlier letters argue against Paul's authorship of Ephesians. There is even more agreement that the "Pastoral Epistles," 1 and 2 Timothy and Titus, were written by a later member of the Pauline school close to the year A.D. 100, for some, even later.

The first written gospel, Mark, appeared between 65 and 70. Matthew, Luke, and Luke's Acts of the Apostles were written between 85 and 90, John perhaps a little later.

A number of letters, not included in the New Testament canon, but important for understanding the developments taking place at the end of the New Testament period, appeared around 100. 1 Clement is a letter (with concerns similar to those of 1 Corinthians) written around 96 from a leader of the Church of Rome to the Church of Corinth. The seven letters of Ignatius, bishop of Antioch, were written between 107-117. The *Didache* or the "Teaching of the Twelve Apostles," written around 100, is a collection of instructions on Christian morality and church order. These works are considered part of the tradition of the "Apostolic Fathers." For an overview and probable dates for the other New Testament books, see the chart, "the Development of the New Testament" on the following page.

The first step towards the development of a Christian canon was made by the heretic Marcion around the year 150. Under the influence of Gnosticism, Marcion argued that the wrathful God of the Jewish scriptures was very different from the loving God of Jesus. Consequently he rejected entirely the Jewish scriptures. Furthermore, in accepting only ten letters of Paul and an edited version of the gospel of Luke he was in effect establishing his own canon. In response, the various churches reaffirmed the value of the Jewish scriptures as well as that of the other gospels and apostolic letters which they recognized as having apostolic authority. This was an important step in the development of a New Testament canon, based on the discernment and practice of the churches. Some scholars suggest that the subsequent practice of distinguishing between the Old and the New Testaments may be rooted in Marcion's rejection of the Jewish scriptures, even though the term "New Testament" was first used by Tertullian some years later.

Evidence for the acceptance of other gospels as well as the

DEVELOPMENT OF THE
NEW TESTAMENT

```
          33   Apostolic preaching
    A
    P
    O
    S    40
    T
    O
    L
    I
    C
          50
    A          1 Thessalonians, Philemon
    G          1 & 2 Corinthians, Galatians, Philippians
    E          Romans
               Colossians (?)

          60
               James

               MARK
          70
    S          Ephesians (?)
    U          2 Thessalonians (?)
    B
          80                                                NON CANONICAL
    A                                                          WORKS
    P          1 Peter 1-4:11
    O          Hebrews (?)
    S
    T    90    MATTHEW, LUKE, Acts, Revelation
    O          JOHN
    L          1 & 2 Timothy, Titus                         1 Clement
    I
    C

    A   100    1 Peter 4:12-5:14                            Ignatian Epistles
    G          1, 2, 3 John                                 Didache
    E

               Jude
         110   2 Peter
```

Old Testament comes from the writings of a contemporary of Marcion. In describing a Eucharist celebrated around the year 155, Justin Martyr mentions that "the memoirs of the Apostles or the writings of the Prophets are read" (*Apology* 1, 67). Later he adds that these memoirs "are called gospels" (*Apol.* 2, 33, 66). Here the gospels are recognized as having apostolic authority and are being read in the liturgy like other scriptures.

Marcion was not the only gnostic influence at this time in the life of the church. Gnosticism in its many forms was a sectarian movement, partly religious, partly philosophical, which promised its adherents salvation through the secret knowledge (*gnōsis*) possessed only by those initiated into the sect. Some of the Gnostics found in Christian symbols and concepts an apt vehicle for expressing gnostic doctrine; thus there developed in the second and third centuries a heretical, gnostic expression of Christianity. A gnostic literature, modeled on orthodox Christian writings, soon followed. These gnostic books claimed to possess the secret teachings of Jesus and the apostles. Typical was the gnostic Gospel of Thomas (2nd-3rd century) which begins: "These are the secret words which the living Jesus spoke and which Didymus Thomas wrote down."

From the second century on, the problem of false teachers grew and the number of pseudo or apocryphal gospels, epistles, and acts proliferated. Many were gnostic in origin. Some, rich in extravagant miracles, represent pious speculation on the childhood of Jesus or on the lives of Mary and Joseph. Mary's presentation in the Temple as a child, marvelous details of her engagement to Joseph, her account of the annunciation, various miracles which supposedly occurred during the flight into Egypt, including a chance meeting of the infant Jesus with the two robbers who would later be crucified with him, stories about the death of Joseph in the presence of Jesus and Mary and of the death and assumption of Mary, these and other stories enlivened the apocryphal books. Some no doubt were used for a time by one or another orthodox community. However the early church was sensitive to the problem of false teachers; if a book was judged as lacking apostolic origin or contrary to the faith of the church, it was rejected as heretical.

By the end of the second century, various collections began to appear. The Muratorian Canon, perhaps from Rome, lacked only five of the later epistles (Hebrews, James, 1 and 2 Peter, 3 John), though it also contained two other books subsequently rejected. In the third century Tertullian in the West and Origen in the East distinguished between the accepted works and those still disputed. In 367 Athanasius, bishop of Alexandria, described the New Testament canon as it exists today. Some twenty years later Jerome followed the canon of Athanasius in his Latin translation of the New Testament (the "Vulgate") which became the standard for the West. Thus the canon of scripture emerged as a result of a process of recognition and discernment on the part of the church as it struggled to defend its apostolic tradition against the threat of false teachers and heterodox books.

Conclusion

In its deepest sense tradition, that which is handed on, is the faith experience of the Christian community, its shared experience of the Lord. That tradition comes to official expression in the community's worship and sacraments, in its creeds, and especially in its scriptures. Because scripture is the word of God expressed through the words of believers it needs to be interpreted. Historical-critical scholarship is of great assistance in recovering the historical or "literal sense" of a text. When that text, intelligently interpreted, is received in faith by a community it can become again God's living word. Those books which the early Christian community recognized as authentic expressions of its faith experience became part of its official canon of sacred writings which remain the normative expression of the faith of the apostolic church.

2. THE TRADITION OF ISRAEL

> After John's arrest, Jesus appeared in Galilee proclaiming the good news of God: "This is the time of fulfillment. The reign of God is at hand: Reform your lives and believe in the gospel!"
>
> Mark 1:14-15

It is interesting how few Christians today are able to say in detail what Jesus actually spoke about during his earthly ministry. So many of the themes we associate with his preaching actually come from the post-Pentecost church and from the various writers of the New Testament. The word "church" itself is a post-Pentecost word, appearing in only two gospel passages, both of them in Matthew (16:18; 18:17). What dominates the preaching of Jesus is the proclamation that God's reign is at hand. For a Gentile congregation that message needed some translation, but Jesus' Jewish contemporaries were not unfamiliar with the concept. For Jesus was a man of his times. He spoke in the language and images of a first century Palestinian Jew. Therefore, before we can begin to consider more closely his message, it is essential to understand the tradition out of which he came and thus to know something about the history of his people.

The History of Israel

The story of the people of Israel begins with the patriarch Abraham. According to Genesis, Abraham migrated with his family from Mesopotamia to Canaan or Palestine in response to God's call (Gen 12:1-4). Much of the patriarchal material in Genesis consists of family traditions and originally independent stories brought together around the figures of Abraham, Isaac, and Jacob. Whatever history may once have been part of them has probably been very much reshaped in the retelling and later theological editing. But most scholars agree that Abraham represents an historical figure who lived between 1500 and 2000 B.C. and came to Canaan as part of a larger migration of semi-nomadic peoples early in the second millennium.

Biblical faith really begins with Abraham. Abraham's God was probably once a tribal or clan deity. Yet each of the patriarchs came to know this God personally and entered into a relationship with him, so the "God of Abraham" was also known as "the Fear of Isaac" or "the Mighty One of Jacob." As the God of a seminomadic people rather than a local deity, this God of the patriarchs was one who traveled with the clan, suggesting a relationship which was dynamic and personal, a relationship which would later be expressed by the concept of covenant.

When the ancestors of the Hebrews settled in the land of Canaan their understanding of God was expanded through their contact with the Canaanites who worshipped a universal God, El, under various names at the different Canaanite sanctuaries; it was El Elyon (God Most High) at Jerusalem, or El Olam (God Eternal) at Beersheba. As they settled in the land, the patriarchs also began to address their God under the name of El. An early name was El Shaddai (God of the Mountain), translated in the Septuagint as God Almighty. Thus long before they knew God as Yahweh the ancestors of Israel worshipped a God who combined the personal characteristics of a clan god, the God of the Patriarchs, with the universal characteristics of El, the head of the Canaanite pantheon.

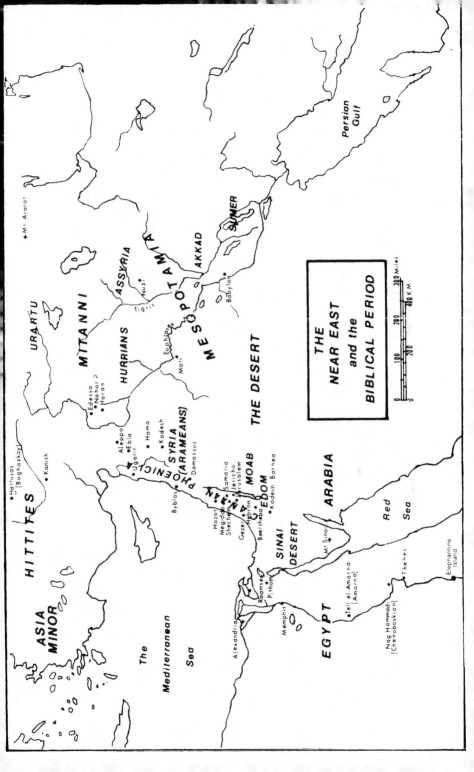

THE
NEAR EAST
and the
BIBLICAL PERIOD

Exodus and Covenant. It is difficult to reconstruct just how the ancestors of Israel arrived in Egypt. According to Genesis, the descendants of the Patriarchs migrated there because of a famine. Probably the move was the result of a number of causes and over a period of time. Some may have migrated there; others may have been brought to Egypt as slaves or prisoners of war. But it is clear that as early as the fifteenth century B.C. there was a sizable Hebrew (*Habiru*) population in Egypt who were in a state of bondage. Sociologically, these people —among them those who would later be called Hebrews — were an exploited minority, migrant workers forced to labor in the building projects of the pharaohs and reduced to virtual slavery within an oppressive empire.

Nor is there any doubt that the Exodus of this group from Egypt was an historical event, with a probable date around 1250. The Exodus is foundational to the entire Old Testament tradition. It was experienced and remembered as God's great act of salvation that delivered the Israelites from Egypt with great demonstrations of his power and made them a people.

The figure of Moses dominates Exodus and the remaining books of the Pentateuch. The biblical tradition credits him with leading the people out of Egypt and during the course of their wanderings in the desert. But perhaps even more important was his role as the founder of Yahwism, Israel's unique experience of God which was the basis of its identity as a people.

In this sense Moses was the founder of Israel. Prior to the Exodus and the Sinai covenant — the two great traditions of the book of Exodus — Israel did not know God as Yahweh. On the other hand, it is clear that the worship of Yahweh came to Palestine with the conquest. Moses was the mediator of this experience of God to the people. Through him they learned that Yahweh had bound himself to them as a people, that he had established a covenant with them, and that he required of his people certain standards of conduct in imitation of his own holiness.

Much of the history behind the Sinai covenant tradition is

lost in the past. The exact location of the holy mountain is uncertain. Certainly much of the legal tradition in the Pentateuch, attributed to Moses, represents later expansions. Even the origins of the Decalogue, the basic expression of the Covenant (Ex. 20:1-17), are complex. Still a good number of scholars find it highly plausible that the Decalogue — or perhaps a shorter form of it — comes from the time of Moses. There is no doubt that the experience at Sinai established a relationship between Yahweh and Israel which was to remain the fundamental religious experience of the Jewish tradition.

The Conquest. The people who were to become Israel represented a mixed group. Not all were descendants of Jacob. As Exodus 12:38 acknowledges, "a crown of mixed ancestry" departed Egypt with the "Israelites." No doubt there were other fugitive slaves, people of other tribes, even some Egyptians. And other people continued to join themselves to the Israelites during the Exodus and after the conquest. Some scholars see in this swelling of Israel a sociological phenomenon of disadvantaged peoples — seminomads, herdsmen, small farmers — uniting against the established powers of Canaan, the minor kings and overlords who had control of the land. There is probably some truth here, for the saving event of the Exodus itself is inseparable from the liberation of the people from the economic and political oppression they experienced in Egypt. It is important to recognize that the very concept of salvation represented by God's deliverance from Egypt was a political liberation.

The biblical story of the conquest is supported by considerable evidence of widespread destruction which took place in Canaan in the latter half of the thirteenth century. A number of important towns, among them Lachish, Debir, and Hazor mentioned as conquered in Joshua 10-11, are known to have been destroyed during this period. The Bible gives two different pictures of the conquest. Joshua 1-12 reports a rapid, fierce campaign on the part of the invading Israelites leading to a total victory. They crossed the Jordan, destroyed Jericho, and quickly marched to the center, to the

South and to the North, making the land their own. But another tradition, represented by the book of Judges and the later parts of Joshua, presents the picture of a long struggle for the land, with various clans or tribes gradually winning control of different cities or regions. Some towns were won and lost a number of times, others remained in Canaanite hands until the time of David.

Both traditions contribute to our understanding of the conquest, with the truth lying somewhere between them. As Israel gradually gained the ascendancy, other tribes and indigenous peoples were absorbed. Some were of similar stock as Israel's Hebrew ancestors but already settled in Canaan. Others came from various groups entering Palestine at the same time as Israel. Still others were Canaanite peoples who initially resisted the newcomers, but ultimately were incorporated into Israel. Thus Israel's history is very complex. Not all those who were part of Israel had shared the Exodus experience of those who had left Egypt with Moses, nor did they all share the same patriarchal tradition. Certainly social, political, and economic interests were major factors in bringing these peoples together. But the focus of their unity was not tribe or tradition, nor was it a social or political vision. The bond that united them was religious; they accepted the worship of Yahweh and the terms of his covenant, often whole communities entering into the covenant relationship in solemn ceremonies such as the one Joshua 24 describes at the ancient Canaanite shrine of Shechem.

For several hundred years, the unity of Israel remained chiefly religious. Not yet a nation, Israel was a loose federation of tribes, often referred to in the past as an amphictyony. The tribes shared a common faith in Yahweh and a common shrine, probably at Shiloh, although there were other local shrines as well. They would gather at the central shrine for the great annual feasts. During this period, described in the book of Judges, Israel was undergoing a transition from a seminomadic to a more stable, agrarian way of life, learning to farm and building towns. In times of military threat various tribes would rally behind a charismatic leader or "judge" like Othniel, Deborah, Gideon, or Samson, leaders accepted not because of position or office, but by reason of their courage, cunning, or sheer force of personality. Utimately, however, the system broke down. The federation was unable to adjudicate intertribal disputes or prevent the wars that frequently followed them; it could not always maintain the purity of Yahwism against the constant threat of the idolatrous Canaanite fertility cults, and it lacked the organization and military power to provide an effective defense against external aggression. Finally, when the increasingly powerful Philistines defeated Israel's army and occupied the land, the federation collapsed and the tribes were forced to accept a king.

The Monarchy. The man to whom Israel turned was Saul, a warrior from the small and centrally located tribe of Benjamin. Saul was anointed king by the prophet Samuel around 1030. Thus Israel became a monarchy, although this foreign institution was not easily accepted. One tradition, in favor of the monarchy, attributes Saul's election to a divine revelation to Samuel (1 Sam. 9:1 ff.). But another tradition sees the election of Saul as a concession to popular pressure from the elders and people and as a usurpation of Yahweh's rightful role as the true king of Israel (1 Sam. 8; 10:17-27).

Saul's kingdom was a modest one which left the tribal structures largely intact. It did not include all the tribes, for at least Judah in the South remained independent. Saul was successful in driving the Philistines from the hill country but they remained a threat and most of his reign was spent at war. His ultimate downfall was linked to his inability to get along with Samuel who represented the religious authority. When he fell with three of his sons in battle at Mt. Gilboa, the Philistines again occupied much of the land. But they would not hold it, for one of Saul's lieutenants, a man of great courage and personal charism whom Saul had jealously driven into exile, was to succeed him.

That man was David who was to be forever after Israel's ideal king. David was from Bethlehem and of the southern tribe of Judah. At the time of Saul's death he was already a powerful figure, a bandit chief with a large personal following and considerable wealth. With the consent of the Philistines he was chosen as king over Judah in Hebron (2 Sam. 2:1-4). Two years later, after the murder of Saul's ineffectual son Ishbaal, David was chosen by the northern tribes as king over Israel as well. Once ruler of a united kingdom he quickly consolidated his power. He drove the Philistines once and for all from the land and seized the Jebusite city of Jerusalem which he made his capital. With its location midway between the northern and southern tribal areas, Jerusalem was a happy compromise. David's decision to transfer the Ark of the Covenant to Jerusalem gave religious legitimacy to his capital which now became the religious as well as the political center of a united Israel. Under David's inspiration a cult tradition of music and song began to develop; these "psalms" became Israel's Temple liturgy, perhaps the best single expression of Israel's faith as a people for they show us Israel at prayer.

With David's continued conquests, Israel quickly became a powerful state. Along with David's court, Jerusalem acquired the bureaucracy necessary to administer the growing kingdom. The unpopular census mentioned in 2 Samuel 24 was probably used to facilitate taxation, military conscription, and forced labor.

One of the most important Old Testament Davidic traditions is rooted in David's desire to build a Temple in Jerusalem. According to 2 Samuel 7:1-7, the prophet Nathan at first welcomed David's proposal, but learned that night in a vision that Yahweh did not intend that David should build him a house. But the Lord had a further message for David; he promised that he would instead build a house for David, that he would establish an everlasting dynasty for his heir who would be for him a "son" and for whom he would be a "father" (2 Sam. 7:8-16). This "Oracle of Nathan" and its variant expressions (Ps. 89:20-38; 1 Chron. 17:4-14) which many scholars consider as having originated in the Davidic period is the basis for the messianic idea that God's covenant — now established with David — would be fulfilled through the Davidic house and kingdom. However this Davidic covenant in the South tended to overshadow the covenant of Sinai with its clear moral obligations.

David was succeeded by Solomon, the second son of Bathsheba, the wife he had stolen from Uriah the Hittite. Under Solomon the Davidic kingdom reached its zenith, but it was not long able to survive his death in 922. The unity that David had so skillfully nurtured collapsed and the kingdom split into the traditional tribal divisions to become two kingdoms, Israel in the North with the majority of the people and the secessionist Judah in the South. With the loss of unity went the empire as the two kingdoms struggled with each other, with their own internal problems, and with various foreign threats and invasions. The northern kingdom did not endure more than two hundred years. In 721 Israel fell to the power of Assyria under Sargon; many of her people were deported and others from elsewhere in the Assyrian empire were resettled there where they intermarried with the surviving Israelite population. Their descendants were known as the Samaritans.

Along with the name, Israel's tradition (called the Elohist tradition) passed to Judah in the south. Judah managed to survive for another 150 years. Hezekiah (715-687) carried through a comprehensive reform, attempting to restore the nation to strict Yahwism, but the political alliances he entered to support his rebellion against Sennacherib earned him Isaiah's disapproval. Nor was his reform long-lived. Hezekiah's son Manasseh, unable to resist the Assyrians, became their vassal, raising altars to their gods in the Temple. Idolatry, magic, and other pagan practices were again tolerated, including the ritual prostitution associated with the fertility cult.

In its final years a weakened Assyria lost control over its empire and Judah began to recover its independence. The most extensive reform in its history was carried out under Josiah, aided by "the book of the law" discovered in 621 in the course of repairing the Temple. As part of the reform Josiah closed the outlying shrines, centralizing the worship of Yahweh in Jerusalem. Once again, however, the reform was allowed to lapse. After the brief reign of Josiah's son Jehoahaz, his brother Jehoiakim succeeded him. In the meantime Assyria had fallen (612), replaced by the power of Babylon. Judah was unable to maintain its independence. First enthroned as an Egyptian vassal, Jehoiakim later changed his allegiance to Nebuchadnezzar. Still the nation continued to struggle. After several rebellions, the Babylonians sent their army against Jerusalem in 588. After a long siege, the city was taken and burned; its walls were razed, the Temple destroyed, and a large number of Judah's leading citizens carried off to exile in Babylon. Thus the Davidic kingdom came to an end, never to rise again. Meanwhile however, during this long period of crisis for the kingdom, a succession of prophets had been interpreting the experience of Israel in a way which was to give an entirely new direction to its tradition. It is to the prophets that we must now turn.

The Prophets in Israel

Too often the word "prophet" is understood as one who forecasts the future. For the Hebrew word *nabî* the Septuagint consistently used the Greek word *prophētēs,* literally "one who speaks for another," thus "interpreter." The prophets were spokespersons for Yahweh.

The phenomenon of prophecy was common in the ancient Near East. Prophetic messages were frequently mediated by dreams, visions, and ecstatic states, usually self-induced. Israelite prophets are generally divided into two groups. The "early prophets," also known as professional, court, or cultic prophets, appear from the time of the judges and early monarchy. These prophets generally belonged to groups or prophetic guilds. Like the pagan prophets, they specialized in frenetic or ecstatic communications. They were also patriotic nationalists.

More important are those known as the later or classical prophets. Remembered because their teachings have been preserved, usually by books bearing their names, these prophets functioned as spokespersons for Yahweh, seeing in the events of their day the hand of the Lord whose word they proclaimed.

Especially important were the great literary prophets of

the 8th, 7th, and 6th centuries. These lonely figures radically challenged and reinterpreted the Israelite tradition. Though highly individualistic, they were united by their deep conviction that something had gone profoundly wrong in the religious life of Israel. If not actually against the monarchy in principle, as in the case of Hosea, they shared the belief that the people had become blinded because of a complacent overconfidence in Yahweh's election of Israel and his unconditional promise to the house of David. In the southern kingdom of Judah, Nathan's Oracle had become the official state theology, to the detriment of the clear moral obligations specified by the Sinai covenant. As the prophets denounced the resulting sin, their preaching was dominated by the theme of judgment; Yahweh was calling his people to a decisive account, one which was to be a matter of life or death. Along with this constant theme of judgment a second begins to emerge, growing more pronounced as the crisis deepened, but present even in the earlier 8th century prophets such as Hosea, Isaiah, and Micah; it is the idea that Yahweh will manifest his salvation anew in the future.

In proclaiming God's coming judgment several accusations stand out. With Amos begins a tradition of prophetic condemnation of social injustice and the oppression of the poor, a theme which would be continued by Isaiah, Micah, Jeremiah, Habakkuk, Ezekiel, and Malachi. Amos and Isaiah especially assailed the dishonesty, lack of compassion, and mindless pursuit of wealth on the part of the upper classes which trampled the rights of the poor (Isa. 1:12-23; 3:15; 10:1-4; Amos 2:6-8; 5:7-15,21-24; 8:4-6). A second accusation was the worship of false gods. Hosea, a contemporary of Amos, used a powerful image probably based on his own grief over his wife's infidelity to accuse Israel of adultery, forsaking her husband Yahweh for Baal and the fertility cult of the Canaanites. Later Jeremiah and Ezekiel would make the same charge, condemning Israel for her worship of false gods. A third complaint also related to forsaking Yahweh was made by Hosea and Isaiah who inveighed against trusting in armaments and foreign alliances rather than in Yahweh.

Thus the prophets denounced the evil they recognized in

their society and predicted the coming disaster as God's judgment. Isaiah and Jeremiah spoke respectively of the pagan empires of Assyria and Babylon as Yahweh's instruments through which he would chastise his people. Amos and Hosea foretold military defeat and exile for Israel. Jeremiah predicted the loss of kingship, Temple, Ark, and priestly instruction for Judah. The message of coming judgment was overwhelming and consistent, so much so that Jeremiah suffered something like a nervous breakdown, the result of having to proclaim over and over again a message of "violence and outrage" to a nation and people he loved (Jer. 20:8).

Yet the message of the prophets was not merely judgment and condemnation. From the beginning there was also present a message of hope, an assurance of Yahweh's loving kindness and faithfulness to his people and of his ultimate victory over the forces which oppressed them. There is no single image which expresses this hope, faint at first, but growing, that a new manifestation of God's saving power awaits his people in the future. That future is veiled as much for the prophets as for the people. But a variety of images witness to the prophetic conviction that Yahweh's salvation would break forth in a new and definitive way. Before we consider some of those images, we need to note several terms used in reference to the salvific expectations of Israel.

Messianism. This term refers to that complex of ideas concerned with Israel's future salvation. It is broader than the concept of the messiah, although the messiah can be one symbol of messianic hope. Jewish messianism was often interpreted historically and politically, although the concept can also have eschatological or apocalyptic connotations. Late Judaism was familiar with a wealth of messianic images, both personal and impersonal.

Eschatology. Derived from the Greek *eschatos,* "the last," "furthest," eschatology means the teaching concerning the last things. Jewish eschatology looked forward to the fulfillment or consummation of Israel's history, to a new age established by a definitive intervention of God bringing his salvation. Eschatological imagery appears chiefly in post-

OUTLINE: HISTORY OF ISRAEL

DATE		SELECTED LITERATURE by centuries

1750 Abraham

                                       13th early law codes, poetry (Ex 15)

1250 Moses: Exodus from Egypt   11th

           Conquest of Canaan   10th J tradition put in writing
                                                                Davidic court history
                                                                (2 Sm 9-20, 1 K 1-2)

1030 Saul ointed King   Use of Pss in Temple worship

1000 David ᵴ ᵓcceeds Saul   9th E tradition composed, royal annals of
                                                                Judah & Israel (source of 1-2K, 1-2C)

   921 Divisio the Kingdom   8th J and E merged under Hezekiah
                                                                  Amos, Hosea in Israel
                                                                Isaiah, Micah in Judah

       721 ISRAEL falls to Assyria   7th core of Deut. made basis of Josiah's
                                                                reform (621); oracles of Isaiah edited
                                                                 Zephaniah, Nahum, Habakkuk,
                                                                 Jeremiah

                                                     6th P is compiled, Deut. history edited

587 — JUDAH falls to Babylon ─────────┐   Ezekiel, Deutero-Isaiah in Babylon
                                                               Post-exilic oracles of Haggai, Zech-
              Exile   ariah (1-9), Job (?)

538 — Return from Exile by Decree of ─┘   5th Pentateuch completed (c 400?)
       Cyrus the Great   Malachi, Nehemiah, Ezra,
                                                           Obadiah (?)

                                                     4th Jonah (?) Joel (?) Deutero-Zechariah (?)
                                                     3rd Chronicler's History (?)

331 Alexander conquers Persian
       Empire: Palestine comes under
       influence of Hellenistic
       civilization

                                                     2nd Sirach, Daniel, Tobit, 1 Mc (c 100)

167 Maccabean revolt

                                                     1st 2 Mc, Wisdom

 63 Romans under Pompey conquer
       Jerusalem

   4 Death of Herod

exilic Judaism. Popular Christian eschatology speaks of "the four last things: death, judgment, heaven, hell."

Apocalyptic. A particular species of eschatological think-ing, apocalyptic derives from the Greek *apocalypsis*, "uncovering," "revelation." It refers to a type of literature which claims to be a revelation, granted to a seer or vision-ary, expressed in highly symbolic or allegorical language, of what is soon to take place at the end of the world. Apocalyp-tic thinking looks to a new order which transcends the historical, a "clean break" between the old and the new, usually expressed in end-of-the-world language. Apocalyp-tic imagery is frequent in a culture or society no longer confident of its own future. The Golden Age of Jewish apocalyptic extends from the beginning of the 2nd century B.C. to the end of the 1st century A.D. In the New Testa-ment the Book of Revelation represents an example of Christian apocalyptic writing.

The historical and eschatological imagery used by the prophets to express Jewish messianic hope frequently gave way in the late Old Testament period to the apocalyptic. Among the more important messianic images were the following.

Day of Yahweh. Appearing for the first time in Amos 5:18-20, the Day of Yahweh may have originally recalled Yahweh's saving interventions in the past as in the Exodus and conquest. However, Amos associates it with the fall of Israel, thus with Yahweh's coming judgment. In Isaiah 2:11 ff. the concept of the day of judgment is broadened to include others without excluding Israel. In Ezekiel and Zephaniah the image takes on a cosmic dimension, for all the earth will be subjected to Yahweh's judgment. In the writings of some of the later postexilic prophets, the Day of Yahweh begins to have eschatological connotations. In Joel 4:14 ff. and Deutero-Zechariah 14:1 ff. the Day of Yah-weh is seen as a day of judgment and defeat for the nations and of vindication for a purified Israel.

The Remnant. This tradition, appearing frequently in the prophets, speaks of a "remnant" which will survive God's judgment. In the earlier prophets the term is used more as a threat, or at least in a neutral sense. Isaiah named one of his sons *"She'ar jashub"* ("a remnant shall return") to remind the people of the coming judgment (Isa. 7:3). The image of a remnant radically challenged a nation which had become complacent regarding God's continuing favor. In what are probably exilic or postexilic additions to Isaiah (10:20-22; 11:11, 16; 28:5), Jeremiah (31:7), Micah (1:12; 5:6), and Zephaniah (2:7, 9; 3:13), as well as in Zechariah 8:10-12, remnant is used in a messianic sense of the survivors of Israel who will be gathered from among the nations and again experience Yahweh's blessings.

The Davidic Messiah. The Hebrew word *mashîaḥ* (Gk. *christos,* anointed) refers to one "anointed" for an office, here the anointed king of the house of David. The prophetic tradition prior to the exile looked forward to a new king in the Davidic line who would govern Israel righteously and deliver the nation from its enemies, thus an historical figure in the political life of the nation based on the Oracle of Nathan with its promise of an eternal Davidic dynasty. Isaiah speaks of a successor of David who would bring about a kingdom of justice and righteousness (Isa. 9:16). Micah describes an ideal ruler who will come from Bethlehem (Mi. 5:1-5). Jeremiah proclaims the coming of "a righteous shoot to David" who shall reign and govern wisely (Jer. 23:5).

During and after the exile, with the loss of the kingdom, the ideal king becomes increasingly a figure in the indefinite future through whom God himself would establish a new order of justice, peace, and righteousness. Ezekiel promises a restoration and spiritual renewal of the people in which "my servant David shall be prince over them" (Ezk. 37:24). Similar passages such as Amos 9:11 ff., Isaiah 11:1-9, and Jeremiah 30:9, considered by most scholars to have been added during the exile, represent a messianism which is more eschatological than historical in the sense that they look forward to a decisive intervention of Yahweh in history manifesting his salvation. A later passage in Zechariah 9:9 ff. looks to a future king who will bring peace, though this time the king is identified not with the pomp of the mighty, but with the meekness of the poor who made up so great a part of postexilic Judaism. In these passages a contrast emerges between the righteousness of the future king and the injustice and oppression of the poor practiced by their predecessors and so often condemned by the prophets. In this way justice, peace, and the vindication of the poor and the powerless become characteristics of the messianic age (Isa. 45:8; 54:14), a theme echoed in the later books of the Old Testament, particularly in the psalms (Pss. 12:6; 18:28; 22:27; 76:10).

Still the development of the concept of the messiah should not be oversimplified. In the apocryphal books of late Judaism the messianic theme has frequently been politicized into an earthly kingdom established by Yahweh, sometimes seen as immediately preceding the consummation of the world. The messiah is often seen as a superhuman figure coming from heaven. Some strands of late Jewish thought under the influence of a strong priesthood looked forward to two messiahs, a royal Davidic messiah and a priestly messiah, a tradition present at Qumran.

New Covenant. The word covenant does not appear frequently in the writings of the classical prophets of the 8th century, perhaps because the idea of covenant had been transformed into a false guarantee of divine favor or because it was too closely linked to the official theology of the Davidic kingdom. In either case, the prophets found the people too secure in the belief of their divine election. But with Jeremiah the word covenant reappears, though in a radically new sense. For Jeremiah the covenant no longer existed; the people had abrogated it by their conduct. But Jeremiah did not abandon the notion of covenant. Rather his messianic vision saw Yahweh establishing a new covenant with his people in the future, not a covenant of law but one which would work a change in the heart of each individual (Jer. 31:31-34). In a similar way Ezekiel used the image of Yahweh establishing a covenant of peace (Ezk. 27:26; 34:27). In language even more anthropological than Jeremiah's he speaks of Yahweh cleansing his people from their sins and placing a new spirit within them, giving them natural hearts in place of their hearts of stone (Ezk. 36:24-28). Here Yahweh's future is imaged as an interior purification and regeneration touching the individual in a way which goes beyond the old covenantal relationship.

Servant of Yahweh. The enigmatic figure of the Servant of Yahweh appears in Second Isaiah (Isa. 40-55) in the so-called Servant Songs (Isa. 42:1-4; 49:1-6; 50:4-9; 52:13-53:12). In some of the passages, the Servant is clearly a collective image for the people, Jacob and Israel (41:8 ff.; 44:1 ff.; 44:21; 48:20). But in other passages the Servant appears as a single figure who will gather the people to the Lord (Isa. 49:5), bring his salvation to the ends of the earth (Isa. 49:6), and give his life as an innocent victim who takes upon himself the sins of the people (Isa. 53:4-5, 12).

While acknowledging that the concept of the Servant includes both collective and individual dimensions, an increasing number of scholars agree that the figure of the servant cannot be reduced simply to a collective image of Israel. The very elasticity of the concept suggests that the figure of the servant in some way represents the mission of the people of Israel; yet particularly in the final song the servant stands apart from the people in his innocence. Here the prophet images a future in which salvation comes through the suffering of one who offers himself as a victim for sin (Isa. 53:10-12).

Son of Man. This last expression, though frequently used by Ezekiel in a non-messianic sense, first appears in a messianic context later in the Old Testament period in the book of Daniel (c. 165). Here the eschatological imagery of the late prophetic period has given way to the apocalyptic. In a vision Daniel sees "one like a son of man coming on the clouds of heaven" to receive an everlasting kingdom (Dan. 7:13). In this passage the son of man is a collective image for the redeemed of Israel. However in the subsequent tradition the emphasis shifts frequently from kingdom to king and the Son of Man, particularly in apocalyptic works such as the books of Enoch, becomes a figure who will come in the last days as ruler and judge.

From a pastoral point of view the prophets were not terribly successful, for they failed to bring about the conversion of the nation they sought through their preaching. Yet it is difficult to overestimate the importance of their role in shaping the biblical tradition. What they effected was a shift in the religious imagination of the people, away from what God had done for them in the past and to the future, to the expectation of a new manifestation of his saving power which would surpass his great works of old.

In Second Isaiah this shift becomes explicit. In the context of the Exodus event itself he proclaims: "Remember not the events of the past, the things of long ago consider not; See, I am doing something new!" (Isa. 43:18-19a). The emphasis and imagery in the prophets vary but the theme is remarkably constant. As the prophets reinterpreted the religious tradition, what emerged was a growing expectation of a new and definitive act of God establishing a messianic age. The results of that expectation are evident in the Judaism of the time of Jesus.

Postexilic Judaism

The fragmentation of the Jewish community began with the deportations and exile that followed the fall of the northern kingdom of Israel in 721 and the southern kingdom of Judah in 587. These events initiated the "Diaspora" or dispersion of the Jews from their homeland. The Babylonian exile came to an end in 538 when Cyrus the Great of Persia conquered the Babylonian empire and issued an edict which allowed the Jews to return to Palestine and reestablish their cult (Ezra 1:2-4; 6:3-5). As the exiles made their way back to the land in groups, they set about rebuilding the Temple, though on a modest scale. An effort to restore the monarchy under Zerubbabel failed, perhaps because the Persian imperial administration to which Israel was subjected saw in this the beginnings of a movement for independence. Without a king, the political power of the priesthood increased as the high priest became the effective ruler of the community. At the same time, as prophecy disappeared, the interpretation and observance of the law or Torah assumed an increasingly central role in the community's religious life.

In 332 Alexander the Great of Macedonia conquered the Persian empire, thus bringing Palestine under his control and under the influence of the Hellenistic culture which spread with his victories. When Alexander died some eight years later, his generals divided up his empire. Egypt came under the control of Ptolemy Lagi who after considerable struggle with his rival Seleucus added Palestine to his domain. The Ptolemies ruled Palestine for almost a century. In 198 the Seleucid ruler Antiochus III finally triumphed over Ptolemy V and Palestine became part of the Seleucid Syrian kingdom.

When Antiochus IV Epiphanes succeeded to the throne he attempted to unify his kingdom by fostering its Hellenization. After some years during which relations with the Jews worsened, he finally abrogated the religious concessions they had previously enjoyed. Temple sacrifices, traditional festivals, Sabbath worship, and the rite of circumcision (the sign of the covenant) were forbidden. Torah scrolls were to be destroyed, sacrifices were to be offered to the Greek gods, and the cult of Zeus was introduced in the Temple itself. Disobedience was punished by death.

Though a number of Jews, comfortable with the new Hellenistic ways, complied with Antiochus' decree, many others refused and paid the price with their lives. Among them were members of a group of believers known as the Hasidim (the pious ones), from whom both the Essenes and the Pharisees are descended. One expression of Jewish resistance was the book of Daniel, written about 165; the apocalyptic language in chapters 7-12 reflected the desperate situation of the times. The author of Daniel counseled fidelity to the Law and assured the people that God's intervention was at hand. For those who had died for their faith he expressed the hope that the coming apocalyptic judgment would see the dead raised to everlasting life (Dan.

12:1-3). Here for the first time the concept of the resurrection of the dead comes to expression in the Jewish tradition.

The other reaction to Antiochus' persecution was much more violent. Even as Daniel was being written a revolt broke out, started by a man named Mattathias who slew at the altar a Jew about to offer a pagan sacrifice and then fled to the hills with his sons, to be followed by a number of the Hasidim. Under his son Judas "Maccabeus" ("the hammer") the revolt turned into a war which resulted finally in victory for the Maccabees. Judas purified and rededicated the Temple, a day commemorated since then by the Feast of Hanukkah, and established the Maccabean or Hasmonean kingdom. The Hasmonean rule lasted until 63 B.C. when Roman intervention in a quarrel between two Hasmonean rivals brought Palestine under Roman control, to be administered by the imperial province of Syria. Herod, a member of the Idumean family forcibly converted to Judaism by the Hasmonean John Hyrcanus, became king of Judea under the Romans in 37 B.C. A cruel but capable tyrant, one of his achievements was the rebuilding of the Temple in Jerusalem, adding the Fortress Antonia at one corner. Herod died in 4 B.C. Jesus of Nazareth was born towards the end of his reign.

First Century Palestinian Judaism

Too often there is a tendency to oversimplify the picture of the religious life of the Jewish community in the time of Jesus. But Palestinian Judaism was by no means monolithic; it was made up of many different groups and parties, often with different messianic expectations and irreconcilable doctrines based on their different interpretations of the Jewish tradition.

The Essenes, like the Pharisees, were descendants of the Hasidim. They emphasized rigid observance of the law, ritual purity, and the study of the scriptures which they interpreted in an apocalyptic context. In protest to the assumption of the office of high priest by the Hasmoneans, the Essenes withdrew from the mainline Jewish community under a leader called "the Teacher of Righteousness" and moved to the desert where they lived by themselves along the western shore of the Dead Sea at a place called the Wadi Qumran.

Thus the Essenes had become a sect. They lived a monastic life under a strict discipline, rising for worship at sunrise, spending the day in manual labor, and devoting part of the night to prayer, reading, and the study of the law. Only full members, wearing the white robe of the community, could share in the communal meals. New members were admitted only after a probation of two or three years. In their scriptorium they produced the writings known as the Dead Sea Scrolls; these documents, sealed in earthenware jars and hidden in a cave above the wadi, were discovered in 1947 by two Palestinian shepherds. Qumran is only a few miles from where the Jordan empties into the Dead Sea, very near the site where John the Baptist exercised his ministry. It is quite possible that John was familiar with the sect. There are also a number of parallels between the life of Qumran and that of the early Christian community. Both groups studied and interpreted the Jewish scriptures in an apocalyptic context, both practiced a community of goods and celebrated a communal, ceremonial meal, at Qumran most probably a liturgical anticipation of the messianic banquet. *The Manual of Discipline*, found at Qumran, shows the apocalyptic character of the sect. The members of the community sought to prepare themselves for the final eschatological war and awaited the coming of two messiahs, a Davidic messiah and another priestly messianic figure, the Messiah of Aaron, who took precedence over the former, reflecting the importance of the priestly order at Qumran.

The Pharisees also developed out of the Hasidim. A deeply religious party, the Pharisees saw Jewish religious life as centered on the exact observance of the law. They studied the oral traditions of the elders and sought to erect a "fence" of binding traditions around the law so that observing the former would insure the perfect observance of the law itself. Politically the Pharisees wanted a state governed according to the precepts of the law not unlike the Islamic fundamentalists of today. For this reason the Pharisees opposed the Hasmonean rulers as well as Herod, though they tolerated the Romans who generally respected the religious practices of those they ruled and allowed the Jews to regulate their life according to the law.

Theologically the Pharisees were more liberal, believing in certain doctrines which had developed in the later Jewish tradition such as the existence of angels and demons, free will, judgment after death, and the resurrection of the dead. Among the more important Pharisees mentioned in the New Testament were Nicodemus, Paul's teacher Gamaliel, and of course, Paul himself. The Judaism which emerged after the destruction of Jerusalem and the Temple in 70 A.D. was largely the work of the Pharisees. At the coastal town of Jamnia they established the Jewish canon of scripture, collected the oral traditions, and reorganized the Jewish religious community around the Law, the synagogue, and the leadership of the rabbis.

The Sadducees, the rivals and the opponents of the Pharisees, made up the party of the priests along with their dependants and supporters among the wealthy and aristocratic Jerusalem families. They sought good relations with the Roman authorities on whom they were dependent for the power they exercised through the Temple and the Sanhedrin while their considerable economic interests led them to favor political stability. Theologically conservative, they accepted the authority only of the Pentateuch and rejected ideas which developed later in the postexilic books such as angels and demons and the resurrection of the dead.

The scribes, sometimes called lawyers, were originally the transcribers of the religious texts; from this they gained a familiarity with the law which established their authority as its teachers and interpreters. In the New Testament they represented a group of scholars and intellectuals, many of whom were Pharisees, though some of the Sadducees were also scribes.

The Zealots were the revolutionaries, fanatic Jewish nationalists who used the tactics of assassination and terrorism against those, Romans and Jews alike, who stood in the way of a free and independent Jewish state. The Zealots interpreted Jewish messianic hope politically, a fact which no doubt led to misunderstandings when Jesus began proclaiming that the kingdom of God was at hand (cf. John 6:15). One member of the Twelve, Simon the Zealot (Lk.6:15) had been a member of this group; there may have been others among the disciples. The Zealots were largely responsible for the rebellion which broke out in 66 A.D. against the Romans and the war that followed which led to the destruction of Jerusalem and the Temple. But they were not the only ones who were eager for a revolution against the Romans; many other Jews shared their desire for Jewish independence and joined their revolt when it finally came.

The Herodians were the political supporters of King Herod, and thus of the Roman rule which was the source of Herod's power.

The Samaritans, considered by the other Jews in New Testament times as schismatics and heretics, were the descendants of the survivors of the northern kingdom of Israel and of those peoples brought in by the Assyrians to resettle the land after 721. The roots of the schism may lie even deeper in the old tension between the tribes of the north and the south.

When the Jews returned to Jerusalem from Babylon, the offer of the Samaritans to assist in the rebuilding of the Temple was rejected. Later, when they built their own Temple on Mount Garizim (cf. John 4:20), the split became irreparable. They accepted only the Pentateuch and awaited a messianic figure called "the Restorer."

The Galileans, inhabiting the northern part of Palestine, were a mixed population. Isaiah called Galilee "the district of the Gentiles" (Isa. 8:23). Many Galileans had been forcibly converted to Judaism under the Hasmonean kings. At the time of the New Testament the population was still highly mixed, with both Greeks and Jews. Many of the Jews of Galilee were fiercely nationalistic.

The supreme religious authority in the Jewish community at the time of Jesus was the Sanhedrin or Council. Composed of seventy-one members, the Council was divided into three classes: the elders, made up of members of the chief families and clans; the high priests, mostly former high priests; and the scribes, most of whom were Pharisees. The Council was presided over by the ruling high priest. At the time of Jesus the jurisdiction of the Council in both religious and secular matters was limited to Judea; still it was very influential and the far-flung Jewish communities of the Diaspora looked to it for guidance.

Conclusion

At the center of the Jewish tradition stand the two great signs of God's choice of Israel, the exodus and the covenant. The exodus was an experience of salvation from bondage and oppression. Covenant expressed the unique relationship between Yahweh and his people.

The national history of Israel reached its highpoint under David and especially Solomon but the united kingdom did not long survive the latter's death. In the centuries that followed the prophets rebuked the people for their growing infidelity, for worshipping false gods and oppressing the poor. The disaster they foretold was realized in the destruction of both kingdoms but their promise of a future manifestation of God's salvation effected a shift in the religious imagination of the people, away from what God had done in the past to an expectation of future deliverance. The Judaism into which Jesus was born was a diverse community with different messianic expectations and sometimes irreconcilable doctrines.

3. THE DEVELOPMENT OF THE GOSPEL TRADITION

> Jesus toured all of Galilee. He taught in their synagogues, proclaiming the good news (*euangelion*) of the kingdom, and cured the people of every disease and illness.
>
> Matt. 4:23

> Here begins the gospel (*euangelion*) of Jesus Christ, the Son of God.
>
> Mark 1:1

The English word "gospel" comes from the Anglo-Saxon god-spell, "good tidings," which in turn is a literal translation of the Greek *euangelion*, "good news." In its primary sense, the Gospel or good news is what God has done in Jesus, however that might be expressed. Only later, in a secondary sense, did the word gospel come to mean a particular written account of that good news such as that of Matthew, Mark, Luke, or John.

The four canonical gospels represent the end product of a long process of proclamation, celebration, and interpretation of the life, death, and resurrection of Jesus. Deepened by constant reflection on the meaning of the mystery of Christ for the life of the community, this process also reflects different moments in the faith and life of the early Church.

Thus the gospels cannot be read simply as biographies or histories. They tell us something about the Jesus of history, but they are far more concerned with the Christ of faith. The distinction is an important one, and is basic to christology, that area of theology concerned with the question, "who is Jesus?" that same crucial question for every Christian which the gospels tell us Jesus himself asked of his disciples: "Who do people say that I am?" (Mk. 8:27). As we examine the various stages in the development of the gospel tradition we will use this basic christological question as a focus.

The Jesus of history is a technical expression used by theologians for Jesus of Nazareth as he was known and experienced by his contemporaries during his historical life. It considers Jesus from the standpoint of his unfinished life, without knowing the end of the story. The Christ of faith refers to Jesus from the standpoint of his finished life, the Christ as he was recognized and confessed in faith by the disciples who witnessed to his resurrection, by the early Christian communities which proclaimed him as Messiah, Lord, and the Son of God, and by the evangelists who gave us that good news in written form. In short, the Christ of faith refers to Jesus as he is presented to us by the faith of the early church, for the gospels are already expressions of Christian faith. They represent the proclamation of the early church in written form; they are written in light of the resurrection, not to record past history but to proclaim the risen Christ present in the community.

Thus the gospels belong to the category of preaching; they are written sermons. Their authors, like good preachers everywhere, frequently adapt their material so that their gospels will speak more directly to their respective communities. Similarly each evangelist shapes his gospel according to his own insight and point of view. Therefore, the gospels cannot be understood as biographies or histories in our modern sense.[1] They are not carefully researched and docu-

---

[1]The 1964 *Instruction on the Historical Truth of the Gospels* of the Pontifical Biblical Commission acknowledges that the gospels are not literal accounts of the words and deeds of Jesus. For the document and a commentary see Joseph A.

mented accounts of the words and deeds of the historical Jesus. We know for example that the divinity of Jesus was not perceived during his public ministry, and that the earliest Christian communities did not immediately proclaim him as the eternal Son of God.

In the same way, if one takes the evidence of the earlier gospels seriously, it is highly unlikely that Jesus himself openly claimed to be the Messiah from the very beginning of his ministry (John 4:26), or proclaimed his divinity with statements such as "before Abraham came to be I AM" (John 8:58), or included in his preaching long theological lectures on the meaning of the Eucharist even before he had instituted it (John 6:52-59), to take only a few examples from the gospel of John. John presents the good news with a theological depth that suggests long years of contemplation on the mystery of Christ. His style combines the sensitivity of the poet and the mystic. But he is not an historian.

This is not to suggest that there is no history to be found within the gospels, including the gospel of John. If this were the case, there would be an unbridgeable chasm between the Christ of faith which the gospels give us and the Jesus of history. Christology would be simply a product of faith, without any historical foundation. A difference between history and proclamation exists, but not an insurmountable obstacle, for the gospels themselves are intended to hand on the Jesus tradition. Therefore to reach the Jesus of history one must begin with the Christ of faith presented by the gospels. Using the results of historical-critical biblical scholarship it is possible to move backwards through the various levels or layers of the gospel tradition to the historical Jesus. At the same time, to fully grasp the meaning of Jesus it is important to consider also how the church's understanding of Jesus developed as it continued to proclaim and celebrate the mystery of his death and resurrection.

Fitzmyer, *Theological Studies* 25 (1964) 386-408. Also see the Dogmatic Constitution on Divine Revelation, *The Documents of Vatican II*, ed. Walter M. Abbot (New York: America Press, 1966).

The gospel tradition developed through three basic stages, from the original words and deeds of the historical Jesus, through the oral preaching of the early church, to the actual writing of the gospels by the evangelists. We will consider, first, the preaching of Jesus, second, the Christ proclaimed, and third, the written gospels.

The Preaching of Jesus

Form criticism's greatest contribution to biblical scholarship has been its recovery of the Jesus tradition from the gospels in which it has been imbedded, usually in a form modified and reshaped by its use in the preaching and catechesis of the early Christian communities. This section will focus on the preaching of Jesus from which the gospel tradition developed. At the risk of seeming too brief or superficial in our treatment, we will try to confine our discussion to those sayings and parables which can be reasonably claimed by critical scholarship as authentic.[2] In this way we will settle for a critical minimum which can anchor the gospel tradition in the actual words and deeds of the historical Jesus.

The synoptic accounts of the public ministry of Jesus begin with his baptism at the hands of John the Baptist; John's gospel suggests that Jesus himself may originally have been part of the Baptist's movement (John 3:22-23). We do not know exactly what happened to Jesus at his baptism; the gospel accounts are colored by a symbolic story of a vision and later theological reflection. But the experience for Jesus must have been profound, for not long afterwards the carpenter of Nazareth began to proclaim publicly that the reign of God was at hand (Mk 1:14).

While the roots of the concept of the kingdom of God lie deep in the Old Testament, the term itself is of more recent

---

[2]See especially Rudolf Bultmann, *The History of the Synoptic Tradition* (Oxford: Basil Blackwell, 1963) and Norman Perrin, *Rediscovering the Teaching of Jesus* (London: SCM Press, 1967).

origin. The idea originates in the Old Testament notion of the Kingship of Yahweh. In the ancient world the power of the king over life and death frequently led to the monarch's divinization, as in Egypt, or at least to the recognition of the monarchy as a divine institution, as was the case in Mesopotamia. At the same time, the power of the king frequently led the ancient peoples to conceive of their gods as kings. In both Mesopotamia and Canaan various gods were worshipped as heavenly monarchs.

Israel did not turn its king into a god. But it is quite probable that even before the monarchy was established Yahweh was understood as king of Israel (Dt. 33:5; 1 Sam. 8:7). Later the concept of Yahweh's royal power was expanded, the result of a natural theological reflection on his saving deeds as well as on the attributes claimed for the gods of Israel's neighbors. In this way Yahweh came to be seen as king over the other nations as well (Pss. 22:29; 47; 99) and finally as king over all creation in virtue of his work as creator, an idea which developed later in Israelite theology (Pss. 74:12; 93; 95-99). In some of the later prophets (or in later additions to earlier prophets) the royal rule of Yahweh was seen in an eschatological perspective, something to be established in the messianic future (Isa. 24:23; Ob. 21; Zeph. 3:15; Zech. 14:16).

Though the expression "kingdom of God" is rare in the earlier tradition (Pss. 103:19; 145:11-13), it appears more frequently in the late Old Testament period, in Tobit 13:1, in Daniel who refers both to the throne of God's reign (Dan. 3:54) and to the kingdom which will be given to the saints in the apocalyptic future (Dan. 7:14, 18, 22, 27), and in Wisdom 6:4 and 10:10. In some of the intertestamental (non-canonical) writings, including works like the Assumption of Moses which is contemporary with the New Testament, the kingdom or reign of God is associated with apocalyptic displays of God's power and judgment, and with the establishment of Israel's rule over the nations.

Thus the concept of the kingdom of God was a familiar one to the Jews of Jesus' time; it was especially popular with the Zealots who interpreted it in terms of freedom from

Roman rule. Generally, however, it was understood in the context of the Messianic hope of Israel. Jesus does not seem to explain it. Nevertheless his proclamation of the kingdom of God was not simply dependent on the imagery and theology of his day; it was unique, rooted in his own religious experience. What then does the kingdom of God mean in Jesus' preaching? We will consider four dimensions of his preaching.

First, the expression kingdom of God (*basileia tou theou*) should generally be translated "reign of God." In Jesus' preaching the concept is dynamic; it refers not to a place but to an event, God's saving power breaking into history in a new way. It means the coming of the messianic age of salvation.

Second, there is an eschatological tension in Jesus' preaching of the reign of God; it is both present and future. From the beginning Jesus proclaims that the reign of God is at hand, at least in an initial way (Mk. 1:15; Matt. 4:17; 10:7). This present dimension, what Joachim Jeremias calls "the dawn of the reign of God,"[3] means that God is now manifesting his salvific activity, his rule in human affairs. Jesus illustrates and makes present this dawning of the age of salvation in his preaching and parables, his miracles, his proclamation of the forgiveness of sins, and in his sharing meals both with his friends and with sinners and others who were despised by the religious establishment.

Too often the miracle tradition has been interpreted apologetically as "proofs" for the divinity of Jesus. Jesus changed water into wine; therefore, Jesus is the Son of God; so went the argument. Yet in the gospel context, the miracles have a different meaning. For Palestinian Jews of the time of Jesus, physical sickness or infirmity was attributed to demonic power (Lk. 13: 10-16) and sin (Jn. 9:1-3). Jesus' exorcisms (Mk. 1:23-28; 3:23-27) and his physical healings show that with the arrival of the reign of God the power of evil over human beings was being broken. In what is almost

---

[3]Joachim Jeremias, *New Testament Theology*, Part I (London: SCM Press, 1971), pp. 96 ff.

certainly an authentic saying, Jesus makes clear that the reign of God has come: "if it is by the finger of God that I cast out devils, then the reign of God is upon you" (Lk. 11:20).

The proclamation of the forgiveness of sins is more evidence that the age of salvation is at hand. Forgiveness means the remission of debts, a liberation from one's past, and thus reconciliation. Jesus proclaimed forgiveness, not only in words and parables (Matt. 18:23-35; Lk. 15:11-32) but also in deeds. Here especially the table-fellowship tradition, so strong in the synoptic gospels (Matt. 11:19; Mk. 2:15-17; Lk. 15:2), is important. To share a meal with someone in the East even today is an act of communion. In Judaism table-fellowship, sharing the broken bread over which the head of the house has asked a blessing, signified fellowship with God. Not only did Jesus share meals with his friends — joyful occasions which provoked criticism from the Pharisees (Mk. 2:18-22) — but he was also criticized repeatedly for sharing meals with tax collectors, sinners, and others considered outside the law. In this way Jesus proclaimed in sign the participation of all in the reign of God. Finally in parables and figures such as the lost sheep (Lk. 15:3-8) and the lost coin (Lk. 15:8-9) there is the joyful news of God reaching out to establish a new relationship with men and women.

At the same time there is clearly a future dimension to Jesus' preaching of the reign of God. One clear indication of this is to be found in the prayer which Jesus taught his disciples: in the second petition of the Our Father the words "thy kingdom come" (Matt. 6:10; Lk. 11:2) show that Jesus taught his disciples to pray for the coming of the kingdom. The parables of the kingdom — the farmer and the seed, the mustard seed, the yeast kneaded in the flour, the buried treasure, the lost pearl, the net cast into the sea (Matt. 13:1-53) — bring both the present and the future aspects of the reign of God to light. The sayings about the Son of Man coming in judgment also underline the future dimension of God's reign. With only one exception (Acts 7:56), the New Testament always attributes the expression "Son of Man" to Jesus himself. It is recognized today that many of the Son of Man sayings have been reshaped by the post-Easter community which identified the Son of Man with Jesus and spoke of his imminent return in the apocalyptic language then popular in Palestine (Mk. 13:26; Matt. 24:30). Whether or not Jesus himself used the same kind of apocalyptic imagery in talking about the coming reign of God is difficult to establish; a number of scholars conclude that he did not. However, there is general agreement that Jesus did speak of the Son of Man's role in the coming judgment, even if he did not identify the Son of Man with himself (Lk. 12:8-9; Mk. 8:38).

It is clear therefore that Jesus' preaching of the reign of God cannot be reduced either to "realized" eschatology or to "future" eschatology, to the "already" or to the "not yet." To the question, is the eschatology of Jesus' preaching realized or future, the answer can only be "yes"; it is both being realized in Jesus' preaching and ministry and will find its completion in the future. Furthermore, as it became clearer that the opposition to his preaching would lead to his death, the future to which Jesus looked was one quite different from and beyond the present. There is then an eschatological tension in the preaching of Jesus which is reflected in the various levels of the gospel tradition.

A third point to observe about Jesus' preaching of the reign of God is that he calls for an immediate response. Mark summarizes his message as "repent, and believe in the gospel (Mk. 1:15). The English word "repent" used here in the R.S.V. translation has the connotation of being sorry for one's sins. But the word used in the Greek text, *metanoeite*, suggests much more. It means to think again, to change one's heart, one's mind, one's way of life, to assume a new standpoint. To enter the kingdom one must become like a little child (Mk. 10:15; Matt. 18:3; Lk. 18:17). In John's gospel this image is radicalized; John pictures Jesus as saying that "no one can see the reign of God unless he is begotten from above" which through Nicodemus' misunderstanding is turned for many Christian traditions into the positive requirement that a person must be "born again" (John 3:3-4).

Entering into God's reign requires more than sorrow for sins. The sayings and parables of Jesus bring out the magnitude of the decision and the radical nature of the conversion he demands. The stories of the treasure buried in the field and the pearl of great price compare the news of the reign to a discovery of something of such value that a person gladly gives up everything in order to possess it (Matt. 13:44-46). The parable of the marriage feast stresses the urgent nature of the invitation (Matt. 22:1-14) while that of the unjust steward teaches in a practical way the need for immediate action. Responding to God's reign involves a conversion, a fundamental reordering of one's ways of thinking, responding, and acting. Jesus calls for a disinterested love of both friends and enemies (Matt. 5:44-48) and for a radically different way of responding to insult or injury: "When a person strikes you on the right cheek turn and offer him the other. If anyone wants to go to law over your shirt, hand him your coat as well. Should anyone press you into service for one mile, go with him two miles" (Matt. 5:39-41). The commitment to this new way of living must be total: "whoever puts his hand to the plow but keeps looking back is unfit for the reign of God" (Lk. 9:62).

The beatitudes belong substantially to the Jesus tradition, with Luke's version probably closer to the original. In them Jesus echoes the prophetic tradition in teaching God's special love for the poor and the powerless (Lk. 6:20-21, Matt. 5:3-9). He also warned against the danger of wealth (Mk. 10:23-25). He challenged the religious legalism of his day, reinterpreting the law when he felt it necessary (Mk. 7:15) and denouncing the scribes and Pharisees, the religious leaders of his day, for "neglecting the weightier matters of the law, justice and mercy and good faith" (Matt. 23:23). This unique sense for what was essential in the tradition and what was oppressive religious legalism or mere social convention gives a liberating dimension to Jesus' message. As Leonardo Boff emphasizes, Jesus' preaching "implies a revolution of the human world," for in ignoring the social stratification of his society, secularizing its principle of authority, breaking its social conventions, and showing a special concern for its marginalized, Jesus challenged the very foundation of traditional society and called for a new order based on the norm of a universal love (Matt. 5:43-48).[4]

Unfortunately, as the parable of the marriage feast makes clear, most were too busy with their own affairs to hear his message, not really "into" the radical commitment to God, the very definition of religion, that Jesus demanded (Lk. 14:16-24).

A fourth and final point concerns the relation between the reign of God and Jesus himself. What was the relation between the message and the messenger? Jesus did not preach himself, and in the opinion of an increasing number of scholars today he probably did not claim or accept any of the "higher" christological titles such as "Messiah," "Lord," "Son of Man," or "Son of God" later used by the New Testament church.[5] Jesus was totally concerned with proclaiming the reign of God. The expression kingdom of God appears some 122 times in the gospels, mostly in the synoptics; yet in the rest of the New Testament the term is much less frequently found. While Jesus proclaimed the reign of God, the early Church from the beginning proclaimed Jesus. Thus the early Christians must have grasped instinctively the connection between Jesus and his message.

Even if Jesus did not make explicit christological claims in his own regard, many commentators recognize an implicit christology in the way he spoke and acted. Although a thorough examination of this question is beyond our purpose here, there are two expressions coming from the preaching of the historical Jesus we should consider briefly. The first offers an insight into how Jesus understood the relationship between himself and the reign

[4]Leonardo Boff, *Jesus Christ Liberator* (New York: Orbis Books, 1978), pp. 72 ff.

[5]Walter Kasper reviews Jesus' possible use of the christological titles in his *Jesus the Christ* (New York: Paulist Press, 1976), pp. 104-111.

of God. The second provides a clue to the more difficult mystery of his self-understanding.

The sayings of Jesus about the role of the Son of Man as judge are especially significant. While many of the Son of Man sayings have been shaped and adapted in the early preaching, scholars today generally regard the statement in Luke 12:8-9 as substantially authentic: "I tell you, whoever acknowledges me before men — the Son of Man will acknowledge him before the angels of God. But the man who has disowned me in the presence of men will be disowned in the presence of the angels of God." Several things are to be noted here. First, Jesus does not explicitly claim to be the Son of Man in this statement. The same is true in a parallel in Mark 8:38 although here the saying may have been colored by Palestinian apocalyptic thinking. But both look forward to the coming role of the Son of Man on the Day of Judgment. Second, there is an important claim here; the statement says that on the Day of Judgment those who reject Jesus will themselves be rejected, or in other words, a decision for or against Jesus is the same thing as a decision for or against the reign of God.

Thus the reign of God cannot be reduced to some message about God, to a revelation of his unconditional love, to his personal closeness or his concern for the poor, to the new life he offers through the service of others, or to any other message separated from the messenger. There is an incredible claim to authority discernible in Jesus' preaching: one encountered the reign of God in the person and work of Jesus. As the miracle tradition makes clear, to accept him was to experience God's saving power in body and spirit, to reject him was to reject that saving power.

A second expression of Jesus, the word "abba," raises the question of his self-understanding. All four gospels as well as the sayings from Q show Jesus addressing God as "my father," especially in his prayers. In addition, Mark's account of the prayer of Jesus in Gethsemane tells us specifically that he use the Aramaic word "abba" (Mk. 14:36). Both usages were highly unusual for a Jew at that time. Joachim Jeremias who has surveyed the entire Old Testament and the postcanonical Jewish literature reports that the Old Testament never addressed God as father.[6] In the time of Jesus, pious Jews out of respect generally avoided pronouncing the word "God," using instead paraphrases such as Matthew's "kingdom of heaven" and Mark's report of the high priest's question to Jesus at his trial, "are you the Messiah, the Son of the Blessed One?" (Mk. 14:61). Yet the gospel tradition clearly shows not only that Jesus addressed God as "my father," but also that he used the Aramaic "abba," a word used by sons and daughters of their father within the family relationship. We know that this unique way of addressing God was taken up by the early Christians (Rom. 8:15; Gal. 4:6). Therefore Jesus' use of this intimate form of address to God, something no other Jew of his time presumed to do, is highly suggestive of the way he understood his own relation to God. The least we can say is that he experienced himself related to God in a uniquely close, even filial way, and that this experience must have been the source of the message he proclaimed. The efforts to express and formulate that relationship are evident in the proclamation of the Christian community from its earliest days.

The Christ Proclaimed

The second stage in the formation of the gospel tradition is the oral proclamation of the early church. The community of disciples, scattered by the death of Jesus, is assembled again by the Easter experience. The Christian community exists from this time, and at the center of its life is the proclamation of the astonishing news that God has raised Jesus from the dead. This early preaching, often called the "apostolic kerygma" (*kerygma* means "proclama-

---

[6]See J. Jeremias, *New Testament Theology*, Part I, pp. 63 ff. The only exceptions are several instances where God is spoken of as the Father of the people Israel (Isa. 63:16, 64:7; Jer. 3:4), an oracle in Psalm 89 concerning the Davidic dynasty which recalls Yahweh's promise to be a father to David's descendant (Ps. 89:27), and several isolated examples in postcanonical Jewish works.

tion," from the Greek *kērux,* "herald," "one who proclaims") is the nucleus around which the New Testament
tradition developed.

Although the New Testament documents themselves date
from considerably later in the life of the early church, it is
possible to discern within them fragments of the early
preaching, originally separate traditions preserved from the
earliest communities. These traditions witness to the efforts
of the early communities to formulate answers to the
obvious question raised by the disciples' Easter experience:
who is this Jesus? Their answers could only be expressed in
terms of the images and concepts which constituted their
collective religious imagination, formed by the religious
tradition out of which they came. They interpreted the
mystery of Jesus in the language and imagery, the "models"
of Jewish messianic hope, especially in terms of the apocalyptic tradition with its salvific figures and its image of the
resurrection of the dead. Their religious tradition provided
the interpretative framework, the horizon against which the
Easter experience of the disciples could be interpreted and
expressed, even if the mystery itself constantly overflowed
the boundaries of any particular image or interpretative
figure and increasingly challenged the very tradition used to
express it. In the early theological formulas we find preserved in the New Testament the communities are already
struggling to express their experience and their faith. Here
we find examples of the church's early christology, though
we can sometimes discern behind them even earlier traditions, just as the New Testament books in which they appear
also represent later interpretations. Some examples of the
early preaching:

> This is the Jesus God has raised up, and we are his
> witnesses. Exalted at God's right hand, he first received
> the promised Holy Spirit from the Father, then poured
> this Spirit out on us . . . . Therefore let the whole house of
> Israel know beyond any doubt that God has made both
> Lord and Messiah this Jesus whom you crucified.
>
> Acts 2:32-33, 36

> The God of our fathers has raised up Jesus whom you put
> to death, hanging him on a tree. He whom God has
> exalted at his right hand as ruler and savior is to bring
> repentance to Israel and forgiveness of sins.
>
> Acts 5:30-31

> The gospel concerning his Son, who was descended from
> David according to the flesh but was made Son of God in
> power according to the spirit of holiness, by his resurrec-
> tion from the dead.
>
> Rom. 1:3-4

> If you confess with your lips that Jesus is the Lord, and
> believe in your heart that God raised him from the dead,
> you will be saved.
>
> Rom. 10:9

> I handed on to you first of all what I myself received, that
> Christ died for our sins in accordance with the Scriptures;
> that he was buried and, in accordance with the Scrip-
> tures, rose on the third day; that he was seen by Cephas,
> then by the Twelve.
>
> 1 Cor. 15:3-5

> The Lord has been raised . . . He has appeared to Simon.
> Lk. 24:34

The careful reader will have noted a number of interesting
points about these early christological statements. First, the
resurrection is described as something that happens to
Jesus. Second, there is no expression of his divinity. Third,
in several of the statements, christological titles such as
"ruler," "savior," "Lord," "Messiah," and "Son of God"
(used in the Old Testament of the king as a divine representative) are predicated of Jesus *after* his exaltation or resurrection; he receives the Holy Spirit and becomes Lord and
Messiah (Acts 2:33, 36) and Son of God (Rom. 1:4) only
after his death when he is "exalted" to God's right hand.
Fourth, several of the formulas associate Jesus' death with
the forgiveness of sins. Fifth, in two of the texts Peter is
mentioned as the first witness to the resurrection. Sixth, the

statements read as though they were composed for recitation. And they were. They are brief, binding, communal formulations of belief whose original *Sitz im Leben* must have been preaching or liturgy. Yet behind them lie even earlier traditions.

Scholars today reconstruct several strata in the development of christology, based on different moments in the life of the early church. The earliest is represented by Palestinian Jewish Christianity. These early congregations interpreted Jesus in the context of their own apocalyptic tradition. They saw the earthly Jesus as a prophetic servant like Moses and moved easily from his own Son of Man sayings to the proclamation that Jesus himself would soon return as the Son of Man in glory. This apocalyptic parousia (second coming) or Maranatha (Aramaic for "Come Lord" — 1 Cor. 16:22) christology appears both in the Q tradition and in Mark.

The second stratum is found in the christology of the Hellenistic Jewish mission. As the Greek-speaking Jewish Christians proclaimed the Gospel in the Diaspora several things happened. First, these Hellenistic Jewish Christians began to draw their christological titles from the Septuagint. One of them, to become increasingly important, was the title *Kyrios*, a Greek title of respect meaning "Lord" or "Sir," used in the LXX to translate the name Yahweh. Second, they brought forward the titles Messiah and Lord from the parousia to the exalted life of the risen Jesus who was now seen as reigning at God's right hand, prior to his second coming. Thus there was a shift from a parousia to an exaltation christology. The formulas we considered above generally reflect this stratum. They are certainly modest in what they affirm about Jesus, if judged from the perspective of the later New Testament; they represent a "low" christology as compared to a "high" christology such as Thomas' profession of faith in Jesus as "my Lord and my God" at the end of the gospel of John (20:28). But already present in these early kerygmatic formulas are various soteriological interpretations of the death and resurrection of Jesus; the Christ event means that God has poured out the Holy Spirit

(Acts 2:33), one of the signs of the messianic age of salvation; the death of Jesus means the forgiveness of sins (Acts 5:31; 1 Cor. 15:3).

These interpretations would find deeper expression as each early community continued to live and celebrate the mystery of Christ from which its life flowed. St. Paul stressed God's mysterious plan of salvation, revealed in "Christ Jesus," accomplished through his sacrificial death and resurrection, and leading to new life in his body the church, formed by his life-giving Spirit. Later the evangelists would express in a different way the meaning of the good news in their different gospels. This brings us to the third stratum, the christology of the Gentile mission in which our more familiar threefold christology of pre-existence, incarnation, and resurrection-ascension developed. We will see this in more detail when we turn to the gospels. But first we must ask what else became part of the growing gospel tradition as the various communities proclaimed what God had done in Jesus?

As the good news spread, details from the life of Jesus and examples of his teachings were called forth "by the original eyewitnesses and ministers of the word" (Lk. 1:2). Adapted for memorization and oral transmission by means of rhythm, rhyme, repetitions, and catchwords, originally independent stories and traditions were collected and assembled even as they were being reshaped by the different communities in which the Gospel was being proclaimed. Nor was preaching the only source upon which the evangelists would later draw. Each community was a fully functioning church, preparing neophytes for baptism, praising God with hymns and songs, using various liturgical formulas in the celebration of baptism and the Eucharist, developing structures of ministry and authority as well as catechetical material and official creeds or formulas of faith. Thus the growing gospel tradition included the following:

Stories about Jesus. Before any ordered narrative of the life of Jesus existed, various originally independent stories about him were handed down in the different communities. They included stories about his birth, his baptism, temptations, his disciples, transfiguration, triumphal entry into Jerusalem, and so on. Some of them such as the story of the Magi in Matthew or Luke's story of Jesus at the age of twelve carrying on a conversation with the teachers in the Temple are considered to be legends, used by the evangelists to foreshadow or illustrate some gospel theme. The Passion Narrative is also related to this general category of stories. This oldest continuous narrative in the gospel tradition is generally considered to have been composed prior to Mark (though some recent studies argue that it is a Markan composition.)

Miracle stories. Also circulating in the early communities were stories recounting the miracles of Jesus. As the miracle stories were passed on they were frequently magnified, expanded, and gradually gathered into collections. Some are probably legendary, but the basic miracle tradition, particularly the Sabbath healings, cannot be denied. The stories of the exorcisms also belong here. These stories generally have been shaped according to a three-point literary pattern adapted for oral transmission. Each states the circumstances ("a bad squall blew up"), the miracle itself ("Jesus awoke and rebuked the wind"), and the reaction ("a great awe overcame them" — Mk. 4:35-41).

Parables and images. Collections of the parables used by Jesus, possibly in his table conversations, also circulated. As they were retold by the early communities they were also reinterpreted to suit local situations and often allegorized.

Sayings of Jesus. Originally isolated, various sayings of Jesus were also handed down and collected. The great German form critic Rudolf Bultmann distinguished three main groups of sayings: *logia* or sayings of the Lord in the narrow sense (subdivided into declaratory principles, exhortations, and questions), prophetic and apocalyptic sayings, and laws or community regulations.[7] Among the authentic words and sayings of Jesus can certainly be included the beatitudes, the Our Father, the word abba, the expression king-

[7]Rudolf Bultmann, *The History of the Synoptic Tradition* (Oxford: Basil Blackwell, 1963), pp. 69 ff.

dom of God, and some of the sayings about the Son of Man coming as judge (Lk. 12:8-9). The sayings of Jesus may have been gathered into a written collection quite early. Because Matthew and Luke share about 230 verses not found in Mark, virtually identical, scholars have postulated the existence of a source called Q (from the German *Quelle*, "source"). This source, probably a document, is thought to have originated in Palestine or Syria within two generations of the death of Jesus.

Liturgical traditions. Other units of tradition came from or were shaped by the liturgical and sacramental life of the early church. Early Christian hymns appear in the Prologue to John's gospel (John 1:1-18) and in Paul's letters (Phil. 2:6-11). Last Supper narratives are found in the synoptic gospels (Mt. 26:26-29; Mk. 14:22-25; Lk. 22:17-19). The trinitarian baptismal formula attributed by Matthew to the risen Jesus (Matt. 28:19) has its original *Sitz im Leben* in the baptismal liturgy of the church of the second or third generation. Liturgical formulas of the early communities are incorporated into the Last Supper narratives in the synoptic gospels and 1 Corinthians 11:23 ff. and into the retelling of the story of the miracle of the loaves. In this way the catechetical and liturgical life of the church as well as the missionary activity of those whom Ephesians calls "apostles, prophets, and evangelists" (Eph. 4:11) provides a rich source of material. Soon other evangelists would draw upon these traditions in giving the church written gospels.

The Written Gospels

The final stage in the formation of the gospel tradition is the actual writing of the gospels themselves. With different traditions to draw upon, writing a gospel involves a process of selection and synthesis. At the same time selection and proclamation in a specific context imply the task of theological interpretation. Each evangelist has a unique point of view, based on his own particular insight, experience, and background. Each is writing for a distinct community. And each is writing in a different historical situation. Mark, the name given to the unknown author of the first gospel, was probably a Jewish Christian with ties to Palestinian Jewish Christianity. His gospel was probably written at Rome shortly before the destruction of Jerusalem; it reflects the threat of persecution. Matthew was probably a Christian scribe from the Jewish Christian scribal school at Antioch. While his gospel reflects much of the conflict between the Jewish Christians and the Jewish reform movement of the Pharisees at Jamnia, it was probably written after the final break which saw the excommunication of Jewish Christians from the synagogues (c. 85).

Luke is considered to have been a Gentile Christian, a product of the Hellenistic Jewish Christian mission. He wrote around the year 85 for a church learning to live within the Roman Empire. The literary history of the fourth gospel is complex. Scholars suggest the following development.[8] The gospel is based on the tradition handed down by "the Beloved Disciple." Originally a disciple of John the Baptist, this disciple was a follower of Jesus from the beginning of his ministry, though not one of the Twelve, and hence not John the Son of Zebedee. The gospel itself was written by a later disciple within the Johannine community and given its final form still later by a redactor who added some additional material.

The problem of the literary relationship between Matthew, Mark, and Luke — known as the synoptic gospels because of their common perspective — has puzzled scholars since the question was first raised at the end of the eighteenth century. Today it is generally agreed that Mark was the earliest gospel, and that Matthew and Luke are dependent on Mark as well as on the sayings source Q. Matthew contains all but 40-50 of Mark's 660 verses. Luke is more selective, using some 350 verses of Mark in addition to the 230 verses he shares with Matthew and another 548 from his own sources. John is relatively independent of the

[8]See Raymond E. Brown, *The Community of the Beloved Disciple* (New York: Paulist Press, 1979), pp. 20-34.

synoptics. Discovering how a particular evangelist has used or "edited" his material by comparing it with the original tradition is the task of redaction criticism (the German word *Redakteur* means "editor"). However, each evangelist is also an author in a true sense, and so redaction criticism also involves the broader methods of analysis used by literary criticism. A sensitivity to organization, literary structure, imagery, and recurring themes is crucial for the task of discovering the unique purpose and theological viewpoint of an evangelist. For an illustration we will consider the synoptic accounts of the baptism of Jesus (R.S.V. translation):

Matthew 3:13-17	Mark 1:9-11	Luke 3:21-22
Then Jesus came from Galilee to the Jordan to John, to be baptized by him. John would have prevented him, saying, "I need to be baptized by you, and do you come to me?" But Jesus answered him, "Let it be so now; for thus it is fitting for us to fulfill all righteousness." Then he consented.	In those days Jesus came from Nazareth of Galilee	Now when all the people were baptized,
And when Jesus was baptized, he went up immediately from the water, and behold, the heavens were opened	and was baptized by John in the Jordan. And when he came up out of the water, immediately he saw the heavens opened	and when Jesus also had been baptized and was praying, the heaven was opened

and he saw the Spirit of God descending like a dove, and alighting on him; and lo, a voice from heaven, saying, "This is my beloved Son, with whom I am well pleased."

and the Spirit descending upon him like a dove; and a voice came from heaven, "Thou art my beloved Son; with thee I am well pleased."

and the Holy Spirit descended upon him in bodily form, as a dove, and a voice came from heaven, "Thou art my beloved Son; with thee I am well pleased."

Mark's account, the earliest, is a very straightforward report of Jesus' baptism by John and the vision that followed it. Matthew follows Mark's text closely, but interpolates a dialogue between John and Jesus, the effect of which is to indicate that John already knows who Jesus is and therefore feels that it is inappropriate for him to baptize Jesus. Perhaps this indicates a certain hesitancy on Matthew's part about describing Jesus submitting to a baptism for repentance (Matt. 3:11). Luke's version is quite different but he also seems uncomfortable with the story of John's baptism of Jesus. He tones it down by dropping John's name from his account and subordinates the actual baptism by calling attention to the fact that Jesus was praying. Thus Luke situates the vision as something that happens to Jesus in the context of his prayer, introducing an emphasis on the prayer of Jesus that will recur many times in his gospel, usually at decisive moments in Jesus' life (Lk. 6:12; 9:18; 11:1; 22:41; 23:46). All three accounts attribute to the voice from heaven the words spoken over the Servant of Yahweh in Isaiah 42:1, changing the word Servant to Son. In Mark and Matthew only Jesus sees the vision. In regard to the toning down of John's role in the baptism of Jesus in the later accounts, it is interesting to note that in John, the last gospel, the actual baptism of Jesus is not even mentioned.

Mark. The gospel of Mark was written shortly before the destruction of Jerusalem in 70 A.D. Mark's christology goes considerably beyond the exaltation christology we noted earlier in several examples of the early apostolic preaching. Yet Mark still reflects the strong apocalyptic tradition of the early Palestinian church in his emphasis on the imminent coming of Jesus as the Son of Man (13:26; 14:62).

For Mark, the Jesus of the ministry is already Messiah and Son of God.[9] In his gospel, without any traditions concerning the birth of Jesus, the baptism of Jesus becomes the moment in which he is revealed as God's Son, even though the disciples do not grasp this during his life. The inability of the disciples to understand Jesus and his teaching is a Markan theme. In fact the only ones who seem to grasp Jesus' true identity during his life are the evil spirits whose power was threatened by his appearance (Mk. 1:24; 3:11; 5:7). Mark is more concerned with the person of Jesus than with his teachings; his gospel can be seen as a progressive revelation of who Jesus is culminating with the exclamation of the Roman centurion, a pagan, at Calvary: "clearly this man was the Son of God" (Mk. 15:39).

The first half of the gospel focuses on the mystery of the Messiah; in spite of the incomprehension of the disciples and the efforts of Jesus to conceal his true identity, his messiahship is revealed in his activity, especially in his miracles. A turning point is reached when Peter identifies Jesus as the Messiah in response to his question, "Who do people say that I am?" (Mk. 8:27-29). In acknowledging Peter's answer, Jesus begins to prepare his disciples for his death, using the image of the Son of Man who must suffer. This becomes the occasion for an extended instruction on the nature of discipleship and the way of the Son of Man (Mk. 8:27-10:52).

The second half of Mark's gospel has been described as the mystery of the Son of Man whom Jesus seems to identify with the suffering Servant of Isaiah 52:13-53:12. The gospel

[9]Raymond Brown describes the gradual revelation of Jesus' divine sonship from the exaltation christology of the early preaching in Acts to the preexistence christology of John in his *The Birth of the Messiah* (New York: Doubleday & Co., 1977), pp. 29 ff.

lacks any resurrection appearance stories and probably ended originally with the discovery of the empty tomb and the message of the angel to the women that the disciples would see the risen Jesus in Galilee (Mk. 16:8). An appendix (Mk. 16:9-20), missing in some of the earliest manuscripts, was added later.

Mark writes in unpolished Greek. His vocabulary is simple and repetitive (note the overuse of the word "immediately"); he sometimes includes two versions of the same story as he does with the two cycles of stories recounting in order the miracle of the loaves, a crossing of the lake, a controversy with the Pharisees, and a teaching concerning food or bread (Mk. 6:30-7:23; 8:1-21). But he also adds personal details missing in the other gospels and calls attention to the feelings of Jesus and others in a way that gives his gospel a particularly vivid and moving character. Only Mark tells us that Jesus was asleep "on a cushion" during the storm on the lake (Mk. 4:38) or that when he met the rich young man he "looked at him with love" (Mk. 10:21).

Matthew. For Matthew, with his account of the virginal conception, Jesus is the Son of God from the moment of his conception. The evangelist's high christology is evident in his addition to Peter's confession "You are the Messiah" the words "the Son of the living God" (Matt. 16:16 cf. Mk. 8:29). Matthew wrote his gospel for a community in transition.[10] The church of Antioch in the 80s was a church in which the formerly dominant Jewish Christians, now cut off from the synagogue, were becoming a minority as the number of Gentile Christians continued to increase. Like the typical pastor trying to hold a diverse community together, Matthew had to show the Jewish Christian group how deeply rooted in their own Jewish tradition they were while the Jewish community from which they came, reshaped by the Jamnia reform, was rapidly moving in a

[10]See John P. Meier, pp. 45 ff. in Raymond E. Brown and John P. Meier, *Antioch and Rome: New Testament Cradles of Catholic Christianity* (New York: Paulist Press, 1983).

different direction. At the same time he had to reexpress the Antiochene tradition to deal with the changes taking place. Thus his gospel is concerned with the rejection of Israel (Matt. 8:11-12), with justifying the Gentile future, and with showing how the authority of the church was tied to the person and institution of Jesus.

The genealogy which begins Matthew's gospel roots Jesus within the history of Israel. A central purpose of the gospel is to show how Jesus is the Messiah of the Old Testament, the fulfillment of the law and the prophets. To this end Matthew quotes the Old Testament more than any other evangelist, usually introducing the passage in question with the formula "that it might be fulfilled." Most scholars see in Matthew's division of the teaching of Jesus into five great discourses a reflection of the five books of the Torah which Jesus fulfills. The Matthean discourses include the Sermon on the Mount, the Missionary Sermon, the Parables of the Reign, the Sermon on the Church, and the Eschatological Sermon. In contrast to Paul, Matthew's attitude towards the law is much more reverent (Matt. 5:17-19). Yet the coming of the Gentiles is foreshadowed from the very beginning of the Gospel by the coming of the Magi to adore the infant Jesus.

Besides being very much a Jewish Christian gospel, Matthew is also a gospel of the church. Matthew interprets the reign of God for which he generally uses the Jewish paraphrase "kingdom of heaven" much more as a present reality: frequently he identifies it with the church (Matt. 11:11; 13:38; 16:19; 21:31). His is the only gospel in which the word "church" actually appears (Matt. 16:18, 18:17). Particularly significant is the link he establishes between Jesus, the church, and the church's authority. Jesus founds the church on Peter (Matt. 16:18), Peter is given the authority to bind and loose, thus to make binding decisions in Jesus' name (Matt. 16:19b), local communities are given power for disciplinary action including excommunication (Matt. 18:15-18), Jesus himself is present wherever two or three are gathered in his name (Matt. 18:20), and he gives the disciples after his resurrection authority to baptize and teach all nations (Matt. 28:18-20).

Luke. Like Matthew, Luke also presents Jesus as Messiah and Son of God from the time of his conception. Here also reflection on the mystery of Jesus has reached back to his "hidden life" and to the events preceeding his birth. The extensive infancy narrative which begins Luke's gospel includes the announcement of the birth of John the Baptist, the annunciation and virginal conception of Jesus, the canticles of Zechariah and Mary, the birth of the Baptist and the nativity, the adoration of the shepherds, the presentation of the child Jesus in the Temple — witnessed by Simeon and Anna — and the story of Jesus in the Temple at the age of twelve. In keeping with Luke's high christology, people address Jesus with the christological title Lord even during his public ministry.

The most literate of the evangelists, Luke wrote his two-part work, gospel and Acts, in polished Greek, imitating both classical and Hebraic styles. Selective in his presentation, he generally eliminates double traditions, Semitic expressions, and material irrelevant to his Gentile readers or not in keeping with his theological and literary purposes. Thus, he omits anything that could suggest a limitation of Jesus' human knowledge (cf. Mk. 4:40, 13:32), "cleans up" the image of the disciples, and out of a sense of reverence and respect drops a number of the more distasteful details of the passion, such as the actual kiss of betrayal from Judas (Lk. 22:47-48), the flight of the disciples, the scourging and mocking of Jesus by the soldiers, and the cry before his death "my God, my God, why have you forsaken me?" (Mk. 15:34; Matt. 27:46), substituting the more dignified "Father, into your hands I commend my spirit" (Lk. 23:46).

Paralleling the ministry of Jesus in the gospel with the ministry of the apostles in Acts, Luke presents a history of salvation which is foretold through Israel, fulfilled in Jesus, and made available to all people through the church. Both gospel and Acts are structured by a geographical movement towards a place of fulfillment. In the gospel Jesus moves from Galilee to Jerusalem where he will "enter into his glory" (Lk. 24:26). Luke mentions repeatedly that Jesus is on a journey to Jerusalem. After Pentecost the apostles journey as witnesses to Jesus "even to the ends of the earth" (Acts 1:8), represented by Rome where the book of Acts ends.

Luke's gospel is addressed primarily to Gentiles and reflects the universalism of its author. His genealogy of Jesus begins with Adam rather than with Abraham as in Matthew. He avoids Semitic expressions and references to Jewish practices unfamiliar to Gentile readers, frequently alludes to the universal significance of salvation (Lk. 2:14, 32; 24:47) and shows a special concern for marginalized groups — women, Samaritans, lepers, public sinners, and especially the poor. His gospel has frequently been called "gospel of the poor." The special relevance of the gospel for the poor and the oppressed is evident from the unique way in which Luke presents the first preaching of Jesus. While Mark and Matthew represent him as proclaiming the reign of God (or "kingdom of heaven" in Matthew's case) Luke — perhaps to translate the Jewish concept into concrete terms his Gentile readers could grasp — shows Jesus beginning his ministry by reading a passage from Isaiah describing the Messiah as one who brings good news to the poor, liberty to captives, sight to the blind, and release to prisoners (Lk. 4:18-19). The Isaiah text well characterizes Luke's interpretation of the preaching of Jesus and his attitude towards poverty and wealth. Luke alone gives us the parable of the rich fool (Lk. 12:13-21) and that of the rich man and Lazarus (Lk. 16:19-31); he states the first beatitude simply as "blest are you poor" rather than addressing the "poor in spirit" as in Matthew; Jesus tells the wealthy not to forget to include the poor in their feasts (Lk. 14:12-14) and counsels his disciples to practice a total renunciation (Lk. 5:11, 28; 14:26, 33).

Some of the parables and stories unique to Luke are among the most powerful in the gospel tradition: in addition to the infancy narrative they include the Good Samaritan, the Prodigal Son, the rich man and Lazarus, the Pharisee and the Publican, Zacchaeus, the Good Thief, and Jesus' prayer for his executioners. He frequently shows Jesus at prayer and sees in his practice a model for Christian life. Similarly he adds the word "each day" to the sayings of Jesus about taking up one's cross and following him (Lk. 9:23). The reign of God, a Jewish Palestinian concept, is less emphasized; generally for Luke it refers to the now more distant eschatological future. For the present reality of salvation he constantly calls attention to the Holy Spirit, possessed by Jesus from the beginning and poured out on the disciples after Pentecost; in Acts he shows the Spirit at work in the growth of the church. Other Lukan themes include the mercy of God and the joy occasioned by the coming of salvation.

John. In many ways John's gospel represents a mystical theology centered on Jesus. In his pre-existence christology the christological development of the New Testament reaches its completion. In the Prologue Jesus is the eternal Word of God through whom all things were created (John 1:1-3), the Word become flesh and only Son of the Father (John 1:14). The whole gospel is written from the point of view of the resurrection and the deeper understanding of Jesus to which it led. Jesus openly claims to be the Messiah (John 4:26); he identifies himself as the Son who has come into the world (John 3:17), doing only the work of the Father (John 10:37) with whom he is one (John 10:30) and bringing eternal life to those who believe in him (John 3:16, 36; 4:21). In the Johannine discourses Jesus frequently uses the formula "I AM," usually with a predicate such as "I am the bread of life" (John 6:35), "I am the good shepherd" (John 10:11, 14), "I am the resurrection and the life" (John 11:25), sometimes using the formula without modification: "When you lift up the Son of Man you will come to realize that I AM" (John 8:28). The I AM formula is used in the Old Testament and rabbinic Judaism as a divine name for Yahweh.

John's high christology also influences his eschatology.

The kingdom of God plays little role; instead he generally reinterprets or historicizes the future and apocalyptic aspects of the kingdom found in the synoptics. Rather than a future reality, judgment is now, in the encounter with Jesus (John 3:19); the future coming of the kingdom and the apocalyptic images of the coming of the Son of Man give way to an emphasis on eternal life which for the believer is a present reality, and to the believer's sharing in the divine life through the indwelling of Father, Son, and Spirit (John 14:23-26). Yet the eschatological tension we noted earlier in the preaching of Jesus and which is evident in the synoptics is present also in John. A typical example occurs in the discourse on the Bread of Life; here both present and future dimensions of the life Jesus offers become apparent: "He who feeds on my flesh and drinks my blood has life eternal and I will raise him up on the last day" (John 6:54). Thus there remains an element of future eschatology which John interprets in light of the resurrection.

The gospel is divided into the Prologue, the Book of Signs (John 1:19-12:50), the Book of Glory (13:1-20:31), and the Epilogue. The style of the author is very different from that of the synoptics. Where the latter seem to tell the story of Jesus in a carefully detailed narrative, John reads more like a selection of stories, highlighting some episodes and omitting others. For example, John follows the miracle of the loaves with a long discourse on the Bread of Life but omits the institution of the Eucharist from his account of the Last Supper. His narrative is broken by long discourses, often marked by double meanings, misunderstandings, and irony which have the effect of moving or spiraling the dialogue into more penetrating depths of meaning. Consider Nicodemus' misunderstanding of what it means to be "begotten from above" (John 3:3 ff) or the Samaritan woman's failure to grasp what Jesus means by "living water" (John 4:10 ff). John frequently will re-express in a different way a tradition appearing elsewhere. Peter's confession of Jesus as the Messiah in the synoptics appears in John as his response to the unbelief of many of the disciples at the end of the Bread of Life discourse: "Lord, to whom shall we go? You have the words of eternal life. We have come to believe; we are convinced that you are God's holy one" (John 6:68-69). Or where Luke tells us that Jesus at the Last Supper gave his disciples an instruction about serving one another as he has served them (Lk. 22:27), in his account of the Last Supper John portrays Jesus washing his disciples' feet (John 13:1-10).

In contrast to Matthew and Luke, John does not appear to reflect a concern for the developing structures of the apostolic church. The emphasis is on the role of the Spirit rather than upon apostolic authority within the community. Furthermore the Beloved Disciple seems to play as important a role as does Peter. Yet an important Petrine tradition appears in the Epilogue to John which probably represents a variant of the tradition of an authoritative commission to Peter found in Matthew 16:18. In Matthew Peter is described as the rock on which Jesus will build his church. In John the imagery is more pastoral; not the juridical language of the keys but the image of the shepherd commissioned by the risen Jesus to feed his flock (John 21:15-17). However the basic message is the same.

Another passage in John with important ecclesial significance appears towards the end of the Bread of Life discourse in chapter 6. Verses 51-58 move the dialogue from a sapiential understanding of Jesus as the "bread of life" come down from heaven to reveal the Father (John 6:35-50) to a specifically eucharistic focus. Here the emphasis is not on believing but on eating and drinking the flesh and blood of the Son of Man. Verses 51-58 may originally have been part of the Johannine account of the institution of the Eucharist, reworked by the final editor of the gospel into its present position in the Bread of Life discourse, building on the eucharistic connotations already present in the story of the multiplication of the loaves (John 6:1-13) and the earlier part of the Bread of Life discourse itself.

Conclusion

The four gospels represent the end product of a long process of development. Jesus himself taught that the new age of salvation had already begun. The power of God's reign was evident in the miracles of Jesus and his proclamation of the forgiveness of sins, while his practice of table-fellowship with his friends and with those outside the law extended the offer of salvation to all people. Though Jesus spoke much more of the one he called "abba" than of himself, it is still clear from his preaching that a decision for or against himself was the same thing as a decision for or against the kingdom.

From the time of the resurrection the disciples proclaimed the good news that God had raised Jesus from the dead and struggled to express the meaning of the Jesus story in the language and images of Jewish messianic hope. But as the early church's christology developed it quickly overflowed the very tradition used to express it. The four written gospels witness to this christological development and reflect different stages in the process. Each gospel proclaims anew the good news of the Christ event; each reflects the unique point of view of its author and the situation and needs of the communities to which it was directed.

4. Meeting Jesus

> The Lord said . . . Should not this daughter of Abraham
> here who has been in the bondage of Satan for eighteen
> years have been released from her shackles on the
> Sabbath?
>
> Luke 13:15-16

When Jesus looked out over the congregation in the synagogue and saw this woman, stooped under the burden of
her infirmity, he approached her and laid his hand on her
to heal her. "Immediately," Luke tells us, "she stood up
straight and began thanking God" (Lk. 13:13). For the
woman, meeting Jesus meant being set free from a physio-
logical affliction, a physical healing which also touched her
spirit so that she broke forth in praise of God.

The gospels tell us many stories of people who were transformed by their encounters with Jesus. The experience of
meeting him was something special, an experience which
made real for each of them the concrete meaning of the reign
of God. So also those who encountered the risen Jesus were
incredibly affected by that experience, whatever it was. They
too were changed, transformed, empowered, so that those
few disciples who had fled in terror from the garden at Jesus'
arrest had within a few years turned his movement into a
world religion. In trying to convey the meaning of that
experience of meeting the risen Jesus the New Testament
writers speak of peace (Matt. 28:9; Lk. 24:36; John 20:19, 21,
26), the forgiveness of sins (Acts 5:30-31; 1 Cor. 15:3-5, 17-18;

Lk. 24:47; John 20:23), and the gift of the Spirit (Acts 2:32-33; Lk. 24:47; John 20:22). Both the fragments of the resurrection kerygma (Acts 2:32-33; 5:30-31; 1 Cor. 15:3-5) and the later, more detailed and dramatic appearance stories in the gospels are more than simple reports; they represent theological interpretations of the disciples' "Easter experience."[1] This is especially true of the Easter appearance stories; they are highly theological in character, composed around the themes of the risen Lord manifesting himself to his disciples, their acknowledgment, and their apostolic commission to witness to what God had accomplished. These themes are themselves theological interpretations of an experience which cannot be expressed in a literal way. Certainly the appearance stories cannot be taken as literal descriptions of what the disciples saw and heard. For all their concreteness of detail, they remain symbolic, expressing through image and story the meaning of the disciples' Easter experience.

What is more important for us and for the church's proclamation today is to recapture something of the experience of meeting Jesus which has been communicated by the stories themselves and by the themes so frequently associated with them, forgiveness, peace, and the gift of the Spirit. Without denying either the uniqueness of the disciples' Easter experience or the priority of the risen Lord who manifests himself, we want to try and make more concrete the experience of that encounter. Furthermore, we can speak of the experience of meeting Jesus either in regard to his earthly life or in regard to his making himself known to his disciples after his death. The mode of his presence was certainly different in each case, but his effect on those who met him must have been similar. Indeed, just as the presence of someone we love has a unique effect on us, leaving as it were a unique signature of that person's presence on our experience, so also the disciples must have been able to recognize the risen Lord's presence at least in part because they were already familiar with how his presence touched

[1]The term "Easter experience" is from Edward Schillebeeckx, *Jesus: An Experiment in Christology* (New York: Crossroad, 1981), pp. 379 ff.

and affected them. Thus we are concerned with the effect of his presence — with what we call "meeting Jesus," and not just with the Easter experience as such.

What then can we learn from the New Testament about the experience of meeting Jesus? Monika Hellwig has stressed that Jesus, as the evangelists present him, mediated redemption through the quality of his own faith and ministry; he was able to open the eyes and hearts of others by his presence, his healing touch, his ability to release them from their burdens, refocus their imaginations, and give them new possibilities, new life through his love.[2] Most important, through his ministry the reign of God took on a personal, salvific meaning in the life of each person who encountered him. Salvation was not an abstract theological idea, but a vivid personal experience, healing people of physical infirmities and psychological compulsions, freeing them from their sins — in short, liberating all who opened themselves to him of whatever prevented them from receiving the divine gift he offered. By way of illustration we will begin with Paul, since he alone among the New Testament writers has included in his letters something of his personal experience. Then we will consider some stories told by the evangelists of others who encountered Jesus. Here especially we must let the symbolism of the gospel stories speak to us.

Paul

The man known to history as St. Paul was born Saul at Tarsus in what is now Turkey. Educated as a Pharisee, Saul was well versed in the law, by his own admission so zealous to live out all the traditions of his ancestors that he "made progress in Jewish observance far beyond most of my contemporaries" (Gal. 2:14). It is not difficult to imagine the same passion and strong feeling so obvious in his letters consuming him in his efforts to live the life of a Pharisee. He was a man of strong character and passionate single-

---

[2]Monika K. Hellwig. *Jesus: The Compassion of God* (Wilmington, Delaware: Michael Glazier, 1983), p. 83.

mindedness, so obsessed with his own religious quest and his tradition as he understood it that he became a persecutor of those who threatened it. According to the Acts of the Apostles Saul was implicated in the stoning of Stephen (Acts 7:58) and afterwards began a persecution of the disciples that was to be long remembered (Acts 9:1-2). Thus there was something of the fanatic in Saul the Pharisee; his extreme reaction to the challenge presented by the early disciples suggests that he shared some of the narrowness and inflexibility of the compulsive religious personality.

This compulsive dimension of Paul's personality should not be minimized. The rigidity and even fanaticism he displayed as a Pharisee cannot be attributed simply to the influence of that particular religious tradition. The Pharisees were not all fanatics. However much they opposed the early disciples, they could also produce men of discernment like Gamaliel who advised the Sanhedrin not to use violence against the disciples, arguing that if their movement was not from God it would not long endure (Acts 5:38). This wise man, according to Acts 22:3, was Paul's teacher: The legalism of the Pharisees may have reinforced Paul's own personal rigidity, but it did not cause it; that rigidity, the shadow side of his own strength of character, was rooted in the structure of his personality and in his personal religious needs.

Still, for all his intolerance. Paul was a deeply religious man. The great issue of his life, both as a Pharisee and later as a Christian, was righteousness before God. This "quest for righteousness" — at root a quest for divine acceptance — is the thread that runs through his life story.[3] He thought he had found the way to righteousness in the teaching of the Pharisees on the perfect observance of the law, and he prided himself in being "above reproach when it came to justice based on the law" (Phil. 3:6). But his religious security was shaken by his contact with the early Christian disciples, for it was precisely his concept of salvation which was challenged by their proclamation of "Jesus is Lord," espe-

---

[3]See John S. Dunne, *A Search for God in Time and Memory* (London: Macmillan, 1967), pp. 36-37.

cially when this was proclaimed by the Hellenist Jewish Christians who were already beginning to distance themselves from the obligations of the law. The fact that in speaking of his former persecution of the church Paul twice calls attention to his zeal for the traditions of his ancestors (Gal. 1:13-14) or for the legal observance of the Pharisees (Phil. 3:5-6) suggests that it was the more "liberal" Hellenist Jewish Christians who first aroused his hostility. They were a direct threat to his concept of righteousness, and he responded with violence.

The experience of meeting the risen Jesus (Gal. 1:12-16) totally changed Paul's life. His conversion did not take away his great concern for righteousness, or as it is often called justification, but it turned the state of the question upside down. It was to emerge as a central theme in the Good News as Paul proclaimed it: justification was not something to be earned; it was a free, unmerited gift of God, accomplished for us through the death of Jesus and ours through faith. Paul's theology of justification by faith rather than by observance of the law (Rom. 3:28; Gal. 2:16) is well known. It was a message of liberation for the infant church rapidly outgrowing its cradle in Judaism as it moved into the pagan world. But it was also a message of liberation for Paul himself. His meditation on sin and death in Romans 7 is eloquent testimony to his own struggle to live righteously, and to the tragic discovery of the vitiating power of sin working within him, revealed by the very law he was unable to live up to (Rom. 7:7-25). Paul ends his meditation with the cry, "What a wretched man I am! Who can free me from this body under the power of death?" (Rom. 7:24).

The answer was Jesus Christ; through him Paul began to experience a new kind of freedom, and so the freedom of the Christian, like justification by faith, becomes another central theme in his preaching. The freedom that comes with faith in Christ Jesus is for Paul threefold: freedom from the obligations of the law (Rom. 7:3 ff), freedom from sin (Rom. 6:18-23), and finally, as a consequence, freedom from death (Rom. 6:21 ff). Even the world of nature will one day share in what Paul calls "the glorious freedom of the children of God" (Rom. 8:21).

Paul writes about freedom because he first came to experience it in his own personal life. His encounter with the risen Lord was the beginning of a profound conversion, a complete reordering of his ideas, values, and commitments. He writes, "Those things I used to consider gain I have now reappraised as loss in the light of Christ. I have come to rate all as loss in the light of the surpassing knowledge of my Lord Jesus Christ. For his sake I have forfeited everything; I have accounted all else rubbish so that Christ may be my wealth" (Phil. 3:7-8). Specifically that meant giving up a religious tradition to which he was passionately attached and the vision of God which it mediated. However his conversion affected more than his religious vision; it also touched his affectivity. The experience of meeting Jesus left him a changed man, gentled in spirit and freed from the tyranny of his own inner need to win God's approval by what he could accomplish through his observance of the law. His own inner freedom can be sensed in his letters and in the manner of his guidance of the communities over which he watched as an apostle. He can accept his own weakness and even boast of it, for it becomes an occasion for experiencing Christ's "power" (*dynamis*) within him (2 Cor. 12:9-10). Power is a word he used frequently in connection with his experience of the risen Lord. He speaks of knowing the power of Christ's resurrection (Phil. 3:10) and frequently refers to the power of the gospel (1 Thes. 1:5; Rom. 1:16; 1 Cor. 1:18). To preach the gospel is the only compulsion left to him (1 Cor. 9:16 ff).

Thus Paul's message that a person "is not justified by legal observance but by faith in Jesus Christ" (Gal. 2:16) was a gracious personal discovery just as the freedom he proclaimed to a church undergoing an immense cultural transition — a freedom in the Spirit against the letter of the law — was not the result of a theological deduction but flowed from the inner freedom he gained from his own encounter with the risen Jesus.

Stories from the Gospels

The gospels tell the stories of others whose lives were changed by the experience of meeting Jesus. Some of these stories are based on what was remembered about some of the early disciples of Jesus while others were created by the evangelists from their own experience of the risen Lord's transforming power in the lives of men and women. It is generally unquestioned that the first (male, thus official) witness to the resurrection was Peter (1 Cor. 15:5; Lk. 24:34; cf. Mk. 16:7), the Peter who had denied Jesus on the night of his arrest. [4] Of course the New Testament cannot convey just how Peter came to experience the risen Jesus. But for this man who loved Jesus and who must have been tortured by his denial, meeting the risen Jesus must have been an experience of forgiveness and reconciliation. This is affirmed by an old tradition of an Easter appearance to Peter in Galilee which is preserved in the form of reworked fragments in chapter 21 of John; here the commission to pastoral leadership he receives implicitly rehabilitates him to his position of leadership among the disciples (John 21:1-19). The redactor of the passage sharpens the relation between Peter's denial and his rehabilitation; both take place near a charcoal fire (John 18:18; 21:9), while for each of the three times Peter denied him Jesus asks, "Simon, son of John, do you love me?" and instructs him, "feed my sheep" (John 21:15-17).

The Peter who was restored to his place among the disciples must have been a different man from the blustery Peter of the gospels so little aware of his own weakness; more important than the self-knowledge he gained was the depth of his experience of Jesus' love for him in spite of his limitations. He went on to become a leader of the early Christian community and ultimately to give his life in witness to his Lord.

Still others were profoundly changed by meeting with Jesus during his historical ministry. The story of the tax

[4]At that time in the Jewish tradition a woman was not accepted as a valid witness.

collector Zacchaeus (Lk. 19:1-10) may represent a type of those "tax collectors and offenders against the law" (Mk. 2:16) so despised by the self-righteous among the scribes and Pharisees. Permitted by Roman law to keep for themselves whatever they were able to gain over the fixed annual sum they paid for the right to collect the customs tax, they were themselves caught in an economic system that encouraged abuse and extortion. Jesus went out of his way to minister to them, eating with them and calling them also to God's reign. The story of Zacchaeus illustrates the case of one who through meeting Jesus was moved to repentance and enabled to break out of a position of privilege in an exploitative system, making retribution beyond what the law required.

One whose memory has left a deep imprint on the gospel tradition was Mary Magdalene. Not to be confused with the sister of Martha, Mary of Bethany, who according to John anointed Jesus shortly before his death (John 12:1-8), the other Mary was from Magdala in Galilee. Her meeting with Jesus must have been a powerful experience of personal healing and liberation for the gospels tell us that Jesus had driven from her seven demons (Mk. 16:9; Lk. 8:2). She was deeply touched by her meeting with Jesus and became one of his most faithful disciples. She was among those women who assisted Jesus during his ministry and was one of the few disciples courageous enough to follow him to his crucifixion (Mk. 15:40) and burial (Mk. 15:47). The synoptic tradition lists her first among the women who discovered the empty tomb. A tradition, very possibly historical, that she was the first to whom the risen Jesus appeared (Mk. 16:9; John 20:11-18; cf. Matt. 28:8-10) testifies to her great love for Jesus.

One who was not changed by his encounter with Jesus was the traitor, Judas Iscariot. The figure of Judas has long fascinated novelists and playwrights. How could one so close to Jesus, a member of the Twelve who had traveled the roads of Galilee with Jesus and shared the intimate fellowship of his meals betray him for a few pieces of silver? Raymond Brown points out that the gospels suggest two possible answers: first, that Judas was an instrument of the devil (Lk. 22:3; John 13:2, 27; also John 6:70), and second, that he was motivated by his love of money. John goes so far as to call him a thief (John 12:6).[5] What actually took place in the heart of Judas remains a mystery, but his story too is instructive. It is proof that grace — the encounter with Jesus himself — cannot take away our human freedom. Those who opened themselves to Jesus were deeply changed by their encounter with him, but there was no magic in the transformation. During his ministry Jesus constantly called for faith on the part of those he healed; where it was lacking he could work no miracles (Mk. 6:5).

A similar dynamic is evident in the stories of the appearances of the risen Lord. The stories strongly suggest that the Easter experience of the disciples did not take away their freedom. Rather than compelling them to believe, it drew upon their faith. First of all, the risen Jesus manifested himself, not to his enemies, but to his friends, to those who had opened their hearts to him. The one exception here might be Paul, but he too however misguided, was honest in his quest and zealous for what he perceived as in accord with God's will.

Secondly, the appearance stories themselves are not descriptions of how the disciples came to their Easter faith; they serve rather to proclaim the Easter faith of the early church. In interpreting theologically the disciples' Easter experience they underline the importance of acknowledgment and faith in the recognition of the glorified Jesus. The stress on the initial non-recognition, confusion, and doubt of the disciples at the appearance of the risen Lord suggests that coming to belief in Jesus' victory over death was more a gradual process than an instantaneous recognition compelling belief. Thus, the disciples doubt the report of Mary Magdalene and the women who were at the tomb (Mk. 16:11; Lk. 24:9-11). In describing the appearance of Jesus to the disciples in Galilee Matthew writes: "And when they saw him

[5]Raymond E. Brown, *The Anchor Bible: The Gospel According to John (i-xii)* Garden City, New York: Doubleday & Co., 1966), p. 453.

they worshipped him, but some doubted" (Matt. 28:17; R.S.V. trans.). In Luke the two disciples on the road to Emmaus only gradually come to a recognition of Jesus (Lk. 24:13 ff); when Jesus appears to the eleven in the upper room the disciples experienced "panic" and "fright" and thought they were seeing a ghost. Jesus must lead them to belief (Lk. 24:37 ff). In John Mary Magdalene does not recognize Jesus, mistaking him for the gardener (John 20:14) and the disciples in the Johannine appendix do not recognize him when he meets them on the shore of the Sea of Tiberias (John 21:4).

Thus even those disciples to whom the risen Jesus manifested himself had to respond in faith. In this, their experience was not so different from our own. Meeting Jesus, whether before Easter, after, or even today always calls for a free human response to his initiative.

Those who opened their hearts to him were touched and changed; they experienced forgiveness, acceptance, love, and an inner healing and empowerment which opened a new vision and suggested a new life and a new Spirit. Furthermore their experience was essentially a shared one. They testified to one another, supported and encouraged one another, and no doubt shared meals together as they had before within the community he had created, perhaps reassembled after his death and their flight (Mk. 14:15) by Peter. Within this context the disciples came to experience Jesus in a new way. And so we must turn to the church.

Conclusion

The stories the New Testament presents of the friends and disciples of Jesus are stories of men and women profoundly changed by their experience of meeting him. Whether historical or symbolic, they illustrate that the personal transformation they experienced from the encounter cannot be reduced to a moral conversion; they were also touched intellectually and affectively and in a way that was deeply personal to each of them. The gospel stories and especially the resurrection appearances also show that grace never takes away human freedom; there remains always a need for a free human response, a response in faith.

5. THE CHURCH IN THE APOSTOLIC AGE

> Those who accepted his message were baptized; some
> three thousand were added that day. They devoted them-
> selves to the apostles' instruction and the communal life,
> to the breaking of the bread and the prayers.
>
> Acts 2:41-42

What is the church? These two verses, coming towards the
end of the second chapter of the Acts of the Apostles,
suggest an answer. Verse 41 closes Peter's great Pentecost
sermon, a Lukan composition. Verse 42 is part of a Lukan
summary (Acts 2:42-47), an ideal sketch of the life of the
early community which links the Pentecost sermon with
Peter's cure of a cripple which follows. We can see in these
two verses a theological outline or summary of the church's
constitutive elements. They include:

1. *baptism.* A rite of initiation into the Christian community, baptism "in the name of Jesus" incorporates
   one into the salvation he proclaimed and bestows the
   Spirit (Acts 2:38).

2. *the apostles' instruction.* Literally the apostles teaching (*didachē*), the expression points to the pivotal role

of the apostles in the early church which remains bound to their teaching.

3. *the communal life.* The Pauline term *koinōnia,* communion or fellowship, appearing here for the only time in Luke, refers to the shared life of the disciples, here expressed as a sharing of material goods (cf. vv 44-45). The church is essentially a community of believers.

4. *the breaking of the bread.* Generally accepted as a Lukan term for the community's sacramental meal or Eucharist (cf. Luke 24:30, 35; Acts 20:7, 11). The church is not just a community; it is essentially a eucharistic community.

5. *the prayers.* Prayer also is essential to the life of the church.

Thus in a few lines Luke sketches an ideal theological picture of the church. Yet how close does this picture come to the life of the earliest Christian communities? Recovering that history is a difficult task. The only New Testament author who seems to be concerned with describing it is Luke, but his Acts of the Apostles, written as an apology for the growth of early Christianity, is much more dominated by theological concerns than by the care for careful reconstruction and exact reporting of the modern historian. Luke wants to show how the movement of the gospel from Jerusalem "to the ends of the earth" (Act 1:8), thus the development of Christianity out of Judaism and into a world religion, is the work of the Holy Spirit. To accomplish this he tends to idealize the story; problems are smoothed out, complex developments are condensed, traditions are not infrequently recast for theological reasons, and later church structures are sometimes retrojected into earlier history.

At the same time there is more history contained in the Acts than some of the more skeptical German scholars are willing to recognize. Therefore in considering the earliest communities we will follow Luke's account, though somewhat cautiously, checking it when possible with Paul and expanding it with what can be learned from the exegetical and historical studies of contemporary scholars.

Early Palestinian Communities

In describing the life of the early Jerusalem church Luke writes "They went to the temple area together every day, while in their homes they broke bread" (Acts 2:46). His picture underlines the obvious; these early Christians are still very much Jews. They are still participating in the cult of the Temple, though they gather in their homes for the communal meal. The church begins as a sect within Judaism. It was not, however, the only one. The discovery of the Dead Sea scrolls reveals the existence of another sect within first century Palestinian Judaism, the apocalyptic community at Qumran. There are some striking similarities between this Jewish movement and the early Jerusalem church as Luke describes it. Furthermore, the reconstruction of the Q source used by Matthew and Luke illustrates that primitive Palestinian Christianity, broader than the Jerusalem community, also represented an apocalyptic movement.

Q is dominated by an apocalyptic eschatology. It suggests a movement which continued Jesus' proclamation of the reign of God and awaited his return as the Son of Man. The members of this movement, many of them wandering charismatic missionaries, proclaimed his message in the different villages, using a collection of his sayings. The majority of these sayings preserved in Q are apocalyptic in form, looking forward to a sudden and unexpected return of Jesus "like the lightning that flashes from one end of the sky to the other" (Luke 17:24). As in the early Jerusalem community (Acts 2:17-18), the members of these communities considered the revival of prophecy in their midst as a sign of the end times.

Although the Q source does not have a passion narrative, certainly the early Jerusalem community had its own traditions concerning Jesus' crucifixion and death, the Jerusalem resurrection appearances, and the Last Supper. These also became part of the inheritance of the later church from Palestinian Christianity. That inheritance includes elements of the church's worship, specifically baptism, the sacramental meal, and various liturgical acclamations which kept their Hebrew or Aramaic forms even in the Greek-speaking communities, expressions such as "Amen," "Alleluia" (praise Yahweh), and "Maranatha"(Our Lord, come!), generally presumed to have been used in the celebration of the Lord's Supper.

Since the discovery of the Dead Sea scrolls, the parallels between the Qumran community and the early Jerusalem church have been carefully noted. Though there are significant differences, both practiced ritual purification, a ritual communal meal, and some form of a community of goods. Both saw their own community as the renewed Israel and gave prominence to a leadership group of twelve, a symbolic representation of the twelve tribes. Both shared an apocalyptic eschatology focused on the Day of the Lord. And both saw themselves as the legitimate heir to the Jewish scriptural tradition. Recently several authors have stressed this, calling attention to the fact that both of these Jewish sectarian movements shared a similar method of interpreting the Jewish scriptures, seeing them as being fulfilled within their own respective communities.[1]

But while the Qumran community could only point to itself and await the divine intervention, the early church proclaimed the fulfillment of the Jewish scriptures in Jesus and thus saw itself as the true people of God. Here is the crucial difference that gave the early Christian community its own unique identity. Christian baptism in the name of Jesus was not a sign of ritual purity but of moral regenera-

[1]Norman Perrin and Dennis C. Duling, *The New Testament: An Introduction* (New York: Harcourt Brace Jovanovich, Inc., 1982) (Second Edition), pp. 97 ff. Daniel J. Harrington, *God's People in Christ* (Philadelphia: Fortress Press, 1980), pp. 35 ff.

tion and new life in the Spirit. The communal meal was not merely anticipation of the eschatological banquet; it was also the joyful celebration of the presence of the risen Lord (cf. Lk. 24:35). Most importantly, the inner logic of the community's faith in what God had accomplished gave a completely different orientation to their way of life. Rather than withdrawing into a monastic isolation as a preparation for the coming apocalyptic struggle like the community of Qumran, the Christian community was from the beginning inspired with a missionary spirit. The good news was to be shared, even if initially its missionary effort was to be directed only towards the Jewish community of which it remained a part.

Our knowledge of the organization of the early Palestinian community is minimal. According to Luke the earliest community at Jerusalem was led by the Twelve (Judas having been replaced — Acts 1:15 ff) functioning as a council or college, with Peter acting as a leader and spokesman (Acts 1-6). This view is partially confirmed by Paul who reports that several years after his conversion he "went up to Jerusalem to get to know Cephas," referring to Peter by his Aramaic name "rock" (Gal. 1:18). Again, some fourteen years later he returned to see the "leaders" in Jerusalem about his missionary policy; he mentions meeting the three "pillars, James, Cephas, and John" who confirm his practice and his mission among the Gentiles (Gal. 2:1-10). We know less about leadership in the other Palestinian communities represented by Q; their leaders seem to have included wandering missionaries and charismatic prophets, perhaps also the heads of the house churches in the local communities (Lk. 10:5 ff; Matt. 10:12 ff).

An important turning point in the life of the early Jerusalem church lies behind the story of the institution of the Seven (Acts 6:1-6). On the surface the story concerns a dispute between the disciples "who spoke Greek" and those "who spoke Hebrew" because the widows of the former were being neglected. The solution is the appointing of seven assistants who will help with the distribution of food, freeing the Twelve to concentrate on "prayer and the ministry of the word." The story has been traditionally associated with the institution of the diaconate, but it actually represents the memory of something far more significant. The passage contains an early historical tradition, joined by the redactor of Acts to the Stephen episode[2], concerning a dispute early in the history of the community between the "Hebrews," the Hebrew or Aramaic speaking members of the original Jerusalem community, and the "Hellenists," Greek-speaking Jews from the Diaspora, a more liberal, cosmopolitan group without the same commitment to the Temple cult and Torah of the Jewish Christians of Jerusalem and Palestine. The problem is resolved by giving the Hellenists their own leaders. The Seven are authoritatively appointed to their office, the nature of which is evident from the following chapters. They are seen exercising the same ministry of the word that the Twelve were said to have reserved for themselves. Thus the passage is witness to an early sharing of the original apostolic leadership.

According to Luke's account, after this several events happened in rapid succession. First, as the Hellenist Jewish Christians began preaching in Jerusalem — represented by Stephen whose great sermon in chapter 7 of Acts reinterprets the history of Israel in terms of disobedience and culminates with an attack on the Temple (Acts 7:45-50) — a violent persecution breaks out which leads to Stephen's death and the scattering of the community. Yet Luke notes that the apostles (and probably other members of the original Jerusalem community) remained in Jerusalem (Acts 8:1). Secondly, Luke situates the story of Paul's conversion within the time-frame of this persecution (Acts 9:1 ff), around the middle of the 30s or earlier. Apparently it was during this time that some of the Hellenist Jewish Christians began to distance themselves from the law, judging from Paul's comments that he had once persecuted the church out of zeal for the traditions of his ancestors, as we

---

[2]See Joseph T. Lienhard, "Acts 6:1-6: A Redactional View," *Catholic Biblical Quarterly* 37 (1975) 228-236, p. 236.

noted earlier. Thirdly, Luke shows us the word of God spreading through Samaria, Phoenicia, Cyprus, and ultimatley to Antioch, preached by the Hellenists driven from Jerusalem by the persecution.

When the word reaches Antioch it is welcomed by some Greeks, that is by non-Jews as well, leading "the church in Jerusalem" to send Barnabas to investigate (Acts 11:22). Luke's story of Peter receiving the Gentile convert Cornelius in chapter 10 — like his raising of the good woman Dorcas (Acts 9:36 ff) — no doubt reflects theological concerns more properly than history; it is important for Luke to show that an initiative as important for the future of the Church as the admission of the Gentiles could only come about through the leadership of Peter. However many scholars believe that it was the Hellenists at Antioch who first accepted Gentiles into the faith.

It is difficult for us to appreciate the magnitude of the challenge the conversion of the Gentiles presented to the original Jewish Christians. After almost two thousand years of Christian history we take it for granted. But for a first-century Jewish Christian, whose whole identity was still very much tied up with being a member of a unique people united by a covenant symbolized by circumcision, by the cult of the Temple and the observance of the law, it was profound. The experience of God was mediated by these forms. The precise question was not so much could a non-Jew share in the blessings promised to God's chosen people, but could he or she do so without becoming a Jew. If the answer was to be yes, and of course it was, thanks to the clarity of people like Paul, what then did that mean for the self-understanding of the Jewish Christians? They certainly must have felt that not just their tradition but their own personal identity was being called into question. When we realize how great an obstacle our attachment to our own confessional traditions — whether we are Catholics or Lutherans or Methodists or evangelicals — is to the ecumenical movement today, then perhaps we can appreciate a little more the difficult transition through which the early church had to go.

The transition began at Antioch. This church, founded in the late 30s, was the first significant community of both Jews and Gentiles. It was here, even before Paul, that the Gentile mission began, though Paul himself would soon be intimately associated with it. It is significant that it was at Antioch that the disciples were called "Christians" for the first time (Acts 11:26).

We don't know much about Paul's activities during this period. A few years after his conversion he made a visit to Jerusalem and spent several weeks with Peter (Gal. 2:18). Some time after this he became involved in missionary work, probably in Syria, evangelizing the Gentiles and receiving them into the church without the requirements of circumcision and the observance of the law. But the question about Gentiles and the law had become critical; it was an issue the entire church had to face. Another major turning point in the life of the early church was at hand.

The "Council" of Jerusalem

The issue was resolved by what has become known as the "apostolic council" of Jerusalem. The New Testament gives us two separate accounts of this meeting (Gal. 2:1-10; Acts 15). In Galatians Paul stresses his own initiative in bringing his solution before the leaders in Jerusalem for their confirmation. And in spite of some opposition from those "false brethren" who insisted on circumcision, he received it; he writes that he and Barnabas received the "handclasp of fellowship" (*koinōnia*) from James, Cephas, and John and the acknowledgment of their mission to the Gentiles (Gal. 2:1-10). Paul goes to some lengths to parallel his own mission and authority among the Gentiles with that of Peter in his mission to the Jews, no doubt because members of the circumcision party had been busy among his communities in Galatia trying to undermine his authority.

Luke's account in Acts 15 leaves a somewhat different impression. He describes Paul and Barnabas as being delegated by the church in Antioch to bring the question before "the apostles and presbyters" in Jerusalem (Acts 15:2). The church in Jerusalem gathers to consider the question; Luke pictures a model conciliar assembly, with debates taking place before the authorities, the apostles and presbyters, and the entire church. Paul doesn't mention presbyters; it is not clear when this structure emerged in Jerusalem but about the time of the council or shortly after James, sometimes called "the brother of the Lord," became the leader of the church in Jerusalem, exercising his authority over a council of elders (*presbyteroi*) whose function seems to have been governmental and administrative.

According to Luke, Peter and James play the crucial roles in arguing for the Gentiles' freedom from circumcision and the law (Acts 15:6-21). They carry the day, but not without a compromise which Paul doesn't mention, for the decision of the council includes an "apostolic decree" added at the request of James requiring that the Gentiles abstain from meat sacrificed to idols, from foods prepared with blood, from the meat of animals which had been strangled, and from illicit sexual unions (Acts 15:29). In other words, the council did not require circumcision of the Gentiles of Antioch, but it did impose on them some "kosher" regulations. In the opinion of many scholars, this compromise was probably worked out sometime after the council.

In Galatians the same issue surfaces in Paul's account of Peter's visit to Antioch. At first Peter was eating with the Gentile converts there, but when others "from James" protested he ceased. Paul objected violently, accusing Barnabas of joining in their dishonesty and challenging Peter: "If you who are a Jew are living according to Gentile ways rather than Jewish, by what logic do you force the Gentiles to adopt Jewish ways?" (Gal. 2:14). Apparently, however, Peter and Antioch adopted a compromise enabling Jewish and Gentile Christians to preserve some kind of *koinōnia*. Paul himself parted company with Barnabas after this and shook the dust of Antioch from his feet, returning only once to this important church (Acts 18:22) and not mentioning it again in his writings.[3] However, as he began the extensive missionary work reflected in his epistles, he was careful to maintain *koinōnia* with the mother church in Jerusalem, as his efforts to have his churches contribute financially to assist the poor of that community attest (Rom. 15:25-26; 1 Cor. 16:1-4; 2 Cor. 8:1-5).

The Pauline Churches

The years following the council of Jerusalem were to be Paul's most productive. Within less than a decade he had established a number of churches in Galatia, crossed into Europe founding churches at Philippi, Thessalonica, Berea, and Corinth, and returned to Asia Minor to establish a church at Ephesus, the capital of the Roman province of Asia. Because of his letters and the fact that Paul is the focus of the second half of Acts, we are more familiar with this period than perhaps any other.

Paul's method, described in Acts, was to go first to the synagogue to preach to the Jews. Some would join him but eventually there would be opposition and he would be forced to turn to the Gentiles. Among his converts were many associated with the synagogues described as "God-fearers" (cf. Acts 18:7); these were Gentiles attracted by the Jewish understanding of God and Jewish moral teaching but prevented from full membership by the requirements of circumcision and the observance of the law. They welcomed Paul's preaching that in Christ Jesus both Jews and Greeks were "descendants of Abraham" and inheritors of all that was promised, thus members of God's people (Gal. 3:28-29). During his stay within a community Paul refused the support due him as a missionary apostle (1 Cor. 9:1-18), prefer-

[3]In their important study *Antioch and Rome* (New York: Paulist Press, 1982) Raymond E. Brown and John P. Meier argue that it was not a purely Pauline Christianity that dominated the NT and post NT times, but rather a more conservative Christianity better able to accommodate diverse approaches, such as that which emerged at Antioch and Rome in connection with Peter. See especially Preface, p. viii.

ring to support himself by his trade as a tentmaker. His conviction that the risen Lord would soon return in glory gave a certain urgency to his missionary work (cf. 1 Cor. 7:26 ff) and his churches shared his apocalyptic outlook.

Paul refers to his communities as "churches." The word church, *ekklēsia*, appears some sixty-five times in his writings, more frequently than in the rest of the New Testament combined. From the Greek *ex* (out) and *kaleō* (to call), *ekklēsia* means literally "those who have been called out," thus an assembly or congregation. The secular Greek word ekklesia, used for a civic assembly of the people, was used in the Septuagint to translate the Hebrew expression *Kehal Yahweh,* the assembly of the Lord, used for a religious or cultic assembly of the people.

Contrary to the generally accepted view that *ekklēsia* at first always means the local community and only later, in the Deutero-Pauline letters, comes to stand for the whole church, Paul uses *ekklēsia* in several senses. First, he sometimes uses the expression *hē kat oikon ekklēsia* meaning "church in their house" or house church (1 Cor. 16:19; Philemon 2; Rom. 16:5).[4] A house church was a local assembly of Christians who gathered regularly in a private home for worship, catechesis, and fellowship. The host or householder would have been the leader of the community and possibly on the basis of the parallels with Jewish practice the one who presided at the Eucharist. The many women whom Paul acknowledges in his letters as playing important roles in the early communities raise the interesting possibility that some of them also may have been householders with churches meeting in their homes (cf. Rom. 16:1; 1 Cor. 1:11). Certainly Nymphia in Col. 4:15 seems to have been a woman, though some versions translate the name and following adjective as masculine.

Secondly, Paul uses *ekklēsia* for the local or regional

---

[4] Raymond E. Brown discusses the NT house churches in "New Testament Background for the Concept of Local Church" in *The Catholic Theological Society of America: Proceedings of the Thirty-Sixth Annual Convention* 36 (1981) 1-14, pp. 4-8; see also Hans-Josef Klauck, "The house-church as a way of life," *Theology Digest* 30 (1982) 153-57.

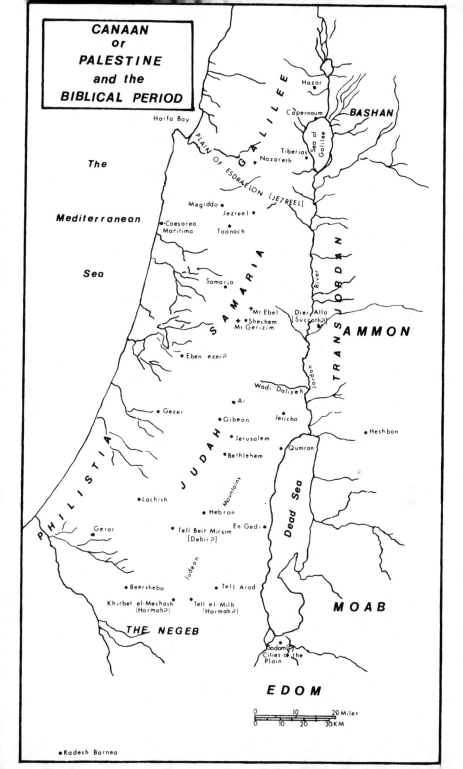

CANAAN
or
PALESTINE
and the
BIBLICAL PERIOD

The

Mediterranean

Sea

Haifa Bay

PLAIN OF ESDRAELON [JEZREEL]

G A L I L E E

Hazor

Capernaum

BASHAN

Tiberias

Sea of Galilee

Nazareth

Megiddo

Jezreel

Caesarea Maritima

Taanach

S A M A R I A

Samaria

River

+ Mt Ebel

+ Shechem
Mt Gerizim

Dier Alla
[Succoth?]

T R A N S J O R D A N

A M M O N

Eben-ezer?

Wadi Daliyeh

Jordan

Gezer

Ai

Gibeon

Jericho

Heshbon

J U D A H

Jerusalem

Bethlehem

Qumran

Lachish

Mountains

Hebron

En Gedi

Dead Sea

Gerar

Tell Beit Mirsim
[Debir?]

Judean

Beersheba

Tell Arad

Khirbet el-Meshash
(Hormah?)

Tell el-Milh
(Hormah?)

M O A B

THE NEGEB

Sodom?
Cities of the
Plain

E D O M

0   10   20 Miles
0   10   20   30 KM

Kadesh-Barnea

church. He speaks of "the church of God which is in Corinth" (1 Cor. 1:2) or "the churches in Galatia" (Gal. 1:2). This is his most common usage.

Finally, he occasionally uses church in a more general sense which approaches its universal meaning in the Deutero-Pauline letters. From Paul's statement in 1 Corinthians that "God has set up in the church first apostles, second prophets, third teachers" (1 Cor. 12:28) or the one in Galatians in which he speaks of having persecuted "the church of God" (Gal. 1:13) it is not so long a way to the statement in Colossians that Christ "is the head of the body, the church" (Col. 1:18). Here the church has come together with the image of the body of Christ, a concept which is fundamental to Paul's understanding of church as we shall see below.

Paul insists that his churches remain faithful to the *paradosis,* the tradition he has "handed on" to them (2 Thes. 2:15; 3:6). Christian teaching for Paul is tradition. But in instructing his communities he is generally careful to distinguish teaching which represents the apostolic tradition itself from decisions he makes on the basis of his own judgment or preference, and from his occasional appeals to the practice of other churches. Thus he points out that his teaching on the Lord's Supper (1 Cor. 15:3) is a handing on of what he received; so also he identifies the prohibition of divorce as "from the Lord" (1 Cor. 7:10). He identifies as his own interpretation his teaching on mixed marriages, granting a believer freedom from an unbelieving spouse not willing to live together in peace (1 Cor. 7:12 ff). Similarly his counsel in favor of celibacy (reflecting his expectation of the imminent parousia) he states as his own opinion (1 Cor. 7:25). On other questions he sometimes appeals simply to the customs and practices of the churches — traditions in the popular sense. Some of these, such as the insistence that women were to wear veils and had to keep silence at the religious assemblies (1 Cor. 11:16; 14:34), were clearly culturally conditioned customs with no lasting value for the church.[5]

[5]According to Jerome Murphy-O'Connor Paul teaches that a woman's hair is a symbol of a new power which women in Christ share with men. See his "Sex and Logic in 1 Corinthians 11:2-16," *Catholic Biblical Quarterly* 42 (1980) 482-500.

To better appreciate Paul's ecclesiology we will focus in the following section on the church in Corinth. Paul founded the church there around the year 50 (Acts 18:1-18). However, there were a number of problems in the community and in the course of dealing with them Paul wrote at least four letters to Corinth. The extent of his correspondence plus the fact that the problems at Corinth required him to deal concretely with issues in the life and structure of the community which do not surface elsewhere in his writings means that we probably know more about this church than we do about any other. The two long letters to the Corinthians can serve as an open window into one of the earliest churches about which we have detailed information.

In many ways the church at Corinth was very like a contemporary parish, divided into competing groups and factions, troubled by a number of serious problems, even scandals, and yet filled with a very real sense of the Spirit's presence. Like the church in every age, the church at Corinth was a sacramental church; it was a spirit-filled church, but it was also a sinful church. In responding to some specific questions referred to him by the community, Paul resembles a modern pastor trying to find the right combination of gentleness and strength to unite a divided community and at the same time safeguard the tradition out of which it lives. In the process he is forced to develop and articulate his understanding of the church as the body of Christ.

A Sinful Church. Situated between two ports, one on the Gulf of Corinth, the other on the Saronic Gulf, Corinth was a typical seaport city, well known in the ancient world as a center of vice and licentiousness. Among other expressions in Greek reflecting the city's reputation was "to play the Corinthian" (*korinthiastēs*), meaning to visit a house of prostitution. Corinth was not the most likely place for a Christian community, and yet the church flourished there even if some of the problems in the environment became evident also in the congregation. Paul's first letter to the Corinthians was precisely a response to certain disorders there about which he had been notified. The problems in

Corinth fall into three main areas: they included offenses against basic Christian morality, offenses against the unity of the community, and problems affecting the community's worship and liturgical life.

Not surprisingly, sexuality was one of the problem areas at Corinth. Christian life demanded of converts a radical break with their pagan past (1 Cor. 6:9-11; cf. 1 Thes. 4:1-8), and for some unable to give up practices incompatible with life in Christ, the transition was not easy. One scandal reported to Paul had to do with a man living in an incestuous union with his stepmother. Apparently the community was unable to deal with the situation. Paul's response, drawing on his apostolic authority, is to excommunicate the offender, though he does so in order to bring him to repentance (1 Cor. 5:1-5; 9-13). His concern is not only for the individual but also for the health of the community. The obverse of his disciplinary action here can be seen in 2 Corinthians where he urges the community to forgive and reaffirm their love for another person who seems to have been excluded from the community for some offense (2 Cor. 2:5-8). In Paul's concern to safeguard the life of the community and to reconcile those who had been disciplined can be recognized the dynamics of "binding and loosing" (cf. Matt. 18:18) which would later be institutionalized in the rite of penance.

Another problem in the area of morality appears in the case of some who are using a slogan ("everything is lawful for me" — 1 Cor. 6:12ff.) in order to justify their visits to one of Corinth's brothels. Many see here one of the factions with gnostic tendencies — perhaps the "Christ party" (see below) — whose members are misinterpreting Paul's principle of Christian freedom or are claiming a right to decide moral questions on the basis of their own supposed superior knowledge. Paul responds that Christian freedom is not license and argues that a union already exists between the Christian and Christ, and hence, any sexual union should reflect the holiness of this relationship. On the other hand another more conservative group at Corinth seemed to feel that even married couples should abstain from sexual relations (1 Cor. 7:1-7).

This problem of rival groups or factions was the most serious at Corinth for it continued to threaten the unity of the community. The different groups probably reflected the social and intellectual differences present in the community. One group claiming allegiance to Paul probably represented the majority. Having founded the community, Paul no doubt was close to many of its members whom he described as lacking in education, influence, and social status (1 Cor. 1:26). A number may have been slaves (1 Cor. 7:21 ff). Another group followed Apollos, a former disciple of John the Baptist, an eloquent orator and trained exegete who had spent some time in Corinth (Acts 18:24-28). Perhaps some of the better educated were attracted to him. The party of Cephas may have represented more conservative Jewish Christians who looked to Peter for leadership. A fourth group is called the "Christ party." Many scholars believe this group claimed a unique relation to Christ on the basis of a special revelation or ecstatic experience. Like the later gnostics, they would have considered that their special knowledge meant that they were not dependent on the recognized teachers within the community. Those we just saw trying to justify sexual immorality with a slogan about freedom may have belonged to this faction. Another offense against unity was the practice of bringing lawsuits against each other in the Roman courts. Paul criticizes them not only for their lack of forbearance but also because they were injuring and cheating each other within the community.

Finally the divisions in the community were adversely affecting the church's worship. The communal meal or agape which accompanied the Lord's Supper at this time had degenerated into little groups or cliques based on social status, to the obvious disadvantage of the poor. While the more affluent were getting drunk, others were going hungry. Paul tells them that "not recognizing the body," that is not recognizing the community as the body of Christ means that they are celebrating unworthily and sinning against the body and blood of the Lord (1 Cor. 11:27 ff; cf. 1 Cor. 10:17). Another problem was a lack of order when they assembled for prayer, coupled with the tendency of some to place too much emphasis on some of the more dramatic *charismata* or spiritual gifts, among them the gift of tongues, contributing not to the building up of the church but only to their own self-importance (1 Cor. 14). To better grasp Paul's concerns here we need to consider how he understands the manifestations of the Spirit within the community and those ritual expressions of its faith which the later church would call sacraments.

A Sacramental Church. The problem of unity which runs like a major theme through 1 Corinthians receives a sacramental focus when Paul turns to address some of the specific questions raised by the community. He grounds the unity of the community in the one Spirit shared through baptism and in the one bread of the Eucharist.

The relation between unity and baptism is already evident in his letter to the Galatians. Paul tells them that as a result of their baptism into Christ "there does not exist among you Jew or Greek, slave or freeman, male or female. All are one in Christ Jesus" (Gal. 3:28). The same language appears in 1 Corinthians, only here, where the context is not the justification of both Jew and Greek by faith as in Galatians but the unity of the church, Paul specifically stresses the relation between the Spirit given in baptism and the community as the one body of Christ: "It was in one Spirit that all of us, whether Jew or Greek, slave or free, were baptized into one body" (1 Cor. 12:13). Similarly a few lines earlier he emphasizes that the community is one body through its participation in the Eucharist: "Because the loaf of bread is one, we, many though we are, are one body, for we all partake of the one loaf" (1 Cor. 10:17). Here we have Paul's basic understanding of church. He may have derived his analogy of the body from Stoicism which spoke of the cosmos as an organic body, but there is a eucharistic dimension to Paul's use of the term; the church becomes the body of Christ through its eucharistic sharing in his body and blood (1 Cor. 10:16).

A Spirit-filled Church. Of all of Paul's churches, Corinth was the most "charismatic" in the sense of being preoccupied with dramatic, exuberant manifestations of the Spirit; a similar emphasis was to be found in the ecstatic pagan cults. Paul does not discourage the Corinthians' enthusiasm; at the beginning of his first letter he praises them as being well equipped with spiritual gifts (*charismata*) of every kind as they await the Lord's return (1 Cor. 1:7). But he is careful to develop some criteria for discerning authentic *charismata* in the community and for regulating their use. Chapters 12-14 represent the most extensive treatment of spiritual gifts in the New Testamant. He attributes the diversity of gifts to the one divine source:

> There are different gifts [*charismata*] but the same Spirit; there are different ministries [*diakoniai*] but the same Lord; there are different works [*energēmata*] but the same God who accomplishes all of them in everyone. To each person the manifestation of the Spirit is given for the common good.
>
> 1 Cor. 12:4-7

Paul parallels gifts with ministries (*diakonia* means literally service) and works in a trinitarian structure. Each is a positive manifestation of the inner presence of the invisible Spirit in the life of an individual Christian, a divine gift which enables that person to perform some ministry, function or office in the church. Among the *charismata* he names wisdom, knowledge, faith, the gift of healing, miraculous powers, prophecy, discernment, tongues, and the interpretation of tongues (1 Cor. 12:8-11). To exercise the gift of prophecy was to speak in the name of the Lord, to build up, encourage, and console the community (1 Cor. 14:3). Tongues was a form of praise welling up from within a person which overflowed the constraints of language, resulting in the uttering or singing of unintelligible syllables. Some consider the gift of faith as referring not to ordinary faith but to the extraordinary witness of a person whose whole life becomes a symbol of faith such as a Mother Teresa. A few verses later, after stressing the need for all the members of the body to work together, Paul gives another, ordered list of charisms, situating them within his theology of the church as the body of Christ:

> You, then, are the body of Christ. Everyone of you is a
> member of it. Furthermore, God has set up in the church
> first apostles, second prophets, third teachers, then mira-
> cle workers, healers, assistants, administrators, and those
> who speak in tongues.
>
> 1 Cor. 12:27-28

Among the charisms listed here he ranks first the ministry
of the apostles, and after them, that of the prophets and
teachers, local church leaders whose tasks included preaching, teaching, and most probably the celebration of the
Eucharist. Earlier in the letter he identifies both marriage
and celibacy as charisms. (1 Cor. 7:7; cf. vv. 1-7). Thus he
emphasizes the multiplicity and diversity of the gifts and
ministries within the church.

It is interesting to compare the charism lists in 1 Corinthians with a similar one in Paul's letter to the Romans. Again
the context is the multiplicity of ministries within the body
of Christ. But in Romans there is a difference:

> Just as each one of us has one body with many members,
> and not all the members have the same function, so too
> we, though many, are one body in Christ and individually
> members one of another. We have gifts [*charismata*] that
> differ according to the favor [*charis*] bestowed on each of
> us. One's gift may be prophecy; its use should be in
> proportion to his faith. It may be the gift of ministry
> [*diakonia*]; it should be used for service. One who is a
> teacher should use his gift for teaching. One with the
> power of exhortation should exhort. He who gives alms
> should do so generously; he who rules [*proistamenos*]
> should exercise his authority with care; he who performs
> works of mercy should do so cheerfully.
>
> Rom. 12:4-8

The reader will probably have noticed that what are missing
here are the more dramatic gifts such as healing, miraculous
powers, and tongues that some at Corinth seemed to value
so highly. Instead in Romans Paul stresses the ordinary gifts
of the Spirit, teaching, exhorting, almsgiving, leadership,

and works of mercy so important for the everyday life of the church.

He gives the Corinthians criteria for recognizing authentic spiritual gifts. A charism is always "given for the common good" (1 Cor. 12:7); its purpose is to build up the church (1 Cor. 14:1 ff). He does not forbid the gift of tongues but considers intelligible prophecy more important, and most important of all, the gift of love (1 Cor. 13). Finally he tells the Corinthians to "make sure that everything is done properly and in order" (1 Cor. 14:40).

Although Paul includes the ministries of local church leadership among the charisms, he does not mention appointment to office through the laying on of hands. Many scholars argue that ministries in his churches were not yet "institutionalized" or received through appointment. Some tend to oversimplify the organization of the Pauline churches as associations of free charismatic ministries, arising spontaneously in the Spirit. There is, however, a double principle of order in Paul's churches. There is first of all the authority of the apostle himself, an authority Paul was not hesitant to exercise when it was necessary. Secondly, there were in the local churches recognized ministries of church leadership, preaching, and teaching. Though the ministerial vocabulary is still rather functional and fluid, there is still a certain order. In 1 Corinthians 12:28 Paul ranks under the apostles the prophets, teachers, and administrators (*kuberneseis*), local church leaders, perhaps with a division of functions between the ministry of word and sacrament (prophets and teachers) and that of government and administration. Thessalonica has those "whose task it is (*kopiōntas*) to exercise authority (*proistamenous*) in the Lord and admonish you" (1 Thes. 5:12). In the list of charismata in Romans 12:18 we find "he who rules" (*proistamenos*). In Galatians material support is due to the one "who catechizes" (Gal. 6:6), just as it is to the apostle himself (1 Cor. 9:6-15). The church at Philippi has its "overseers (or bishops) and deacons"(*episkopoi kai diakonoi* — Phil. 1:1). The fact that these terms are almost always given in the plural suggests a collegial dimension to the ministry of church leadership.

In the later New Testament as indeed in the subsequent history of the church there developed an unfortunate tendency to restrict the terms charism and ministry to the ministry of church leaders (Eph. 4:7, 10-12; 1 Pet. 4:10), or to the gift of (ordained) ministry received through the laying on of hands (1 Tim. 4:14; 2 Tim. 1:6). Fortunately this kind of "clericalizing" of charism and ministry is breaking down and we are rediscovering the multiplicity of gifts and ministries so important to Paul's churches: "to *each* person the manifestation of the Spirit is given for the common good" (1 Cor. 12:7).

Conclusion

The early church first appears as a sect within Judaism, but from the beginning the experience of the disciples sets them apart from other Jewish sectarian movements. While sharing with the latter an apocalyptic vision, the disciples proclaim that the age of salvation has already begun in the death and resurrection of Jesus and in his gift of the Spirit. Their community is formed of those baptized in the name of Jesus; they share a common life and a common faith coming from the apostles. They are united in prayer and in the celebration of the eucharistic meal.

The Gentile mission begins almost by accident after a persecution drives the Hellenist Jewish Christians from Jerusalem. The conversion of non-Jews in increasing numbers poses a profound challenge to many of the early Christians but they learn to welcome it as the work of the Spirit. Within less than twenty years there are churches from Jerusalem to Rome.

6. THE CHURCH IN THE SUB-APOSTOLIC AGE

And his gifts were that some should be apostles, some
prophets, some evangelists, some pastors and teachers, to
equip the saints for the works of ministry, for building up
the body of Christ.

Eph. 4:11-12 (R.S.V).

A Church in Transition

The fall of Jerusalem in the year 70 A.D. is the traditional
date for the end of the Apostolic Age. By this time a number
of transitions had taken place which would lead to important developments in the following decades. First, the apostles had died, leaving the churches without the leadership of
the original witnesses and founders. Second, the mother
church in Jerusalem had ceased to exist. Third, an increasing
number of Gentiles were entering the Church. Fourth, the
expectation of an imminent parousia began to fade. As the
communities sought to live out their faith in the midst of the
social, historical, and theological changes taking place, new
problems began to appear. How were Christians to understand themselves in relation to Judaism and the Roman
Empire? How was the faith of the community to be preserved? How were the different communities to be held
together in the face of internal tensions and external challenges? How were the developments taking place seen to
express the apostolic tradition from which the communities

lived? As the Apostolic Age faded into history that tradition was increasingly threatened; books like Colossians and Ephesians, Acts, the Pastoral Letters, Jude, 2 Peter, and the Johannine Letters all reflect a concern for the problem of false teachers.

The Sub-Apostolic Age is usually dated from the year 70 to the end of the New Testament period. It was for the church a period of adjustment and self-definition. But the time-frame is rather fluid since the last New Testament book, 2 Peter, appeared somewhere between 110 and 140. Even before 2 Peter brought the Sub-Apostolic Age to a close, the structures which would mark the post New Testament great church were beginning to emerge; they can be seen developing in many of the late New Testament books and in non-canonical works from the same period like 1 Clement (c. 96) and the letters of Ignatius of Antioch (c. 115). An emphasis in these books on church structure, office, authority, and the apostolic tradition has led to the expression "early Catholicism" as a description of these developments, though some Catholic scholars prefer to avoid the term because of the negative evaluations attached to it.[1] However, it is clear that towards the end of the first century the church was beginning to articulate the structural and institutional aspects of its life in a way that would later characterize the Catholic tradition. To trace these developments in the Sub-Apostolic Age we must continue our survey of the local churches.

In the preceeding chapter we concentrated on Paul's churches largely because the extent of his correspondence makes them so visible. We also know something about later developments in churches related to the Pauline tradition from Colossians and Ephesians, from the Pastoral Epistles, and from Acts. But the Pauline churches were not the only

---

[1] A number of Protestant scholars see early Catholicism as an understandable but unfortunate clericalizing of the church which implied that the Spirit was being "bound" to an institutionalized church office, thus an attempt to limit grace. See Ernst Käsemann's classic essay "Paul and Early Catholicism" in his *New Testament Questions of Today* (London: SCM Press, 1969), 236-51.

expressions of early Christianity. There were others, both in the East and in the West, communities and churches established by different missionary groups, some more conservative in regard to the place of various Jewish observances and traditions than Paul's, others more liberal.

Recently a number of biblical scholars have been attempting to fill in our picture of early Christianity by reconstructing the histories and theologies of these different churches. The task is difficult; it involves considerable detective work, assigning the different New Testament books to the various churches to which or from which they were written and identifying the situations in the lives of the churches which lie behind them. Raymond Brown especially has devoted his research in recent years to this area.[2] His work and the work of others provide the lost pieces necessary to restore the broken mosaic of early Christianity in the Sub-Apostolic Age.[3]

Local Churches

1. *The Church at Antioch.* One of the most important centers of early Christianity was the Church at Antioch in the Roman province of Syria. John P. Meier has reconstructed the first three generations in the life of this church using Galatians 2:11-21 and Acts 15 for the first generation, the gospel of Matthew, most probably written at Antioch (80-90) for the second, and the letters of Ignatius of Antioch (c. 115) for the third. Running through these three genera-

[2]See Raymond E. Brown, *The Community of the Beloved Disciple* (New York: Paulist Press, 1978); Brown and John P. Meier, *Antioch and Rome* (New York: Paulist Press, 1983), and Brown, *The Churches the Apostles Left Behind* (New York: Paulist Press, 1984). Also Daniel J. Harrington, *God's People in Christ* (Philadelphia: Fortress Press, 1980), 67-106. Edward Schillebeeckx has traced the development of ministry in the different post-apostolic communities in his *Ministry: Leadership in the Community of Jesus Christ.* (New York: Crossroad, 1981).

[3]In the following section I am particularly indebted to Brown for the sketches of the church at Rome and the Johannine community and to Meier for the sketch of the church at Antioch. I have given each sketch my own emphasis.

tions like a thread is the problem of unity.

The church at Antioch was a mixed community of Jewish and Gentile Christians. We have already seen that in the first generation a conflict took place between the more conservative Jewish Christians associated with James and ultimately with Peter and other more liberal Jewish Christians associated with Paul and the Hellenists. The accommodation Peter made with the more conservative Jewish group (Gal. 2:11-14) seems to have helped keep the community together; certainly his prominence later in Matthew's gospel suggests his importance at Antioch. But tensions remained and later those on the extremes of both groups may have drifted away from the church, becoming part of the various heretical sects such as the Ebionites or the Christian gnostic groups whose doctrines reflect the orientations of the extreme right and left wings.

Matthew's gospel was especially concerned with helping the more conservative Jewish Christians work out their new identity within an increasingly Gentile church after the final break with the synagogues, somewhere between 70 and 85. Sensing the void left by the break he emphasized certain institutional aspects of the church within a framework of salvation history. He is the only evangelist to actually use the word church (Matt. 16:18; 18:17) and he portrays it as a structured community founded by Christ which continues to exercise his authority. Peter who had been associated with the more conservative Jewish group at Antioch is given authority to make binding decisions for the church based on the authority of Jesus (Matt. 16:18). Local churches have the authority to admit to or exclude from the community (Matt. 18:15-20). When it comes to local church leaders Matthew seems to show a certain ambivalence. While accepting their authority he betrays some misgivings about what appears to be the beginnings of a type of "clericalism," a preference for "ostentatious religious clothing and paraphernalia...first seats at the religious meetings...and the desire to be addressed with special titles" (Matt. 23:5-10).[4]

[4]Meier, *Antioch and Rome*, p. 70.

Matthew's critique, apparently directed at the conduct of
the scribes and Pharisees, must have been occasioned by
similar tendencies on the part of the local church leaders, the
same prophets and teachers (he refers to the latter as scribes
or wise men — Matt. 13.52; 23:34) who appeared earlier as
the local leaders in Acts 13:1.

Within another generation the group of prophets and
teachers at Antioch had evolved into the traditional threefold ministry of bishop, presbyters and deacons. Evidence
here comes from the letters of Antioch's bishop Ignatius; his
letters both indicate the emergence of this threefold structure in other churches of Asia Minor and probably contributed to its spread through what Ignatius calls "the church
catholic" (*hē katholikē ekklēsia* — Smyrneans 3:2). Thus
Antioch holds three "firsts" in the history of the church. It
was here that the disciples were first called "Christians" and
the church was first described as "catholic." Here too we
first find in place the threefold ministry of bishop, presbyters, and deacons which was to become universal in the
church.

2. *Churches Related to the Pauline Tradition.* Following
the observation of scholars like C. K. Barrett and Raymond
Brown we can distinguish three different types of communities in the Sub-Apostolic Age related to the Pauline tradition.[5] They appear to us in Colossians and Ephesians, in the
Pastoral Epistles, and in Luke/Acts respectively.

(a) *Colossians and Ephesians.* Though most scholars
agree that Colossians and Ephesians are post-Pauline, the
two letters are difficult to date. Colossians stands quite close
in time to the genuine Pauline letters; some scholars still
argue for its authenticity. It was addressed to a Gentile
church at Colossae in Asia Minor, to the east of Ephesus;
Paul had worked in the general area though we do not know
if he had ever been at Colossae itself. Ephesians shows
dependence on Colossians and familiarity with the authen-

[5]C. K. Barrett, "Acts and the Pauline Corpus," in *Expository Times* 88 (1966-67)
2-5; "Pauline Controversies in the Post-Pauline Period," *New Testament Studies*
20 (1973-74) 229-45. Raymond E. Brown. *Churches*, 20-22.

tic letters. It may have been written anywhere from the late 70's to the 90's. Because of its style and the lack of a specific address many believe that it was written as a general Pauline instruction, perhaps to accompany a collection of his writings.

Like 1 Corinthians and Romans, Colossians and Ephesians describe the church as the body of Christ. However here the word church is clearly used in a universal sense. The church is composed of both Jews and Gentiles who as "members of the same body" (Eph. 3:6; cf. Col. 3:15) "form a building which rises on the foundation of the apostles and prophets with Christ Jesus himself as the capstone" (Eph. 2:20. Both letters emphasize Christ as the head of his body, the church (Col. 1:18, 24; Eph. 5:23). Ephesians identifies the church with the fullness of Christ's cosmic presence (Eph. 1:22-23) and proposes his intimate love for the church as a model for the love and union of husband and wife (Eph. 5:25-32). One does not find in Colossians and Ephesians the connection between church office and teaching authority that is so obvious in the Pastorals. But Ephesians witnesses to a more developed church ministry than is reflected in the letters of Paul himself as we will see below.

(b) *The Pastoral Epistles.* These letters, 1 and 2 Timothy and Titus, are written in Paul's name to two of his better-known co-workers who are represented as delegates of the apostle working at Ephesus and on Crete respectively. The name "Pastoral" aptly describes the content of the letters, the dying apostle Paul's concern for the continuing well-being of churches he himself would no longer be able to shepherd. It is almost universally agreed that these letters are post-Pauline, written in the 90s or for some even later. Yet the real Paul shows a very similar pastoral concern in sending Timothy to his church at Philippi (Phil. 2:19-23).

The Pastoral Letters present an ecclesiology very close to that of Ignatius of Antioch. In response to the problem of false teachers they stress fidelity to the apostolic tradition and church structure, particularly the teaching authority of the presbyter-bishops (for the two roles are not yet clearly distinguished). The ministry itself has been institutionalized and is in the process of evolving into the traditional three-fold ministry. The church is becoming an institution.

Timothy speaks of the church as "the pillar and bulwark of truth" (1 Tim. 3:15). The letter reads like an early collection of canon law, with liturgical regulations (2:1-15), qualifications for various ministers (3:1-13), rules for widows (5:3-16), and various regulations on the payment, disciplining, and installing of presbyters (5:17-22). The final chapter deals with the relations of slaves and masters and with the obligations of the wealthy. Not every instruction in these letters belongs to the church's permanent heritage; certainly the author's views on women and their role in the liturgical assembly (1 Tim. 2:11-12; 2 Tim. 3:6) are culturally conditioned and should be recognized as such. But the basic message of the Pastorals that a teaching authority belongs to the church's office of leadership is very much part of the Catholic tradition.

(c) *Luke/Acts*. Scholars today are unable to identify the churches to which Luke/Acts was addressed and its connection to the Pauline tradition is not as obvious as that of Colossians and Ephesians or the Pastorals. Besides the claim of authorship, both sets of letters share in the Pauline doctrinal tradition. The author of Luke/Acts, however, seems to be unfamiliar with Paul's epistles and — in spite of an ancient tradition — there is no real evidence that he knew Paul personally. The link is to be found in the kind of Christianity Acts represents, a mostly Gentile Christianity which claimed its own inheritance from the great apostle of the Gentiles.

Acts has often been described as the "Gospel of the Spirit." In reading the story of how the church grew from the first days of the community in Jerusalem, through various internal crises, persecutions, the unforeseen acceptance of the good news by the Gentiles, a council of the church at Jerusalem to resolve the question of the Gentiles and circumcision, Paul's great missionary activity, to finally his arrival in Rome — it is easy to appreciate the great appeal this book still has for evangelical Christians and missionaries. The Church is a Spirit-led community, set within the context of salvation history.

Still the concept of church office in Luke/Acts is a developed one. The Spirit works in a particular way through church leaders. Foundational to the church is the ministry of the apostles, a group Luke restricts almost exclusively to the Twelve (Lk. 6:13). He recognizes the appointment of subordinate ministers, the Seven, through an invocation and the laying on of hands (Acts 6:1-6). Ministry comes from the Spirit; Paul and Barnabas are chosen by the Spirit for missionary work (13:2) and Paul tells the presbyters at Ephesus that the Spirit has made them overseers (20:28). At the same time there is an emphasis on ministers being sent or commissioned by others in authority, in regard to the apostles themselves (1:2-8) and for other ministers appointed by the apostles (6:6; 14:23). Paul and Barnabas are given the title "apostle" in Acts only after the church leaders at Antioch have laid hands on them and comissioned them in the context of what now is generally recognized as a Eucharist (13:1-3).

3. *The Johannine Community.* The uniqueness of John's gospel is a reflection of the distinct character of the Johannine community, so different from other New Testament communities that some scholars have described it as a sect. The gospel suggests that the Johannine Christians formed a community apart; hostile towards the synagogues for expelling and persecuting them (John 9:22; 16:2), the Johannine Christians were also conscious of the differences between themselves and those Brown calls "the Christians of the Apostolic Churches."[6] Though there is no indication that the two groups were not in communion, the Johannine Christians were set apart by their very high christology and by their ecclesiology. Johannine christology leads to a vision of the Christian life as a discipleship centered on Jesus. The realized eschatology of the gospel adds a mystical

---

[6]Brown, *The Community of the Beloved Disciple*, pp. 81 ff.

dimension; the believer already shares in the divine life through the indwelling of Father, Son, and Spirit (John 14:23-26).

Ecclesiologically the fourth gospel presents the church as a community of disciples guided by the Spirit; it lacks the interest in developing church structures that we have seen in other books from this period. The word apostle in the technical sense does not appear, the Beloved Disciple — the founder of the Johannine community — is frequently contrasted with Peter and appears in the more favorable light, and it is difficult to determine from the gospel whether or not there were specific ministries of church leadership in the community (though the Johannine Epistles indicate the existence of presbyters). Rather than calling attention to a teaching authority or to the apostolic tradition, the gospel of John appeals directly to the role of the Paraclete who "will guide you to all truth" (John 16:13; cf. 14:26).

The exact location of the Johannine community cannot be established. Though it seems to have originated in Palestine, many scholars identify it with Ephesus. By the time the Johannine Epistles were written it must have involved a number of house churches with other communities in the surrounding towns and villages. The first epistle mentions a schism from within their ranks; Brown sees this as the beginning of the end for the Johannine Christians' existence as a distinct community.[7] The larger part of the community seems to have travelled the road to Gnosticism, developing a christology so high that it lost sight of the saving significance of the human life of Jesus and became docetic. Through the secessionists Johannine theology was to play an important role in the development of a Christian gnosticism. As a result of the schism those who followed the author of the Johannine Epistles must have come to appreciate the importance of a teaching authority and thus to accept the ministry of the presbyter-bishops then emerging in the other churches. It is possible that the final chapter or appendix to the fourth gospel in which Jesus commissions

[7]Ibid., pp. 146 ff.

Peter to shepherd the flock (John 21:15-17) was added by the Johannine redactor precisely in order to recommend to the Johannine community the pastoral authority exercised in the other churches as an authority instituted by Jesus.[8]

4. *The Church at Rome.* To uncover the strata in the first years in the life of the Roman church we turn again to Raymond Brown's reconstruction.[9] Christianity came early to Rome, at least by the end of the 50s if not before. Most probably it came from Jerusalem and represented the kind of moderately conservative Jewish Gentile Christianity associated with James and especially Peter. One indication of this is Paul's letter to the Romans. Comparing his sympathetic approach to Judaism in Romans with his polemical treatment in the earlier Galatians, Brown makes a good case that Paul felt a need to make himself acceptable to the Christians at Rome by distinguishing himself from the left-wing Hellenist Jewish Christians who rejected all the institutions and traditions of Judaism.[10] He must have been successful for Rome seems to have accepted him. Both Peter and Paul died in Rome somewhere in the mid-60s and were remembered there. Subsequent letters from Rome reflect some of the themes present in Paul's letter to the Romans and 1 Clement mentions him, after Peter, as one of the "pillars" of the church (5:2-6).

For the second generation at Rome Brown turns to 1 Peter and Hebrews. It is generally agreed that 1 Peter was written from Rome in Peter's name to a group of churches in Asia Minor somewhere in the 80s. The author addresses these communities — now largely Gentile — as "a chosen race, a royal priesthood, a holy nation, a people he claims for his own" (2:9), thus using Jewish themes taken from the Exodus and wandering in the desert. Of special interest for understanding the latter development of the Catholic tradition is what Brown points out about the presence of lan-

---

[8]Ibid., pp. 161-62.

[9]See Brown's careful study in *Antioch and Rome*, pp. 89 ff.

[10]Ibid., pp. 111-122.

guage taken from the Jewish cult; he notes that just as Paul in Romans used Jewish cultic language symbolically, perhaps more so than in any other letter (Romans 3:25; 12:1; 15:16), so also the author of 1 Peter applies the language of cultic sacrifice to Christ's saving death ("Christ's blood beyond all price: the blood of a spotless, unblemished lamb" 1:19) and describes the community as "a holy priesthood, offering spiritual sacrifices" (2:5). Thus he argues that the language of the cult was still meaningful to the Christians at Rome even after the Jerusalem Temple and its cult had disappeared.[11]

A renewed interest in the Jewish cult seems to have been the concern of the letter to the Hebrews. This letter, considered by Brown and a number of other scholars as originally addressed to the church at Rome, represents the point of view of the radical Hellenists; it argues that the levitical priesthood, Temple sacrifices, and cult have been superseded by the priesthood and sacrifice of Christ. Since it was probably written after the destruction of the Temple, it seems to have been directed against a renewed interest in the levitical cult on the part of some in the Roman church. But apparently with little effect, for a little more than a decade later in 1 Clement cultic imagery appears again in a more radical form; it is now being used in reference to the functions of church officers. The author of 1 Clement compares the order of the Jewish cult with its high priests, priests, and levites in chapter 40 with the order of the Christian community in chapter 42; God sent Christ who sent the apostles who in turn appointed bishops and deacons for future generations.

Although Clement also speaks of offering sacrifices as one of the roles in the episcopate (44:4) he does not specifically call bishops or presbyters (for him the two terms are still synonymous) priests. But he established the connection and it was not long before others in the Roman church made it explicit. At the beginning of the third century Tertullian

[11] Ibid., p. 137.

(*De Baptismo* 17) speaks of the bishop as "high priest" (*summus sacerdos*) and Hippolytus of Rome (*Apostolic Traditions* 3:5) refers to the "high priestly spirit" of the bishop. A similar development recognizing a priestly dimension to the role of the one who presides at the Eucharist is evident even earlier in Syria. The Didache specifically uses the term "sacrifice" for the Eucharist (14:1-3) and refers to the charismatic prophet celebrants as "high priests." It was not long before the language of priesthood (*hiereus/sacerdos*) was being used of the bishop in recognition of his role as the minister and leader of the eucharistic community, and later by extension also of the presbyters.

The Emergence of the Ordained Ministry

As the different communities in the Sub-Apostolic Age grew, became more organized, and faced the threats of heterodoxy and schism, a consolidation of the church's ministries of leadership took place. If we look at local ministries of leadership in the early New Testament period we find a rather fluid situation; in addition to the presence of the apostles, particularly Peter, Paul, and James, quite early various local leading ministries can be recognized: there are elders or presbyters at Jerusalem (Acts 11:30), prophets and teachers at Antioch (Acts 13:1-3), prophets, teachers, administrators, leaders — among them the heads of the house churches — mentioned in Paul's letters (1 Cor. 12:28; Rom. 12:7-8; 16:5; 1 Thes. 5:12). Shortly after the end of the New Testament period the threefold ministry of a single bishop, assisted by presbyters and deacons has become widespread; it is understood as a ministry succeeding to the leading and teaching role of the apostles and entered through the laying on of hands. How did these institutions which ever since have constituted the basis of ordained ministry in the Catholic tradition develop? The process was neither spontaneous nor uniform and yet certain patterns emerged and coalesced into what was to become the post-apostolic great church. Where did these deacons, presbyters, and bishops come from?

The Greek word *diakonos* (Latin *minister*) meant originally one who served at table, hence a servant. Very early it became the basic term for persons exercising roles of service or ministry within the church. Paul describes the apostles as "qualified ministers of a new covenant" (2 Cor. 3:6) and as "ministers of God" (2 Cor. 6:4); in 1 Corinthians 12:4-6 he parallels ministries with charisms and works as different manifestations of the Spirit, given to all to build up the community. Although Philippians 1:1 addresses the *"episkopoi kai diakonoi"* at the forefront of the community, the special office of the diaconate does not seem to have appeared until later. In Romans 16:1 Paul commends a Corinthian woman Phoebe "who is *'diakonos'* of the church at Cenchreae." *Diakonos* here is usually translated deaconess but could just as well be translated minister or servant.[12] The diaconate as a distinct office is present in 1 Timothy 3:8-13 though without any indication of the deacon's function. It is likely that the deacon's role included a function of serving at the eucharistic meal (cf. Ignatius, Tral. 2:3).

The office of presbyter, literally elder, was an institution borrowed from Judaism. Each synagogue had a group of older men or elders who advised the community and represented its tradition. Christian presbyters appear first at Jerusalem (Acts 11:30), later in Asia Minor at Lycaonia (Acts 14:23) and Ephesus (20:17), at least according to Luke. They appear in letters and communities with strong ties to the Jewish tradition (1 Pet. 5:1; James 5:14). In the development of church office at Rome, 1 Peter represents a midpoint between the situation in Romans which mentions the function of presiding or leading (*proistamenos*) among the charisms (12:8) and indicates the existence of house churches (16:5 ff) and the presbyters and deacons of 1 Clement. The twofold ministry of the word and of service (*ei tis diakonei*) suggested by 1 Pet. 4:11 seems to be confirmed by 1 Pet. 5:1-5 which shows a ministry of presbyters and

---

[12]Elisabeth Schüssler Fiorenza argues that Phoebe was "an official teacher and missionary of the church at Cenchreae," *In Memory of Her* (New York: Crossroads, 1983), p. 177. For her discussion of Phoebe see 169-71, 181-82.

"younger men," thought by some to be deacons.[13] In the latter passage the presbyters are described with the imagery of pastoral supervision; they shepherd the flock for whom Christ is the chief shepherd, willingly and not for profit.

Ephesians seems also to represent a transitional stage, though one that develops a Pauline pattern of ministry. The section dealing with ministry begins in a way similar to the list of charisms in 1 Corinthians 12:4-11; 27-30 and Romans 12:6-8: "Each of us has received God's favor in the measure in which Christ bestows it" (Eph. 4:7). But here the emphasis is on the church leaders who enable the community itself to be a ministering community: "And his gifts were that some should be apostles, some prophets, some evangelists, some pastors and teachers, to equip the saints for the work of ministry, for building up the body of Christ" (Eph. 4:11-12, R.S.V. trans.). The apostles and prophets are the founders of the first generation (cf. Eph. 2:20); evangelists may refer to their immediate successors, wandering missionaries or perhaps to men like Timothy and Titus.[14] Pastors and teachers, both introduced by a single article, probably refers to a single office of local church leadership, possibly a midpoint in development between the prophets, teachers, administrators, and leaders of Paul's time and the presbyter-bishops of the Pastorals. The function of this office would be similar to that of the presbyters whose ministry is frequently associated with pastor/shepherd imagery (Acts 20:23; 1 Pet. 5:1-4).

In the Pastorals the presbyterate has clearly become an institutionalized office. 1 Timothy seems to presuppose a well-established church at Ephesus with an already existing college of presbyters (1 Tim. 5:17) while Titus shows a more primitive situation as it calls for the establishment of a group of presbyters in each city on Crete (Titus 1:5).[15]

[13]See John H. Elliott, "Ministry and Church Order in the New Testament," *Catholic Biblical Quarterly* 32 (1970) 367-91.

[14]Cf. Reginald Fuller, "The Ministry in the New Testament" in *Episcopalians and Roman Catholics: Can They Ever Get Together?* ed. Herbert J. Ryan and J. Robert Wright (Danville, New Jersey: Dimension Books, 1972) 88-103, pp. 93-94.

[15]John P. Meier, "*Presbyteros* in the Pastoral Epistles," *Catholic Biblical Quarterly* 35 (1973) 323-45, 337-45.

Presbyters are commissioned by the laying on of hands, what the later church would call the sacrament of ordination. It is in this context that the Pauline word charism reappears, though now it is applied to the one who receives the gift of ministry at the hands of the presbyters (1 Tim. 4:14) or from the apostle himself (2 Tim. 1:6). Like the presbyterate, authorization by the laying on of hands seems also to have been an institution borrowed from Judaism.[16]

The role of the *episkopos*, "overseer" or "bishop" was probably a third inheritance from Judaism. The Qumran community had overseers with responsibilities similar to some of the presbyter-bishops in the Pastorals.[17] Because presbyters also exercised a supervisory role, the two terms seem to have been equivalent at least till the time of the Pastorals. In Acts Paul addresses the presbyters at Ephesus (20:17), telling them to watch over the flock in which the Holy Spirit has made them *"episkopoi"* (20:28; cf. 1 Pet. 5:1-4). The two terms are still interchangeable in 1 Clement for the office of the single bishop did not emerge at Rome until close to 150. But in 1 Timothy the twofold office of presbyter-bishops and deacons seems to be in the process of evolving into the threefold office headed by a single bishop. The letter describes some of the presbyters as exercising the particular duties of preaching and teaching, noting that such "presbyters who do well as leaders deserve to be paid double" (1 Tim. 5:17). Here is a group emerging within the presbyteral college in a leadership role, exercising not only supervision but also the liturgical roles implied by the functions of preaching and teaching. These specialized presbyters may well have received the title *episkopos* at Ephesus (cf. 1 Tim. 3:1-7).[18]

A primary duty of the presbyter-bishops in the Pastorals is to guard the faith entrusted to the community, encourag-

---

[16] See Eduard Lohse, *Die Ordination im Spät Judentum und im Neuen Testament* (Göttingen: Evangelische Verlagsanstalt, 1951).

[17] According to Brown the overseers at Qumran had "teaching, admonitory, and administrative roles almost identical to those of the bishops of the Pastorals." *Churches*, p. 33.

[18] Meier, "*Presbyteros*," 344-45.

ing others to follow sound doctrine and refuting those who contradict it (Titus 1:5-14). In stressing fidelity to the truth a more objectified concept of faith begins to appear; faith is described in terms of teaching, doctrine, truths handed down, a deposit of faith. Timothy is advised to "follow the pattern of the sound words" he has heard (2 Tim 1:13-R.S.V. trans.) and to entrust it to others (2 Tim 2:2). False teachers are to be silenced (Titus 1:10-11). This strong emphasis on the teaching authority of the presbyter-bishops needs to be understood against the threats posed to the communities by Gnosticism (1 Tim. 6:20-21) and what seems to have been some ultra-conservative Jewish Christian teachers (1 Tim. 1:3-20; Titus 1:10-16). It has led many to see in the Pastorals a prime example of "early Catholicism" within the New Testament.

In the Antioch of Ignatius (c. 115) the threefold ministry is clearly in place. The differences between the Antioch of Matthew's time and the same church under Bishop Ignatius are considerable. Pastoral and liturgical leadership in Matthew's church came from the prophets and teachers; evidence that they presided at the Eucharist is found in Acts 13:2 which shows them "engaged in the liturgy of the Lord (*leitourgountōn*)" and later in the *Didache*, a work which also seems to have come from Syria and to have been familiar with the Matthean traditions. In speaking of bishops and deacons *Didache* 15:1 states that "they too conduct (*leitourgousi*) the liturgy of the prophets and teachers."

By the time of Ignatius the transition to the single bishop assisted by presbyters and deacons has already taken place. Again the stimulus seems to have been the danger of the fragmentation of the community from false teachers. The principal danger came from a gnostic or docetic group whose high christology all but denied the humanity of Jesus. There also seems to have been a group of Judaizers on the right wing of the church. In trying to steer a middle course Ignatius placed great importance on the role of the bishop as a principle of unity, grounding his office christologically and stressing his right to regulate the sacraments and the life of the community: "Let no one do anything touching the church apart from the bishop. Let that celebration of the Eucharist be considered valid which is held under the bishop or anyone to whom he has committed it. Where the bishop appears, there let the people be, just as where Jesus Christ is, there is the catholic church. It is not permitted without authorization from the bishop either to baptize or to hold an agape; but whatever he approves is also pleasing to God" (Smyrneans 8:1-2).

It is important to note here that the bishop's responsibility for the Eucharist, the sacrament of unity, is based not on some special priestly power but on his role as leader of the local church. According to the ancient tradition reflected in Clement, Ignatius, Justin, Tertullian, Hippolytus and Cyprian those who presided over the life of the church presided over its Eucharists. It would have been unthinkable that a local church could not celebrate the Eucharist; a community would always chose a local leader as presider who would then be appointed with the help of the heads of neighboring churches.[19] Sometimes a person was ordained "unwilling and constrained" by the community's choice[20].

The offfice of the single bishop did not appear at Rome until close to 150. At the time 1 Clement was written the church at Rome was still governed by a group of presbyter-bishops. But in seeking to heal the schism caused at Corinth by the ejection of some presbyters from their office Clement argues that their positions can be traced to apostolic appointment. He states that the apostles themselves, fearing intrigues over the episcopate, had appointed men from among their earliest converts to office and provided that when these died "other approved men shall succeed to their

[19]See Hervé-Marie Legrande, "The Presidency of the Eucharist According to the Ancient Tradition," *Worship* 53 (1979) 413-438, p. 437.

[20]Ibid., 438.

liturgical ministry" (44:1-2; 42:4). Furthermore he describes the office itself as part of a divinely given order, moving from God through Christ to the apostles and then to the presbyter-bishops and deacons (42:1-4). Thus Clement establishes the theological principle of apostolic successsion by appointment.

The Question of Apostolic Succession

Scholars regard Clement's picture here as more theological than historical; he relates the presbyters at Corinth to a divinely established order, providing religious legitimacy to a system which by the end of the first century was widespread. But what history if any may lie behind his picture of the apostles appointing others to carry on their pastoral leadership is an important and hotly debated question which is usually argued along confessional lines. The Roman Catholic Church holds that "by divine institution bishops have succeeded to the place of the apostles as shepherds of the Church."[21] Furthermore, official Catholic teaching generally argues that bishops succeed not merely to the function of leadership once exercised by the apostles, but that this succession is based on a mission or authorization which proceeds from Christ to the apostles and from the apostles to the bishops.[22] Contemporary theology generally regards Clement's picture as unhistorical, and while most Protestant theologians are willing to recognize the episcopal office as one legitimate form of church order, among others, they ground it functionally and not on any special mission distinct from the general mission of the

---

[21] *Lumen Gentium*, no. 20 in *The Documents of Vatican II*, ed. Walter M. Abbott (New York: The American Press, 1966), p. 40.

[22] LG, no. 21, Abbott 40-42. See also the paper of the Vatican's International Theological Commission, "Apostolic Succession/a clarification" *Origins* 4 (1974) 194-200.

church.[23] Since the apostolic succession of the ordained ministry is a fundamental principle of the Catholic tradition we need to raise the question of what biblical and historical support can be offered for Clement's principle of succession by appointment.

The idea that local church leaders succeed to the pastoral ministry of the apostles does not originate with 1 Clement; it is also present in the New Testament. Frequently the emphasis is on a succession which is specifically linked with a responsibility for guarding the apostolic tradition so that the succession of the church in the apostolic tradition becomes equally important. In Acts Paul summons the presbyter-bishops of Ephesus for a farewell address, instructing them to guard the flock against the false teachers who will come after his departure (Acts 20:29-31). 2 Timothy is entirely concerned with handing on the apostolic tradition. Timothy who is represented as having received the laying on of hands from Paul himself (2 Tim 1:6) is told by the author writing in Paul's name to "guard the truth that has been entrusted to you" (2 Tim. 1:14, R.S.V. trans.) and to hand it on to those who will teach it to others (2:2).

At the same time there is a broader concern to link the apostles with those who succeeded to their role of guiding the churches, the presbyter-bishops. In 1 Peter 5:1 an author writing in Peter's name as a "fellow presbyter" to the presbyters of Asia Minor claims for their ministry a continuity with the ministry of the apostle.[24]

Acts represents Paul and Barnabas as appointing (*cheirotonēsantes*) presbyters in each city they visited on their missionary journey (Acts 14:23). While most scholars interpret this passage as a Lukan retrojection of later practice into apostolic times, it does show the author's theological

---

[23]Some theologians go further and see in 1 Clement a prime example of an institutionalization already taking place in the late New Testament which replaced the Spirit-led freedom of the early Pauline congregations with the "clericalism" of the later church.

[24]Elliott, "Ministry and Church Order in the New Testament," p.372.

concern to establish a ministerial continuity between the apostles and the presbyters. Similarly, in the Pastorals Timothy and Titus are delegated by Paul to set up presbyteral colleges in their communities (1 Tim. 5:22; Titus 1:5).

What can be said about apostolic succession by appointment from an historical point of view? Clement's picture of the apostles appointing bishops and deacons in city after city "from among their earliest converts" (42:4) cannot be confirmed by what we know from the New Testament. Therefore we cannot simply accept it. At the same time it should not be rejected out of hand, as though there was no connection between the apostles and the emerging office of local church leaders.

Constitutive for the early church was the ministry of the apostles, and from the beginning this ministry was shared. The early appointment of leaders for the Hellenistic Jewish Christians (Acts 6:1-6) is one example.[25] Paul himself is another. Paul associated others with him in his ministry, acknowledged the authority of those already exercising it in communities others had founded, and most probably left behind local leaders in the communities he established (Thessalonica, Corinth, Philippi). Often his first converts became the leaders of local communities which met in their homes. It is possible that these heads of the house churches were later included among the presbyters. The "*diakonos*" Phoebe in Romans 16:1 may have been the head of a suburban house church at Cenchreae, one of Corinth's ports. Therefore the picture of the apostles appointing leaders who would later be called presbyter-bishops and deacons may have some historical foundation.

On the other hand it cannot be shown to have been the general practice. A number of passages in the New Testament suggest a different development, and other works not part of the New Testament give evidence of different ways into the presbyteral office. The Johannine community

---

[25]Joseph T. Lienhard argues that the tradition behind this passage is basically historical, "Acts 6:1-6: A Redactional View," *Catholic Biblical Quarterly* 37 (1975), 228-236, p. 236.

seems to have accepted the presbyteral-episcopal structure only towards the end of the first century. The communities to which the *Didache* was addressed were told "appoint for yourselves bishops and deacons worthy of the Lord" (15:1). The *Apostolic Tradition* of Hippolytus (9) indicates that a "confessor," someone who had been imprisoned and suffered for the sake of Christ, could be admitted to the presbyterate without the laying on of hands, though his selection as bishop would require it.

Certainly there seems to be more than one form of church order visible within the New Testment, as well as different stories of development. Not all the communities felt that same dynamism towards unity evident in the fourth gospel (John 10:16; 17:20-21); some continued along their own paths and disappeared from history. Yet some of the Johannine communities and probably others with less developed ministries of leadership ultimately accepted the office of the presbyter-bishops which by the end of the century was becoming commonplace. Thus these communities and their ministries were integrated into a ministry of leadership which claimed — not without reason — apostolic succession; similarly whatever *koinōnia* existed between these communities and the other churches took on a visible, institutionalized expression. The real meaning of the apostolic succession of the ordained ministry is to be found here. It is not a guarantee of the church's fidelity nor an unbroken chain which, like an electrical circuit, transmits a sacramental power, but rather a sign which makes visible the link between the church and its ordained ministry today and the original apostolic church. The office of the bishop was also to become a unique ministry serving and expressing the unity of the post New Testament church. The bishop's role was to watch over the unity of the local church and maintain it in the communion of the churches through his communion with the other bishops. By the end of the second century the office of the single bishop was firmly established throughout the church.

Conclusion

As the churches adapted to the changes and challenges of the Sub-Apostolic Age the institutions which would unify the post New Testament church and characterize the Catholic tradition began to emerge. From the various local churches and traditions came different gifts which contributed to the church's developing structure and identity. The tradition reflected by Colossians and Ephesians stressed the universality of the church as the one body of Christ; that reflected in the Pastorals emphasized the teaching authority of the presbyter-bishops, the laying on of hands, and fidelity to the apostolic tradition. Luke/Acts encouraged confidence in the Spirit's guiding presence; the Johannine tradition a life of discipleship centered on Jesus and sharing in the divine life.

From Antioch where the great Gentile mission first began the office of the single bishop surrounded by presbyters and deacons first appeared and spread throughout what Antioch's bishop called "the church catholic." At Rome which claimed the heritages of both Peter and Paul, the relation of that emerging church office to the ministry of the apostles was strengthened by the principle of apostolic succession. Thus the various ministries of church leadership gradually coalesced into the threefold ministry which became universal. However the process was not uniform and the presence of other forms of church order in the New Testament is not without meaning for the church of today.

The continuing interest at Rome in the Jewish cultic tradition seems to have been a major factor in the eventual application of sacerdotal language to the bishop and later the presbyters. The concept of priesthood (*sacerdotium*) was to move to the center of the Catholic understanding of the ordained ministry; in the past this has led to a one-sided emphasis on the cultic and sacramental aspects of the ministry and contributed to its clericalization. But the identification of the church leader as priest has also played an important role in expressing the eucharistic orientation of the ministry of church leadership and hence the nature of the church as a eucharistic community.

7. THE EUCHARIST

> Then they recounted what had happened on the road and
> how they had come to know him in the breaking of the
> bread.
>
> Luke 24:35

A marvelous story is told about Dorothy Day, the woman
who with Peter Maurin founded the Catholic Worker
movement. Dorothy Day was no ordinary Catholic. Always
a maverick, she was a radical, a one-time Marxist, a pacifist,
the inspiration behind a vital movement of men and women
which took root in the urban deserts of inner-city America.
The Catholic Worker communities combine direct service
to the homeless and destitute of America's skid rows with an
uncompromising resistance to militarism, the arms race,
and every recourse to violence. The story concerns a Eucharist celebrated by a priest prominently involved in the peace
movement at the Catholic Worker center in New York. The
liturgy was celebrated around a table with a loaf of French
bread and a cup of wine, simple but dramatic in that kitchen
where so many were fed each day. Afterwards while those
present were standing around chatting with one another
someone noticed Dorothy Day on her hands and knees,
carefully gathering the fragments of the eucharistic bread
that had fallen during the communion.

Contemporary theology could easily allay her scruples
over the crumbs; after all part of the sacramental sign is
bread, and a particle that no longer resembles the bread from
which it came cannot be recognized as the body of Christ.
But her attitude of reverence in gathering both the particles

and the poor is of a piece. It reflects a deeply Catholic attitude which suggests a grasp of Eucharist and church in their essential meaning and relatedness. The Eucharist stands at the very center of the Catholic tradition; it affirms that God in Jesus has truly entered into our history and remains there to be encountered, in the members of the community, in the faces of "these least ones" (Matt. 25:45), in material signs and gestures, and in a special way in sharing the bread and wine of the Eucharist.

The imagination of the Catholic community has been deeply shaped by the centrality of the Eucharist in its life. The Eucharist is the unique worship of the church. It is a service of forgiveness and a celebration of the reconciliation accomplished through Christ which makes us his body. In celebrating the Eucharist our communion with our sisters and brothers is deepened while at the same time we are offered a way of joining our own struggles and sacrifices to the sacrifice of Christ which is remembered and made present. Most of all, the Eucharist is a unique encounter with the risen Christ who comes to nourish and sustain his people.

One of the earliest descriptions of the celebration of the Eucharist appears around the year 150 in the *First Apology* of Justin Martyr (chapters 65–67). Early on a Sunday morning, probably before dawn, Christians assemble in the home of one of the members of the community. Since very early times the first day of the week, the day on which Jesus rose from the dead, has been the day on which the community gathered for the Eucharist (1 Cor. 16:2; Acts 20:7; Rev. 1:10; *Didache* 14:1). The basic structure of the Eucharist Justin describes is remarkably similar to our liturgy today:

1. on the day named after the sun, all who live in city or countryside assemble
2. and the memoirs of the apostles or the writings of the prophets are read as long as time allows (scripture readings)

3. when the reader has finished, the president addresses us, admonishing us and exhorting us to imitate the splendid things we have heard (homily)
4. then we all stand and pray (general intercessions)
5. when we have finished praying, bread, wine, and water are brought up (presentation of the gifts)
6. the president offers prayers of thanksgiving, according to his ability (eucharistic prayer)
7. the people give their assent with an "Amen!" (the Great Amen)
8. next, the gifts over which the thanksgiving has been spoken are distributed, and each one shares in them (communion)
9. while they are also sent via the deacons to [those] absent
10. the wealthy who are willing make contributions, each as he pleases, and the collection is deposited with the president who aids orphans and widows, those who are in want because of sickness or other cause, those in prison, and visiting strangers.[1]

In Justin's description of the liturgy we glimpse the essential structure of the Eucharist. What we call the liturgy of the word and the liturgy of the Eucharist have already been joined. At the heart of the liturgy is memorial (*anamnēsis*) or remembering of what God has done through the death and resurrection of Jesus. In fact for Justin the whole Christian life is a remembering, constantly calling to mind the needs of the poor, the favors of the Creator, the celebration of the Lord's day and the nourishment given in the Eucharist.[2]

In chapter 66 Justin focuses on how the church understands the eucharistic gifts: "For we do not receive these

[1]Justin Martyr, *First Apology* (67), translation taken from Johannes H. Emminghaus, *The Eucharist: Essence, Form, Celebration* trans. Matthew J. O'Connell (Collegeville, Minnesota: Liturgical Press, 1978), p. 36.

[2]Maurice Journon, "Justin" in *The Eucharist of the Early Christians*, trans. Matthew J. O'Connell (New York: Pueblo, 1978) 71-85, pp. 73-74.

things as though they were ordinary food and drink. Just as Jesus Christ our Saviour was made flesh through the word of God and took on flesh and blood for our salvation, so too (we have been taught), through the word of prayer that comes from him, the food over which the thanksgiving has been spoken becomes the flesh and blood of the incarnate Jesus, in order to nourish and transform our flesh and blood." Since only the baptized were permitted to attend the Eucharist, non-Christians were frequently suspicious about what transpired at these "secret rites." With this in mind Justin carefully explains what takes place, defining unfamiliar terms: "This food we call 'eucharist'," "the memoirs which the apostles composed and which we call 'gospels'." In saying that the food becomes the flesh and blood of the incarnate Christ Justin points to the Lord's unique presence. What then is the origin of this rite to which he attaches such extraordinary meaning?

The Liturgy of the Word

The roots of the liturgy of the word lie in the synagogue. The synagogue service consisted in the recitation of the *Shema* (Deut. 6:4 ff.), an opening prayer, two readings, one from the law, another from the prophets, followed by a homily given by one of the members of the congregation. Sometimes other prayers were added and usually some psalms were sung. Luke 4:16-21 shows Jesus reading the scripture and giving the reflection in a Sabbath synagogue service.

Just when a similar word service was joined to the celebration of the Lord's Supper cannot be exactly determined. Some communities of Jewish Christians continued to participate in the synagogue services until the final break with Judaism. For other Christian communities with roots in the Jewish tradition the Jewish pattern of worship would have functioned as a model as they developed their own prayer services. Prophecy, teaching, and the singing of hymns played important roles in their assemblies (1 Cor. 14; Acts

16:25; Eph. 5:19). At Corinth considerable emphasis was placed on the gift of tongues, though Paul argues that this gift should be subordinated to those "that build up the church" (1 Cor. 14:12). Whether or not the Jewish scriptures were read in the early days is not clear; certainly the psalms were used and, as letters and communications from community founders and apostles appeared they were also read to the congregations at the prayer services or their community meals. Paul intended that his letters be read aloud (1 Thes. 5:27) and later the gospels would have been read publicly.

The prayer service apparently closed with the "holy kiss"; a number of Paul's letters conclude with the rubric to share the holy kiss with one another (Rom. 16:16; 1 Cor. 16:20; 2 Cor. 13:11; 1 Thes. 5:26; cf.1 Pet. 5:14) and later in Justin the kiss marks the transition between the prayers following a baptismal liturgy and the Eucharist (65). No doubt there were prayer services without the Lord's Supper but also, particularly on Sundays, there would have been some which concluded with the celebration of the eucharistic meal.[3]

At the end of the liturgy of the word in the early church the usual practice was for the deacon to dismiss from the assembly the non-initiated. This included the catechumens who were preparing for baptism and other non-Christians who were admitted as guests. After the dismissal the doors of the church were closed and the liturgy of the Eucharist began with the presentation of the gifts. This practice lasted until well into the Middle Ages.

The Development of the Eucharist

1. *Jewish Ritual Meals.* Within the Jewish community there was an important religious dimension to meals which was to contribute to the development of the Eucharist. We also know of a number of ritual meals celebrated by Jews in

[3]This is the argument of Gerhard Delling, *Worship in the New Testament* (Philadelphia: Westminster Press, 1962), p. 147.

the time of Jesus, and while the Eucharist itself is unique, the eucharistic tradition of the church reflects the influence of these Jewish ritual meals.

First of all there was the meal associated with the feast of Passover. To celebrate the Paschal supper was to make present through memory, narrative, and ritual the great saving event of the exodus from Egypt (Ex. 12:1-28). In this way the members of the community could enter into and experience God's saving power. Another kind of ritual meal, this one with a future orientation, was celebrated by the Essenes at Qumran. Only full members of the community, dressed in white robes, were admitted to this meal which seems to have been a symbolic anticipation of the eschatological banquet to be celebrated on the Day of the Lord (Isa. 25:6). The imagery of the eschatological banquet appears in Matthew 8:11 to describe the kingdom of God; it is implicit in the parable of the banquet (Lk. 14:15-24) and Jesus himself refers to it in what all the commentators recognize as an authentic saying at the Last Supper (Mk. 14:25).

Finally there was a ritual dimension to ordinary Jewish meals, particularly those which were shared with guests. Such meals opened with the head of the household breaking the bread and distributing it to those at table while saying a blessing (*berakah*) such as "Blessed are you O Lord, our God, king of the universe, who has given us bread from the earth." At the conclusion of the meal the host would pray the elaborate grace after meals (*Birkat Ha-Mazon*), a ritual prayer consisting of another blessing, a thanksgiving which could be expanded, and a supplication.[4] This prayer as we shall see provided the basic ritual structure both for what Jesus did at the Last Supper and later for the development of the church's eucharistic prayer.

2. *Table-Fellowship Tradition.* At the roots of the Eucharist lies the table-fellowship tradition from the historical ministry of Jesus. The gospels frequently show Jesus a guest at meals in the homes of others; he eats with Jewish officials

[4]See Thomas J. Talley, "From *Berakah* to *Eucharistia*: A Reopening Question," *Worship* 50 (1976) 115-37, pp. 120-24.

(Lk. 7:36-50; 14:1-11), with his friends (John 2:1-11; 12:1-11; cf. Lk. 10:38-42), and with sinners (Mk. 2:15-17; Mt. 9:10-13; Lk. 15:2; 19:1-10). Eating with those considered outside the Law was forbidden to Jews, and yet this was for Jesus an important part of his ministry of proclaiming the reign of God: "I have come to call sinners, not the self-righteous" (Mk. 2:17). The story of the miracle of the loaves reflects another meal tradition from the ministry, but one in which Jesus himself is the host, blessing and breaking the loaves in the Jewish fashion and distributing them with what was seen as an eschatological abundance. In the retelling of this story it was to take on eucharistic overtones from its use in early Christian catechesis but the story seems to have its roots in the historical memory of the meals Jesus shared with his friends.[5] These meals were joyful occasions, signs of the nearness of God's reign to which Jesus called all people, inviting them to open themselves to a new, saving relationship with God.

3. *The Last Supper.* Although the synoptic accounts of the Last Supper, especially Luke's, suggest that it was a Passover meal, an increasing number of scholars today doubt that it was. The possibility cannot be ruled out but it seems more likely that the Last Supper was a meal in which Jesus for the last time gathered his disciples to share in the table-fellowship which had been so important during their time together. The fact that he knew that this would be his last meal with them would have given it a much more solemn atmosphere. At the Supper Jesus took the role of host. To open the meal he broke the bread and distributed it, at the same time praying the traditional blessing (*berakah/ eulogia*). The institution narrative in Mark and Matthew preserves the different words describing the prayers over the bread and the cup: Jesus "took bread, blessed (*eulogēsas*) it and broke it" (Mk. 14:22; Mt. 26:26). Then "after the supper" (1 Cor. 11:25) he raised the cup and prayed over it the grace after meals, a prayer which made

[5]Edward Schillebeeckx stresses the "historical recollection" behind the story in his *Jesus* (New York: Crossroad, 1981), pp. 214-15.

provision for a thanksgiving: "He likewise took a cup, gave thanks (*eucharēstesas*) and presented it to them" (Mk. 14:23; Mt. 26:27). At this point, prior to passing the cup, Jesus would have prayed his thanksgiving for the vindication of his ministry that he awaited in faith.

Did Jesus identify the bread and wine with his body and blood? The New Testament accounts of the Last Supper are colored by the liturgical tradition of the later church. But to begin with, they are essentially accurate in reporting that Jesus himself established the Eucharist by relating the blessing over the bread and his words over the cup to his coming death and to a new union with the disciples in the kingdom. The verse "I solemnly assure you, I will never again drink of the fruit of the vine until the day when I drink it new in the reign of God" (Mk. 14:25) reflects his confident trust that God would vindicate him, establishing the eschatological meaning of the Supper. Since it did not play a role in the later liturgy, scholars argue for its authenticity.[6]

But what about the words of institution? Here some scholars, not wishing to go beyond what careful criticism can establish, are more cautious. Schillebeeckx implies that the words of institution are an interpretation, stating "in a more precise and explicit form" what Jesus said about drinking wine once again in the kingdom of God.[7] Others would agree with Jeremias that the words of institution that have come down to us convey substantially what Jesus said at the Last Supper.[8] It is difficult to see how the eucharistic tradition of the early church would have made the connection which the institution narrative expresses between the presence of Christ and the gifts shared in the supper if it was not firmly grounded in a tradition coming from the Last Supper itself. First, there are no models for it in the Jewish

[6] See Günther Bornkamm, *Jesus of Nazareth* (London: Hodder and Stoughton, 1960), pp. 160-61.

[7] Schillebeeckx, *Jesus*, p. 308.

[8] According to J. Jeremias the Markan text (Mk. 14:22-25) "gives us absolutely authentic information." *The Eucharistic Words of Jesus* (Oxford: Basil Blackwell, 1955), p. 132. See also pp. 142-45.

tradition.   Second, the once popular thesis of Hans Leitz-
mann ascribing the sacramental implications of the Eucharist to a meal focused on the death of Jesus which developed
in Paul's communities under the influence of the mystery
cults, different from the joyful eschatological meals celebrated by the disciples in the original Jerusalem community,
has now been largely abandoned.[9] The continuity between
the Lord's Supper and the church's Eucharist is anchored in
the remarkable unity to be found in the different traditions
bearing the words of institution, one represented by Luke
22:15-18 and Paul in 1 Corinthians 11:23-25, the other by
Mark 14:22 and Matthew 26:26-28. In spite of the inci-
dental differences between the two traditions, their fundamental unity is evidence of a common origin.

4. *The Resurrection Appearance Traditions.* It has often
been noted that a number of resurrection appearance stories
associate the experience of the risen Lord with a meal. In a
fragment of the apostolic kerygma preserved in Acts Peter
speaks of himself and the other witnesses to the resurrection
as "us who ate and drank with him after he rose from the
dead" (Acts 10:41). In John 21 the disciples recognize the
risen Lord in the context of a meal of bread and fish which
Jesus offers them on the seashore (John 21:1-14). A somewhat similar story in Luke where two disciples recognize the
risen Jesus in the breaking of the bread is explicitly eucharistic (Lk. 24:30-31, 35).

What lies behind the meal imagery of these stories? One
hypothesis is theological. The appearance stories have been
shaped in light of the church's eucharistic faith to stress that
the members of the community too may encounter the risen
Lord in the eucharistic celebration. Another hypothesis sees
in these stories an historical recollection that it was in
continuing the fellowship meals which Jesus celebrated during his life and to which he gave a new meaning on the night
before his death that the disciples came to experience the
risen Lord. Thus the eucharistic meal becomes the context

[9]Hans Lietzmann, *Messe und Herrenmahl*, 3rd edition (Berlin, 1955), pp. 249-55.

for the resurrection experience.[10] In both approaches there is a common element, the clear recognition of the early church that in the Eucharist the risen Jesus himself becomes present to his disciples just as he did to the original witnesses. Whether these resurrection appearance stories played a role in the development of the Eucharist or are theological reflections of the church's eucharistic faith they testify to the church's belief that the eucharistic assembly is a moment of encounter with the risen Lord.

5. *The Eucharist in the New Testament*

(a) Acts. The term "the breaking of the bread" was used in Jewish circles to describe the ritual of blessing and distributing the bread at the beginning of a meal. Luke uses it several times in reference to the communal meals of the early community (Acts 2:42, 46; 20:7-11; cf. Lk. 24:35). Though he does not seem to distinguish between the communal meal and the Eucharist, several points suggest that "the breaking of the bread" should be understood in the sense of the Eucharist. First, the word *agalliasis*, meaning overflowing joy, in Acts 2:46 gives a special joyous character to these gatherings; they are not ordinary meals. Some commentators thus see these meals as having an eschatological character.[11] Second, Acts 20:7-11 describes the Hellenistic community at Troas gathered in the evening on "the first day of the week" to break bread. Since we know that Sunday was the day on which the community celebrated the Eucharist we have good reason to conclude that Luke intends "to break bread" here in a eucharistic sense. Paul presides, speaking at such length that one of his young listeners falls asleep, with near tragic consequences.

(b) 1 Corinthians. At Corinth the Lord's Supper is joined to a communal meal or agape. Because of the words "after

---

[10] See Raymond Moloney, "The Early Eucharist: An Hypothesis of Development" *Irish Theological Quarterly* 45 (1978) 167-76, pp. 170-71; also M. Kehl, "Eucharistie und Auferstehung," *Geist und Leben* 43 (1970) 90-125.

[11] Cullmann relates it to the certainty of the resurrection and to the community's experience of the risen Lord's presence in "The Breaking of Bread and the Resurrection Appearances," *Essays on the Lord's Supper*, Oscar Cullmann and F. J. Lienhardt (London: Lutterworth Press, 1958), 8-16, p. 12.

the supper" prior to the cup words many commentators consider that the communal meal was framed by the words over the bread and those over the cup.[12] However the communal meal, rather than expressing the unity of the community, had become one more cause of the divisions present in the church. The more affluent members had plenty of food and drink while others, presumably the poor whose work meant that they had to arrive late, were going hungry. In addressing this issue Paul seems to have begun the process of separating the communal meal from the Eucharist, telling the members of the community to eat at home (1 Cor. 11:22, 34).

For Paul the Eucharist is essentially related to the church, for through sharing the cup of blessing and the one loaf the members of the community have a participation (*koinōnia*) in the body and blood of Christ and thus become his one body (1 Cor. 10:16-17). Paul's sacramental realism appears in his rebuke of the Corinthians for celebrating the Lord's Supper unworthily; he argues that whoever receives the bread and wine without "recognizing the body," that is the community as the body of Christ, "sins against the body and blood of the Lord" (1 Cor. 11:27-29). At the same time there is an ethical dimension to the Eucharist evident here that is often lost sight of. "Recognizing the body" means much more than recognizing the presence of Christ in the members of the local community. What would Paul say today about our eucharistic celebrations when we so often seem so little concerned to undo the divisions based on wealth, power, race, confession, and sex which continue to divide the body of Christ throughout the world? Can we share the bread of life before we have shared our daily bread?

---

[12] However Edward Kilmartin has argued that since the beginning of the meal at Corinth was not regulated (cf. 1 Cor. 11:21, 33), the actual Lord's Supper must have followed the agape. *The Eucharist in the Primitive Church* (Englewood Cliffs, New Jersey: Prentice-Hall, 1965), pp. 146-47. Hans Conzelmann also places the Lord's Supper after the meal at Corinth. *An Outline of the Theology of the New Testament*, trans. John Bowden (London: SCM Press, 1968), p. 52.

(c) The Institution Narratives: The liturgical tradition represented by the words of institution in Luke and Paul interprets Christ's death in terms of the Servant of Yahweh and the new covenant. The bread is his body "to be given for you" (Lk. 22:19; cf. Isa. 53:12). The "cup is the new covenant in my blood" (Lk. 22:20; cf. Jer. 31:31). In Paul's account the command to repeat occurs after both the bread words and the cup words, showing the independence of the eucharistic ritual from the meal which here it still frames. Both "body" and "blood" have a certain independence; each stands for the whole Jesus who gives his life.[13] These references to his death and the command to "do this in remembrance (*anamnēsis*) of me" (1 Cor. 11:24-25) bring out the memorial aspect of the Eucharist. There is a similarity at this point between the Eucharist and the Passover Supper. Just as the Passover makes present through ritual recital God's saving acts, so also celebrating the Lord's Supper is to "proclaim the death of the Lord until he comes" (1 Cor. 11:26), making present Christ's redemptive sacrifice.

In the tradition represented by Mark and Matthew the bread words and the cup words have been brought together liturgically into a single ritual moment. Here the terminology is much more explicitly sacrificial. Rather than the asymmetrical reference to "body" and "cup" this tradition uses the parallel terms "body" and "blood," strongly suggesting the elements of a cultic sacrifice.[14] With the expression "the blood of the covenant, to be poured out on behalf of many" (Lk.14:24) the reference to cultic sacrifice becomes explicit; the phrase echoes Exodus 24:8 where Moses sprinkles both altar and people with the blood of the animals sacrificed to ratify the covenant, saying "This is the blood of the covenant which the Lord has made with you." Thus the tradition interprets the death of Jesus as a sacrifice. Matthew adds that the covenant blood is to be poured out "for the forgiveness of sins" (Matt. 26:28). This sacrifice is

[13]Cf. Heinz Schürmann, *Der Einsetzungsbericht Lk 22, 19-20* (Munster: Aschendorff, 1970), pp. 105-07.

[14]Schürmann, p. 107; Moloney, p. 173.

remembered, proclaimed, and celebrated in the ritual action of the community and in the sharing in the bread and wine.

(d) The Gospel of John. The fourth gospel is unique in that it does not have an account of the institution of the Eucharist. Nevertheless there are eucharistic undertones throughout chapter 6 of the gospel, beginning with the account of the miracle of the loaves and continuing through Jesus' discourse on the Bread of Life. In verses 51-59 the discourse becomes explicitly eucharistic; Jesus describes his flesh and blood as real food and drink which give eternal life (6:54-55). These verses have probably been shaped by the institution narrative and may represent a reformulation of the missing Johannine account of the institution.[15] Here belief in the sacramental presence of Christ in the bread and wine is clearly expressed, even underlined by the comment of "the Jews" who understand but cannot accept: "How can he give us his flesh to eat?" (6:52).

6. *The Eucharistic Prayer.* In discussions on the development of the Eucharist one frequently encounters a too easy antithesis between an original festive meal and a later cultic celebration. The fact that the communal meal and the Lord's Supper are distinct is evident from 1 Corinthians where the process of separating them has already begun. But more importantly, the fundamental meaning of the Eucharist does not come from the communal meal itself, for it is precisely this meal that disappears. Its meaning comes from the context in which the bread and wine are shared, and from the institution narrative and eucharistic prayer which interpret that action, both of which were inspired by the ritual prayer of praise, thanksgiving, and supplication of the Jewish blessing after meals. What is common to both rites is the element of worship. A praise of God and thanksgiving for his mighty works in the Jewish table prayer becomes in the Eucharist a thanksgiving for the salvation God has accomplished through the death of Jesus and a joyful cele-

[15]The latter suggestion is made by Raymond Brown in *The Gospel According to John (i-xii)* (Garden City, New York: Doubleday & Co., 1966), p. 287.

bration of his risen presence. At the heart of each is the Jewish practice of memorial.[16]

The eucharistic prayer developed from the prayers said in remembrance of Jesus and his death. The familiar pattern of praise, thanksgiving, and supplication provided the liturgical model. Some scholars see traces of this pattern in Colossians 1:9-11; 12-20 and in 1 Clement 59-61; both passages may have been derived from early eucharistic prayers.[17] Another example of a prayer of thanksgiving specifically related to the Eucharist appears in the *Didache* 9-10. This may very well have been a eucharistic prayer; its close relation to the Jewish blessing after meals has frequently been noted.[18] Justin in his description of an early Eucharist says that "the president offers prayers of thanksgiving, according to his ability" (*Apology* 67). This suggests that the celebrant at this time formulated his own eucharistic prayer but no doubt he would have been dependent on the Christian themes already developed in imitation of the liturgical pattern of the Jewish graces. The relation between the two is evident in the canon or eucharistic prayer of Hippolytus which gives us a fixed liturgical text from Rome around the year 215. The prayer begins with the familiar dialogue between celebrant and congregation:

Bishop:	The Lord be with you.
People:	And with your spirit.
Bishop:	Lift up your hearts.
People:	We have lifted them up to the Lord.
Bishop:	Let us give thanks to the Lord.
People:	It is right and just.

The eucharistic prayer which follows includes a thanksgiving for the great works of creation and redemption, the

---

[16]David N. Power, *Unsearchable Riches: The Symbolic Nature of Liturgy* (New York: Pueblo, 1984), p. 39.

[17]Kilmartin shows the parallels in *The Eucharist*, pp. 156-57.

[18]Talley, *Berekah* to *Eucharistia*, pp. 125-29.

institution narrative, the anamnesis of Christ's death and resurrection, an epiclesis invoking the Spirit on both gifts and people, and the concluding doxology. It has been used as the basis of the Second Eucharistic Prayer in the current Roman Sacramentary.

Later Developments

At the time of Hippolytus (c. 225) the Eucharist was still being celebrated in a private house, probably the home of one of the more prosperous members of the community which was increasing in number. The bishop presided, surrounded by the presbyters in the midst of the congregation. As we noted earlier in sketching the church at Rome, a tendency to introduce cultic language in regard to both Eucharist and ministry is by this time evident. It is already present in the Syrian *Didache* which speaks of the Eucharist as a "sacrifice" (14:1-3) and refers to the charismatic prophet celebrants as "high priests" (13:3). At Rome the author of 1 Clement (c. 96) speaks of offering sacrifice as one of the roles of the episcopate (44:4). By the beginning of the third century at Rome Tertullian can speak of the bishop as "high priest" (*De Baptismo* 17) and Hippolytus refers allegorically to the bishop's "high priestly spirit."

Like the ministry the Eucharist also was undergoing a sacralization. Instead of a community gathered to remember and give thanks for the saving death of Jesus and to celebrate his risen presence in the breaking of the bread the Eucharist was becoming a sacred rite. After the Emperor Constantine's "Edict of Toleration" in 313 the church obtained legal status and began to acquire buildings for its worship. These churches now had stone altars rather than the simple tables of the earlier domestic churches. Latin which had become the language of the people was introduced into the liturgy. The rise of the Arian heresy at the end of the 4th century led to an increased stress on the divinity of Jesus in the liturgy and on reverence towards his eucharistic presence. The reception of communion was becoming less frequent. John Chrysostom complained in the East around 390, "It is in vain that we ascend to the altar; there is no one to participate "(In Ephes. Hom. III, 4). The Synod of Agde in the West mandated in 506 that the faithful should receive communion at least three times a year, at Christmas, Easter, and Pentecost. In the 6th century the presence of large numbers of priests in the monastic communities as well as the desire of the faithful to have Masses offered for their own intentions led in the Western churches to the practice of the private Mass. Hosts of unleavened bread rather than normal bread came into use in the 9th century.

In the following centuries — focusing just on the West — a number of practices were introduced which tended to create more and more of a division between clergy and laity. The priests began to recite the eucharistic prayer silently. Trained choirs increasingly sang the congregational responses. Altar rails were introduced, fencing off the sanctuary as a holy place from the people in the body of the church. The offertory procession disappeared. The people no longer received the bread in their hands and no longer received from the cup. A solemn "high altar" began to appear in the churches, pushed back against the rear wall or apse of the sanctuary, increasing the physical distance between people and priest. The priest was now celebrating with his back to the congregation. Some of these practices were introduced to counter the Albigensian heresy which denied Christ's eucharistic presence, but the cumulative effect was to reduce the people to passive spectators at a mysterious ritual performed by the priest. The requirement of the Fourth Lateran Council in 1215 that communion be received at least once during the Easter season only underlined how far from the ideal the normal practice had become. Shortly before the Reformation one began to see even in some parish churches "rood screens," a wall often found in monastic churches separating the choir or sanctuary from the body of the church, similar to the iconostasis in the East.

The Council of Trent (1545-63) attempted to put an end to some of the abuses; it standardized the liturgy throughout the church in the official Roman rite promulgated under Pius V. The Council made obligatory the practice of reserving the Blessed Sacrament prominently in a tabernacle mounted on the principal altar of every church. The Blessed Sacrament had been reserved for the communion of the sick since the early days of the church, but it was not prominently displayed until the Middle Ages. However many of the reforms called for in the 16th century such as simplifying the liturgical calendar, restoring the chalice to the laity, and putting the liturgy in the vernacular were rejected precisely because they were seen as "Protestant" ideas. Real reform of the liturgy did not really begin until the Second Vatican Council.

Conclusion

By the year 150 the essential structure of the eucharistic liturgy is in place. The liturgy of the word, a Christian form of the Jewish synagogue service, has been joined to the Lord's Supper, now generally called from its central prayer of thanksgiving the Eucharist. Its roots lie in the table-fellowship practiced by Jesus during his ministry and in the new meaning he gave to this tradition at the Last Supper. The basic liturgical form of the Eucharist comes not from the meal itself but from the Jewish blessing after meals which gives to the sharing of the bread and wine its fundamental meaning as thanksgiving (*eucharistia*) and worship. It is the thanksgiving spoken by the church on behalf of all creation.

The Eucharist integrates the past, present, and future dimensions of the history of salvation. Through the anamnesis with its institution narrative the redemptive sacrifice of Christ is proclaimed and made present. The present meaning of the Eucharist is especially clear in Paul; the Eucharist is constitutive of the church as the body of Christ. Thus the Eucharist is a sign of the oneness of all people in God's reign and Christians are called to serve that oneness and to embody it in their lives. Luke stresses that the risen Lord himself becomes present to those who share in the breaking of the bread. In John's theology the eschatological dimension of the Eucharist comes into focus. The eucharistic body and blood of Jesus is spiritual nourishment for eternal life, a life in which we already share.

The history of the liturgy is the story of cultural adaptations and specific responses to particular problems which added gestures, practices, and prayers but frequently obscured the basic meaning of a community gathering to remember and give thanks for Jesus' life and death and to recognize his risen presence in the breaking of the bread. Certainly liturgical reform for the Roman Catholic Church did not come to an end with the close of Vatican II.

8. THE PETRINE MINISTRY

> Jesus replied, "Blest are you, Simon son of Jonah: No
> mere man has revealed this to you, but my heavenly
> Father. I for my part declare to you, you are 'Rock,' and
> on this rock I will build my church, and the jaws of death
> shall not prevail against it."
>
> Matt. 16:17-18

The Roman Catholic Church finds its center of unity as a
worldwide communion in the one who exercises the ministry of Peter, the bishop of Rome. The papacy is Roman
Catholicism's most obvious symbol; it has expressed historically the unity of the church and has anchored its institutional identity. At the same time it has frequently been an
ambiguous sign, an obstacle to the very unity it is bound to
serve. A review of church history shows that the papacy has
not been without fault in the schisms which have divided the
Body of Christ and even today, as Pope Paul VI once stated,
"the Pope...is undoubtedly the greatest obstacle in the
path of ecumenism."[1] For many today the papacy is a
symbol not of unity but of authoritarianism, the source of a
crushing uniformity.

---

[1] Paul VI to the Secretariat for the Unity of Christians, 28 April 1967, Eng. trans.
in E. J. Yarnold, *They Are in Earnest* (Slough, 1982), p. 66.

Thus Catholics and other Christians are still divided today over the origin and meaning of the office of the bishop of Rome. Catholics see this office as rooted in God's will for the church while other Christians generally regard it as being of human origin. And yet considerable agreement has emerged about the role of Peter in the New Testament church and the gradual development of the Roman primacy. The U.S. Lutheran-Catholic Common Statement, *Papal Primacy and the Universal Church*, calls attention to how the understanding of the historical issues involved has changed in recent years: "The question whether Jesus appointed Peter the first pope has shifted in modern scholarship to the question of the extent to which the subsequent use of the images of Peter in reference to the papacy is consistent with the thrust of the New Testament."[2] In developing this chapter I have found two recent ecumenical studies particularly helpful, the Lutheran Catholic work on papal primacy cited above as well as another work sponsored by the Lutheran Catholic Dialogue, *Peter in the New Testament*, a collaborative assessment by Protestant and Catholic scholars.[3] In sketching the origins of the bishop of Rome's ministry we will consider first, Peter in the New Testament, second, the development of the Roman primacy, and finally, the Petrine ministry as a possibility for the church of tomorrow.

Peter in the New Testament

Peter was known to Jesus and the disciples as Simon. He was among the first companions of Jesus and certainly very prominent among the disciples. In each of the four gospels

---

[2] *Papal Primacy and the Universal Church: Lutherans and Catholics in Dialogue* V, ed. Paul C. Empie and T. Austin Murphy (Minneapolis: Augsburg Publishing House, 1974), no 13.

[3] *Peter in the New Testament*, ed. Raymond E. Brown, Karl P. Donfried, and John Reumann (Minneapolis: Augsburg Publishing House and New York: Paulist Press, 1973).

he is the disciple most often mentioned; the Synoptic tradition associates him with James and John in an inner circle of disciples while the Johannine tradition frequently juxtaposes Peter to the Beloved Disciple. From the evidence of both traditions it is probable that Simon confessed Jesus as Messiah (Mk. 8:29) or the Holy One of God (John 6:69). At the same time the stories of Jesus rebuking Simon as Satan (Mk. 8:33) and of his denial of Jesus suggest that Simon did not fully understand Jesus during his ministry.

Very early in the church Simon became known as Cephas or Peter, though whether he received this name during Jesus' ministry or after the resurrection cannot be established. It is quite possible that he received the name Peter from Jesus. There is also strong evidence that Peter was the first to whom the risen Jesus manifested himself (1 Cor. 15:5; Lk. 24:34). He was the first official apostolic witness, though another tradition, possibly very ancient, reports that some of the women disciples were the first to recognize the risen Jesus.

In the early Jerusalem community Peter predominates among the Twelve; again there is history here. Acts represents him as their spokesman and Galatians 1:18 is indirect testimony to his importance. Yet the picture we receive presents Peter as working with others rather than exercising authority over them. There is also evidence that Peter worked as an apostolic missionary, not just "for the circumcised" (Gal. 2:7) but also among the Gentiles (Acts 10; 1 Cor. 1:12).

Theologically Peter seems to have taken a middle course between conservative Jewish Christianity and the more liberal Hellenist Jewish Christianity of Paul and the even more radical Hellenist Jewish Christians and their Gentile converts. This is suggested both by the picture in Acts 15 of the apostolic council at Jerusalem and by Paul's disagreement with Peter at Antioch reported in Galatians 2:11. A study by John Meier argues that Peter won the argument at Antioch and may have consequently played a key role in maintaining *koinōnia* or fellowship between Jewish and

Gentile Christians in that church.[4] In the same study Raymond Brown suggests that the Christianity that took root at Rome was related to the Jerusalem Christianity associated with Peter and James and thus in contrast to those of the Pauline mission the Gentiles converted at Rome were more loyal to the Jewish heritage.[5] It is generally agreed that Peter reached Rome and like Paul was martyred there in the mid-sixties, probably in the persecution under Nero, although there is no evidence that he functioned as the local administrator or bishop of that church.

In tracing the picture of Peter that emerges from the New Testament it has become customary to speak of a "trajectory" of images.[6] Because of his missionary activity Peter is portrayed as the great Christian fisherman (Lk. 5:10; John 21:1-14). The image of Peter as the shepherd or pastor probably reflects the church of the Sub-Apostolic Age when the different communities were becoming more settled and facing the problems of providing for local leadership, pastoral care, and continuity with the apostolic tradition. Peter is represented as the shepherd of the sheep (John 21:15-17) and as a model presbyter (1 Pet. 5). In Matthew's gospel, originating at Antioch where Peter had once played a unifying role, he is portrayed as the unique leader of the whole church, the one on whom the church is founded and to whom Jesus entrusts the power of the keys of the kingdom (Matt. 16:18-19).[7] Other images represent him as a Christian martyr (John 21:18-19), as the receiver of special revelation (Acts 10:9-16), the confessor of the true Christian faith against false teaching, interpreting scriptural prophecies (1 Pet. 1:20-21) and correcting misinterpretations which appeal to the authority of other apostles such as Paul (2 Pet. 3:15-16). Along with these positive images the shadow side of Peter's character is represented; he is a weak and sinful

[4]Raymond E. Brown and John P. Meier, *Antioch and Rome* (New York: Paulist Press, 1983), pp. 39-41.

[5]Ibid, pp.211-12.

[6]*Peter in the New Testament*, p. 163.

[7]See John P. Meier in *Antioch and Rome*, pp. 64-69.

man who frequently misunderstands Jesus (Mk. 8:33; 9:5-6; John 13:6-11) and who denied him, yet afterwards repented and was rehabilitated (John 21:15-17) and was destined to be a source of strength for others (Lk. 22:32).

A review of the New Testament texts and history in regard to Peter does not prove the establishment of a continuing office of supreme church authority based on Peter himself. But neither does it rule out the gradual development of such an office. Tracing the trajectory of the images associated with Peter suggests a development of the ways in which Peter's significance was understood within the New Testament period. Similar trajectories can be shown for the images of Paul and those of the Twelve. But the Petrine trajectory eventually outdistanced the others.[8] For the Roman Catholic Church that later development of the Petrine trajectory represents the Spirit-guided development of a direction already given in the New Testament. In part that development was determined by the accidents of history. And in part it was due to the eventual joining of the Petrine trajectory to a related but separate tradition which was also developing, that of the primacy of the Roman church.

The Roman Primacy

In the year 381 Canon 3 of the first Council of Constantinople testified to the already accepted preeminence of the Roman church when it recognized the bishop of Constantinople as having a primacy of honor second only to that of the bishop of Rome. Certainly the positions of both Rome and Constantinople (the "new Rome") in the Empire contributed to the importance of their respective churches. But Rome's first place was not due solely to its status as the capital city; more important was its unique apostolic heritage, for Rome's was the church where both Peter and Paul

[8] *Peter in the New Testament*, p. 167.

labored and died.[9] Around the year 180 Irenaeus of Lyons identified Peter and Paul as the founders of the church at Rome, and then underlined its unique authority: "For it is a matter of necessity that every Church should agree with this Church, on account of its preeminent authority, that is, the faithful everywhere."[10]

There are already several examples of the Roman church instructing other churches by the end of the New Testament period. One is the first letter of Peter, written from Rome in Peter's name most probably in the 80s to a group of Christians in northern Asia Minor. Another is 1 Clement, a letter sent from the church of Rome around the year 96 to admonish the church of Corinth. It is important to note that the author of 1 Clement was not a single bishop; at that time the church of Rome was still governed by a group of presbyter-bishops, But the church there was exercising an apostolic care toward other churches, teaching and instructing them.[11] Some five to ten years later Ignatius of Antioch acknowledges this in his letter to the Romans: "You have taught others" (3:1).

In the following centuries the importance of the Roman church was increasingly recognized. The city itself—the largest in the world and capital of the Empire—was becoming the most influential Christian center. The authors of *Papal Primacy and the Universal Church* summarize this development: "During the first five centuries, the church of Rome gradually assumed a certain pre-eminence among the churches: it intervened in the life of distant churches, took sides in distant theological controversies, was consulted by other bishops on a wide variety of doctrinal and moral questions, and sent legates to faraway councils. In the

[9]See J. M. R. Tillard, *The Bishop of Rome*, trans. John de Stage (Wilmington. Delaware: Michael Glazier, 1983), p. 75.

[10]Irenaeus, *Against Heresies* III, 3, 2, in *The Ante-Nicene Fathers*, ed. Alexander Roberts and James Donaldson, Vol. I (Grand Rapids, Michigan: Wm. B. Eerdmans, 1979), pp. 415-16.

[11]Brown suggests that the roots of this concern may be religious rather than political. He argues that Rome may have written other churches because it considered itself heir to the pastoral responsibility Peter and Paul had for their Gentile missions. *Antioch and Rome*, pp. 165-66.

course of time Rome came to be regarded in many quarters as the supreme court of appeal and as a focus of unity of the world-wide communion of churches."[12] Some specifics: in the second and third centuries both heterodox and orthodox teachers came to Rome to take up residence. At the same time the Roman church was gaining recognition as the preeminent bearer of the apostolic tradition; Irenaeus (c. 180) and Tertullian (c. 213) both place the Roman tradition first, though they also mention other apostolic churches. Also in this period there is evidence of Roman bishops making demands on distant churches. Both Victor and Stephen apparently broke communion with other churches which refused to observe the Roman practice, Victor in regard to the date for Easter and Stephen because of a controversy over baptism by heretics. Both seemed to presume that the Roman practice was normative even if this was not recognized by their opponents.

In 252 Cyprian of Carthage called attention to Rome's position among the churches when he referred to Rome as "...the throne of Peter... the chief church whence priestly unity has arisen" (Ep. 59:14). Though it is difficult to find a theory of primacy in Cyprian's views, his statement seems to transfer to the Roman church his understanding of Peter's role as the source of episcopal unity.[13] A clear claim to a Roman primacy of jurisdiction based on the authority of Peter does not become evident until the fourth century. But by then such a claim is being made repeatedly by a series of Roman bishops beginning with Damasus (366-384) and finding its most powerful expression in Leo the Great (440-461). Leo emphasized that Peter continued to preside over the whole church through the bishop of Rome. His intervention in the great christological controversy of the fifth century was decisive. He declared null and void the decisions of the Council of Ephesus (449), calling it the "Robber Council" and his famous "Tome" to Flavian of Constantinople

---

[12] *Papal Primacy and the Universal Church* no. 17, p. 17.

[13] See James F. McCue, "The Roman Primacy in the Patristic Era: The Beginning through Nicaea" in *Papal Primacy*, 44-72, pp. 68-69.

became the basis for the christological confession of the Council of Chalcedon (451). It was acclaimed by the bishops at the Council who declared "Peter has spoken through Leo."

The story of the papacy in the Middle Ages is one of the accumulation of great power as the popes struggled to protect the church and their own office from secular rulers and became caught up in the politics of the West. While the eastern churches continued to stress the principle of collegiality Rome became more and more monarchial, following the example of the secular rulers and using the Roman genius for law to codify its power. Although the East recognized Rome's primacy of honor, it rejected the principle that Rome had plenary power and could formulate unilaterally laws binding on the whole church. Relations continued to deteriorate as the East and West grew further apart until a final break came in 1054.

In the West the power of the papacy continued to grow and became more centralized. The False Decretals, forged documents originating in the ninth century, emphasized the primacy of the popes in matters of jurisdiction.[14] Later popes like Gregory VII (1073-85) and Innocent III (1198-1216) used them to describe the church as though it were a papal monarchy. Gregory in his *Dictatus Papae* claimed, among other things, exclusive right to depose or absolve bishops, use the imperial insignia, establish new laws, and to have his name pronounced in all the churches. *Unam Sanctam*, the bull of Boniface VIII (1294-1303) claimed for the pope absolute power, both religious and secular: "We declare, state, and define that it is absolutely necessary to salvation for every creature to be subject to the Roman Pontiff" (DS 875). The movement known as Conciliarism in the fourteenth and fifteenth centuries and the Reformation in the sixteenth were at least in part reactions to the abuses of papal power and Roman corruption which provoked in

---

[14]See Horst Fuhrmann, "From the Early Middle Ages until the Gregorian Reform" in *Papal Ministry in the Church* (Concilium vol. 64) ed. Hans Küng (New York: Herder and Herder, 1971), 54-61, p. 57.

turn further reaffirmation of papal prerogatives on the part of theologians, canonists, and councils.

Vatican I represented the high water mark of this development, even though it must be understood against the background of Gallicanism, the Enlightenment, and nineteenth century liberalism. In the dogmatic constitution *Pastor Aeternus* (1870) Vatican I declared that Peter received a primacy of jurisdiction over the universal church from Christ, that the primacy is passed to whomever succeeds to Peter in the Roman See, and that the Roman Pontiff has full and supreme power over the universal church, not only in regard to faith and morals but also in matters that pertain to the discipline and government of the church throughout the world, thus over churches, pastors, and faithful.[15] Finally the Council declared that the pope when speaking *ex cathedra* "is possessed of that infallibility with which the Divine Redeemer willed that his Church should be endowed for defining doctrine regarding faith or morals."[16]

Vatican II's *Dogmatic Constitution on the Church* (*Lumen Gentium*) marks the beginning of a shift from a monarchical understanding of papal authority to a collegial one. The Constitution is especially concerned to highlight and develop the theology of the episcopal office: "The order of bishops is the successor to the college of the apostles in teaching authority and pastoral rule"; together with the pope as head of the college "the episcopal order is the subject of supreme and full power over the universal Church" (LG 22). The authority of the bishops comes from the Lord who gave them "the mission to teach all nations and to preach the gospel to every creature" (LG 24). When teaching together with the pope they also share in the infallibility promised to the church (LG 25). In governing their dioceses bishops are not "to be regarded as vicars of the

---

[15]For the text see *The Teaching of the Catholic Church*, originally prepared by Josef Neuner and Heinrich Roos and edited by Karl Rahner (New York: Alba House, 1967), pp. 222-227.

[16]Ibid, p. 229 (DS 3074).

Roman Pontiff, for they exercise an authority which is proper to them" (LG 27).[17]

Vatican II did not substantially change the teaching of Vatican I on the papacy; it reaffirmed that "the Roman Pontiff has full, supreme, and universal power over the Church" (LG 22). But a number of shifts of emphasis are evident in the *Constitution on the Church*, setting the teaching of Vatican I in a new context.[18] First, the Constitution moves from an ecclesiology which defines the church as a single institution divided into administrative units called dioceses to one which understands the church as a communion of churches. Second, it describes a collegial rather than a monarchical exercise of authority; the old pyramidal model is gone. Third, it sees episcopacy itself (not papacy) as a sacrament, "the fullness of the sacrament of orders" (LG 26); thus hierarchical authority is grounded sacramentally rather than in delegation from the pope. The result of this is a relocation of the papal ministry within the church rather than over it as its head. As J. M. R. Tillard phrases it, "A pope who was *the* head would be more than a pope."[19]

Tillard relays a story which illustrates how the pope too is limited even though Vatican II did not resolve the tension between papal authority and that of the bishops. During the Council Paul VI had requested that the council fathers add a note to *Lumen Gentium* 22 stating that although the pope has to respect the collegial power of the bishops he himself was accountable to God alone. However the Theological Commission rejected his request, replying: "The Roman Pontiff is bound to abide by Revelation itself, the basic structure of the Church, the sacraments, the definitions of the first councils, etc. It is impossible to list them all."[20]

---

[17]Walter M. Abbott, ed., *The Documents of Vatican II* (New York: America Press, 1966), pp. 42-52.

[18]See Tillard, *The Bishop of Rome*, pp. 34-41.

[19]Ibid, p. 37.

[20]Ibid, p. 41.

The Petrine Ministry

One important result of Vatican II was that it officially committed the Roman Catholic Church to the ecumenical movement. This in turn has made more urgent the question of the papacy's place in the church of the future. In the years since the Council several bilateral consultations between churches and a growing number of non-Catholic theologians have expressed interest in the role a renewed papacy might serve in the cause of Christian unity. The 1974 Lutheran-Catholic Statement *Papal Primacy and the Universal Church* acknowledges "a growing awareness among Lutherans of the necessity of a specific Ministry to serve the church's unity and universal mission, while Catholics increasingly see the need for a more nuanced understanding of the role of the papacy within the universal church" (intro.). To describe this ministry to the unity of the church the authors of the statement observe that they were drawn to the image of Peter both in the New Testament and in subsequent church history, and so they speak—with some qualifications—of a "Petrine function... *a particular form of Ministry exercised by a person, officeholder, or local church with reference to the church as a whole*. This Petrine function of the Ministry serves to promote or preserve the oneness of the church by symbolizing unity, and by facilitating communication, mutual assistance or correction, and collaboration in the church's mission" (no. 4).

Noting that the bishop of Rome has been historically the single most notable representative of this ministry, the statement points out that the sixteenth century Lutheran reformers had hoped for a reform of the papacy (no.5). To the question of how a renewed papacy might function the statement singles out three principles which it would have to respect: the legitimate diversity of the churches in piety, liturgy, theology, custom, and law; collegiality in the area of decision-making; and the principle of subsidiarity which safeguards freedom by insisting that higher bodies or authorities do not make the decisions that can be legitimately made on lower levels (nos. 22-25). The Lutheran participants also suggest that "the pope's service to unity in relation to the Lutheran churches would be more pastoral than juridical" (no. 28). Though they do not wish to understate the remaining differences, the Lutheran participants ask their churches at the end of the statement "if they are prepared to affirm with us that papal primacy, renewed in the light of the gospel, need not be a barrier to reconciliation" (no. 32).

Another important agreement appeared in 1976, the Venice Statement of the Anglican-Roman Catholic International Commission (ARCIC).[21] Drawing on earlier ARCIC reports the statement underlines the need to keep in balance the two complementary elements of *episkope* (oversight), primacy and conciliarity, and it argues that this pattern of complementarity needs to be realized at the universal level. Noting that the "only see which makes any claim to universal primacy and which has exercised and still exercises such *episkope* is the see of Rome, the city where Peter and Paul died," the statement concludes: "it seems appropriate that, in any future union, a universal primacy such as has been described should be held by that see" (nos. 22-23).

Another ARCIC report in 1981 reviewed some of the unresolved problems—the Catholic interpretation of the Petrine passage in the New Testament, primacy by divine right, universal immediate jurisdiction, and infallibility—and found substantial agreement, though there remained different points of view in regard to infallibility.[22] Vatican I's definition of papal infallibility remains an ecumenical problem. It is not the most crucial issue dividing the churches today, but it is certainly one of the most complex and emotional. For many twentieth century Roman Catholics papal infallibility is intimately tied up with their own Catholic identity, yet many would admit to confusion about what their church really means by infallibility. What the

[21]"Authority in the Church I," text in Anglican-Roman Catholic International Commission, *The Final Report* (Washington: U.S. Catholic Conference, 1982), pp. 49-67.

[22]"Authority in the Church II," *The Final Report*, pp. 81-98. *ARCIC* prefers to speak of its "belief in the preservation of the Church from error," p. 97.

Catholic church actually understands by the dogma of infallibility is really much more limited than many—Protestants or Catholics—are aware.

First of all, Vatican I's definition was carefully circumscribed. Infallibility refers to a charism which enables the pope to faithfully expound the revelation or deposit of faith delivered through the apostles; it has nothing to do with new revelations. The pope is infallible—teaches without error—only when he speaks "*ex cathedra*" (from the chair), with the highest authority of his office. His teaching must be regarding faith or morals. And it must be binding on the whole church.[23] As a matter of history papal infallibility has been clearly invoked only twice, in the two Marian dogmas of the Immaculate Conception (1854) and the Assumption (1950).

Second, the dogma of infallibility is fundamentally a statement about the church, not about the pope apart from the church. The statement of the constitution *Pastor Aeternus* that infallible definitions are "irreformable of themselves, and not from the consent of the Church" (DS 3074) means only that papal teachings are not contingent on subsequent juridical approval by national hierarchies, as the Gallican view maintained. In saying that the "Roman Pontiff . . . is possessed of that infallibility with which the Divine Redeemer willed that his Church should be endowed" the Council was pointing to how the church's infallibility comes to expression. Vatican II further clarified the issue by including the college of bishops in the exercise of the church's charism of infallibility. And since bishops and pope can only articulate what is the faith of the church the laity are not excluded; the "*sensus fidelium*" or "consensus of the faithful" can never be ignored. Today some Catholic theologians are reemphasizing the tradition that a dogmatic teaching must be received by the church at large as an accurate expression of its faith.

[23]For an exposition on the limits of papal infallibility see Hans Küng, *Structures of the Church* trans. Salvator Attanasio (Notre Dame: University of Notre Dame Press, 1968), pp. 305-351.

Finally, like any theological or creedal formulation, Vatican I's teaching on infallibility is historically conditioned and therefore subject to reinterpretation. A 1973 instruction from the Congregation for the Doctrine of the Faith entitled *Mysterium Ecclesiae*[24] pointed out that doctrinal definitions are conditioned by the limited knowledge of the time in which they are formulated, by the specific concerns addressed by the definition, by the changeable conceptions (or conceptual framework) of a given epoch, and by the power of the actual language used.

A model ecumenical study on the issues raised by infallibility and their implications is the 1978 Lutheran-Roman Catholic statement *Teaching Authority and Infallibility*.[25] Although the Lutheran participants "continue to question the appropriateness of speaking of the church's teaching office or doctrine as 'infallible' " (III,20), they recognize that the Catholic Church's understanding of papal infallibility is subordinate to the Gospel and that its exercise is becoming more collegial and communal. It is interesting that in reflecting on teaching authority the Lutheran participants are led to point out the need for the Lutheran churches to develop for themselves "an effective magisterium" (III,19). So the statement does not arrive at more than "partial agreement." Yet in relocating infallibility within the broader context of teaching authority in general, the statement has clarified the issues involved for both traditions and led to a surprising consensus on the place and nature of magisterial authority in the church.

[24]Sacred Congregation for the Doctrine of the Faith, *Mysterium Ecclesiae* June 24, 1973. English translation: *Declaration in Defense of the Catholic Doctrine on the Church Against Certain Errors of the Present Day*, (Washington: USCC, 1973).

[25]*Teaching Authority and Infallibility: Lutherans and Catholics in Dialogue VI* ed. Paul C. Empie, T. Austin Murphy, and Joseph A. Burgess (Minneapolis: Augsburg Publishing House, 1980).

Conclusion

Simon Peter was one of the first disciples of Jesus and the first official witness to his resurrection. He played a leading role among the Twelve in the early Jerusalem community as well as an important role in the early missionary work of the church, ultimately reaching Rome where he was martyred. The New Testament represents him as a fisherman, a shepherd, a pastor of the sheep, the receiver of special revelation, and the rock on whom the church was to be built.

The New Testament does not clearly indicate the establishment of a continuing office of supreme authority based on Peter. But neither does it exclude the development of such an office. The gradual emergence of the primacy of the bishop of Rome is considered by Roman Catholics as being according to God's plan for the church, although the essence of the office is not necessarily identical with the papal absolutism which developed historically. Vatican II marked the beginning of a shift to a more collegial understanding of ecclesiastical authority, including that of the bishop of Rome. As the Roman Catholic Church has become more committed to the ecumenical movement the role a renewed papacy or Petrine ministry might play in the cause of Christian unity is becoming increasingly recognized. Even if infallibility remains a problem, ecumenical conversations are beginning to recognize the importance of teaching authority and decision-making structures for the church of tomorrow.

9. MARY IN THE CATHOLIC TRADITION

> For he has looked upon his servant in her lowliness; all
> ages to come shall call me blessed.
>
> Luke 1:48

Devotion to Mary, the mother of Jesus, is deeply rooted in the Catholic tradition. Prayers like the "Hail Mary," the *Angelus*, and the rosary, hymns such as *Alma Redemptoris Mater* ("Sweet Mother of the Redeemer"), *Regina Coeli* ("Queen of Heaven"), and *Salve Regina* ("Hail Holy Queen"), devotions such as The Little Office of Our Lady, the Litany of Loretto, and the May crowning, liturgical feasts such as the Nativity of Mary, the Annunciation, the Purification, and the Assumption, a rich tradition of artistic representations of Mary running from the Madonnas and Pietas created over the centuries to the plaster statues of Mary to be found in almost every Catholic chapel or church, even the solemn dogmas of the Immaculate Conception (1854) and the Assumption (1950)—are all part of the Marian tradition of the Catholic Church.

Although Mary is also venerated in Orthodox Christianity, many Protestants find Catholic devotion to Mary, if not highly problematic, at least difficult to understand. At times Catholicism has supported a sentimental Marian piety which has obscured the central place of Jesus in the economy of salvation. Some examples of Latin American Marian piety come to mind. Others are closer to home. When I moved to the southern United States for graduate studies I frequently heard non-Catholics asking why Catholics "worshipped Mary." Catholics of course always denied that they did. But the parish in which I was living was called "Immaculate Conception Church" and over the main altar where one usually finds the cross, dominating the sanctuary was a massive twenty foot statue of Mary. So it is not difficult to understand why non-Catholics have sometimes been confused. And yet Catholics expect to find Mary occupying a prominent place in their churches for Marian piety is deeply embedded in the Catholic tradition. In what follows we will examine the ancient and complex roots of Catholic devotion to Mary.

New Testament Evidence

Just as biblical scholarship has raised the question of the gap between the Jesus of history and the Christ of faith, so also in recent years similar questions have been asked about recovering the "Mary of history." Specifically biblical scholars have asked, how many of the New Testament stories about Mary are to be considered as historically reliable? And they have generally concluded that the New Testament does not give much historical information about Mary; she generally appears as a symbolic character, and therefore symbolism rather than history may be more important in determining Mary's place in the New Testament.[1] A collaborative assessment by Catholic and Protestant scholars, *Mary in the New Testament*, has summarized a review of the evidence.[2]

[1]See Wolfhart Pannenberg, "Mary, Redemption and Unity," *Una Sancta* 24 (1967) 62-68; also Raymond E. Brown, "The Meaning of Modern New Testament Studies for an Ecumenical Understanding of Mary" in *Biblical Reflections on Crises Facing the Church* (New York: Paulist Press, 1975), pp. 84-108.

[2]Raymond E. Brown, Karl P. Donfried, Joseph A. Fitzmyer, and John Reumann, (eds.) *Mary in the New Testament* (Philadelphia/New York: Fortress Press/Paulist Press, 1978).

The New Testament does not provide a great deal of information about Mary. The earliest New Testament writings, the letters of Paul, mention only that God sent his Son, "born of a woman, born under the law" (Gal. 4:4). Many scholars judge the portrayal of Mary in Mark, the earliest gospel, as a negative one. Mark is ambiguous as to whether or not Mary is to be included among the members of Jesus' family ("his own") who consider him to be "out of his mind" (Mark 3:21). When Jesus is told "your mother and your brothers and sisters are outside asking for you," in Mark's gospel he asks rhetorically, "who are my mother and my brothers?" and then makes it clear that the family of believers takes priority over natural family relationships: "And gazing around him at those seated in the circle he continued, 'These are my mother and my brothers. Whoever does the will of God is brother and sister and mother to me' " (Mark 3:31-35). Because of this, and because Jesus in Mark's gospel complains that a prophet is not "without honor except in his native place, *among his own kindred* (dropped by Matthew and Luke) and *in his own house*" (dropped by Luke), the Protestant and Catholic scholars conclude that Mark's gospel contains a "negative portrait" of Mary, while Matthew represents a middle position and Luke a positive one which includes Mary within the eschatological family of Jesus' disciples who hear the word of God and do it.[3]

The virginal conception of Jesus is mentioned only in the infancy narratives of Matthew and Luke. The majority of scholars consider that many of the details of the infancy narratives represent not so much the reports of eye-witnesses as they do theological constructions based on Old Testament models, used to illustrate particular theological points. To support their view they point out, first that none of the information peculiar to the infancy narratives (such as Luke's report that John the Baptist was of priestly descent and related to Jesus) can be clearly verified elsewhere in the New Testament, and second, that the two infancy narratives show so little agreement with each other.

[3]Ibid, pp. 286-87.

The fourth gospel does not add much. John never refers to Mary by name, though he some fifteen times refers by name to the other Marys. In the two scenes where Mary appears he calls her "the mother of Jesus." The story of the miracle at Cana (like Luke's story of the twelve year old Jesus talking with the teachers in the Temple) may have been based on a popular story representing first century speculation on the "hidden life" of Jesus, reworked by John ("woman, how does this concern of yours involve me? My hour has not yet come" John 2:4) to stress again that doing God's will has priority over any family relationship. This is the same message that one finds in the passages in Mark and Luke dealing with Jesus' family.[4]

In a similar way the Johannine picture of Mary with "the Beloved Disciple" at the crucifixion is contrary to the testimony of the synoptics who mention neither among those present there. It should probably be understood again as a symbolic reinterpretation of family relationships in terms of discipleship, for both Mary and the Beloved Disciple become members of a new family at the foot of the cross.[5] So again, John's gospel seems to offer theological reflection more than historical memory.

Mary in Tradition

Has then modern biblical scholarship rendered Roman Catholic mariological doctrines less tenable by pointing out how little historical knowledge of Mary comes from the New Testament? By no means. Most Roman Catholics are quite aware that the Marian doctrines of their church are not "proved" by scripture; they have developed out of the church's tradition. And thus the theology of Mary plays an ecumenical role in raising the question of the role of tradition as a source of religious knowledge.

[4]See Raymond Brown, "An Ecumenical Understanding of Mary," pp. 97-101.
[5]Ibid, pp. 103-104; *Mary in the New Testament*, pp. 288-89.

As we have seen, tradition is not an objectified body of "truths" handed on from generation to generation; still less is it simply a collection of inherited customs and practices. Tradition is the living faith of the Christian community which comes to expression in scripture, worship, dogmas, and creeds. But that living faith experience of the community is always prior to any of the various forms through which it comes to expression.

What is true for doctrine in general is true for mariology in particular. Official Roman Catholic dogmatic teaching includes only four solemn declarations concerning Mary: perpetual virginity, the title Mother of God, the Immaculate Conception, and the Assumption. But these Marian definitions are the dogmatic expression of a long history of Catholic devotion to Mary which emerges out of the faith experience of the early Christian community. The history of the growth of this devotion is a complex one in which Christian imagination and piety, heterodox tendencies, and doctrinal developments have all played a part. The fact that Mary appears so frequently in the apocryphal writings of the second and third century shows that she held a fascination for the imagination of the early Christians. These writings often include examples of pious speculation, attempts to fill in, as it were, details about the life of Mary not provided by the gospels. Many elements of the church's Marian tradition first appear in these apocryphal writings.

The Ascension of Isaiah, a Christian revision of a Jewish apocalyptic writing, probably dating from the early second century, suggests that the birth of Jesus came about miraculously. Some see this as the first statement of the belief in Mary's virginity *in partu,* in other words, that Jesus was born miraculously.[6] The *Odes of Solomon,* another second century work with gnostic tendencies, describes Mary as a powerful "mother with many mercies" who brought forth Jesus without any pain. The *Protoevangelium* or *Gospel of James,* from the middle of the second century, is the source

[6]See Hilda Graef, *Mary: A History of Doctrine and Devotion,* Vol. 1 (New York: Sheed and Ward, 1963), p. 34.

for much of the traditional biographical material relating to Mary; it names for the first time Joachim and Anna as the parents of Mary, and tells, often with fantastic details, the story of her birth, her presentation in the Temple, and her betrothal to Joseph. The work seems to be the first to assert the perpetual virginity of Mary and explains the "brothers and sisters" of Jesus mentioned in the gospels as the children of Joseph by a previous marriage. A later apocryphal work known as the *Transitus* or "passing" is the literary source for the story of Mary's death and assumption into heaven. Probably originating towards the end of the fifth century, the *Transitus* circulated widely in Greek, Latin, Syriac, Coptic, and Arabic versions. It played a major role in the development of the feast of the Assumption of Mary, already celebrated by some churches in the East by the end of the sixth century.

The apocryphal writings were not recognized by the church as official, "canonical" expressions of the tradition. Many of them were the products of heretical groups and schismatic movements. Yet there is also the chance that they may sometimes express what was already part of a popular piety that would later obtain official recognition.

What the early theologians have to say about Mary is in contrast to the apocryphal writings much more sober. Much of their teaching is christological in focus. At the beginning of the second century Ignatius of Antioch (d. 110) emphasized that Mary truly carried Jesus in her womb and truly gave him birth, to counter the docetist teaching that Christ only "seemed" to have a real human body and thus was not truly human. Strangely enough, though it is not really consistent with his anti-docetist polemic, he also refers to the virginity of Mary. Justin Martyr (d. 165) and especially Irenaeus of Lyons (d. 202) developed the parallelism between the virgin Eve and the virgin Mary, a corollary to Paul's symbolism of Christ as the new Adam. Irenaeus, stressing Mary's active role through her obedience in the work of redemption, associated her with the church, a theme which was further developed by Tertullian, Hippolytus, and especially Augustine. Mary was increasingly coming to be seen as a type of the church.

Perhaps the most important mariological development in the early church was the gradual acceptance of the term *theotokos*, "Mother of God" (literally, "God-bearer"), as a title for Mary. *Theotokos* also expressed christological concerns; it was used as early as 324 by Alexander of Alexandria in a letter against the Arians, and until the definitions of Ephesus in 431 and Chalcedon in 451 determined its universal acceptance, the title was an important issue in the fierce christological controversies which troubled the Church of the fourth and fifth centuries. But here again, theology was giving expression to what was already part of the faith experience and popular piety of the Christian community. Jaroslav Pelikan has stated that the sources for calling Mary *theotokos* "are almost certainly to be sought neither in polemics nor in speculation, but in devotion, perhaps in an early Greek version of the hymn to Mary, *Sub tuum praesidium.*"[7] Some scholars trace this prayer to the third century; the more general opinion ascribes our present version of it to the fourth. The Greek manuscript fragment asks the "mother of God" for protection, "to deliver us from danger."[8] The prayer is early evidence of Christians turning to Mary as an intercessor. Another form of this prayer appears in the opening petition of the medieval *Memorare*: "Remember O most gracious Virgin Mary, that never was it known that anyone who fled to your protection..."

Thus the theology of Mary emerges out of the interplay of imagination and controversy, faith experience and theological reflection. Imagination led to contemplation, contemplation to veneration and to prayer. And as Christian people turned to Mary in prayer, they found her to be a powerful intercessor. Devotion to Mary is deeply rooted in the church because of a popular piety founded on the experience of generations of Christian peoples. Mariology pre-

[7]Jaroslav Pelikan, *The Emergence of the Catholic Tradition (100-600),* (Chicago and London: the University of Chicago Press, 1971), p. 241.

[8]The text of the prayer is given in Graef, *Mary: A History of Doctrine and Devotion*, p. 48.

sents a clear example of the theological principle *lex orandi, lex credendi* ("the law of praying is the law of believing"). Mariology is therefore not only a question of theology; it is very much and even primarily a question of spirituality.

Unfortunately during the Middle Ages the identification of Mary as a type of the church, which had been so fruitful in the theology of the early church, had given way to an increasingly popular cult of the person of Mary and to an emphasis on her active role in the work of redemption. The result was a tendency to place Mary above the church, gradually obscuring her place within it. Protestantism was not slow in reacting to this. The Reformers of the sixteenth century objected to abuses in the cult of Mary, particularly to any suggestion that Mary shared in Christ's great work of redemption. Thus Luther objected to hymns such as the *Salve Regina* which called Mary "*regina misercordiae*" (queen of mercy) and "*vita dulcedo et spes nostra*" (our life, our sweetness, and our hope).[9]

Yet the early Reformers shared in the Marian piety of the ancient church to a remarkable degree. Luther wrote more about Mary than any other Reformer, continued to defend her perpetual virginity, and kept on the wall of his study a crucifix and an image of the virgin. In Zurich the icono-clastic Zwingli retained the Hail Mary in his instructions for public worship. And in a few Lutheran Church orders, the feasts of the Immaculate Conception and the Assumption, already known by the eighth century, survived well into the later part of the 16th century, even though they had no scriptural basis.[10] But this was not enough to slow the Protestant reaction, so that rather than restoring the proper balance, the place of Mary in the devotional and theological life of the Protestant churches all but disappeared. In his *Church Dogmatics* Karl Barth goes so far as to assert that

[9]See Gottfried Maron, "Mary in Protestant Theology" in *Mary in the Churches* (Concilium 168). ed. Hans Küng and Jürgen Moltmann (New York: Seabury Press, 1983), pp. 40-47.

[10]See Toivo Harjunpaa, "A Lutheran View of Mariology," *America* 117 (1967) 436-41, p. 437; also Walter Tappolet (ed.), *Das Marienlob der Reformatoren* (Tübingen: Katzmann, 1962).

"where Mary is 'venerated,'. . . there the Church of Christ is not."[11] Of course not all Protestants would agree with Barth here.

The balance within Catholicism was restored by Vatican II. One of the more interesting sidelights of the Council was the struggle over the schema on Mary that took place both on the floor of the Council and behind the scenes. The more conservative members among the Council fathers, including the original members of the Theological Commission, wanted the Council to issue a separate document on Mary declaring her to be "Mother of the Church" and "Mediatrix of all graces."[12] This might have done irreparable damage ecumenically. The problem was avoided when by a slim majority the Council fathers voted to have the Council's teaching on Mary included as the final chapter of the *Dogmatic Constitution on the Church.* While the chapter on Mary touches briefly on her relation to the mystery of Christ, its main focus is on the ecclesial aspect of mariology, returning specifically to the theme of Mary as an archetype of the church.

On a popular level Marian piety has proved to be remarkably enduring and elastic; it has been colored by the social, cultural, and political currents of every age. Raymond Brown has sketched the "symbolic trajectory" of Mary's image as it was adapted historically to concretize the ideal of Christian discipleship in different times and places. Mary has taken on the characteristics of an Egyptian nun for the ascetics of the desert in the early church; in the chivalrous culture of the Middle Ages she became "Our Lady" to the knights, a symbol of chaste love; in the twentieth century Mary has been honored as part of the "Holy Family," a model of family life; most recently she has been portrayed as an example of the liberated woman in a letter of the Ameri-

[11]Karl Barth, *Church Dogmatics* Vol. 1/2 (Edinburgh: T. & T. Clark, 1956), p. 143.

[12]For the background to ch viii of *Lumen Gentium* see Otto Semmelroth, "The Role of the Blessed Virgin Mary, Mother of God, in the Mystery of Christ and the Church" in *Commentary on the Documents of Vatican II*, ed. Herbert Vorgrimler (New York: Herder and Herder, 1967), pp. 285-96.

can bishops.[13] Andrew Greeley has argued that in popular religion the cult of Mary has symbolized the feminine dimension of God.[14] Protestant commentators have called attention to "minimalist" and "maximalist" positions in Marian piety; John Hall Elliott points to the contrast between the mariology of Karl Rahner and that of the "Blue Army," a group devoted to the Marian apparitions at Fatima in 1917, teaching that Mary requested prayers for the conversion of Russia, and claiming that all the faithful should make daily sacrifices in reparation for sins against Mary's Immaculate Heart.[15]

The Roman Catholic Church has generally encouraged popular Marian piety. Part of the church's genius historically has been its ability to provide scope for the expression of popular religion and the religious imagination. But it is careful to distinguish between popular and yet essentially private devotions and its public professions of faith, as in the Marian dogmas of the Immaculate Conception and the Assumption. Apparitions and visions such as those at Lourdes and Fatima, even if they are approved by the church, remain private devotions; they are not essential to the church's faith.

The Marian Dogmas

Though they are not at the top of what Vatican II called "the hierarchy of truths,"[16] the dogmas of the Immaculate Conception and the Assumption are proposed for the belief of all. How are they to be interpreted? Traditionally the Immaculate Conception has been understood as affirming

[13]Brown, "An Ecumenical Understanding of Mary," pp. 106-07.

[14]Andrew Greeley, *The Mary Myth: On the Femininity of God*, (New York: Seabury Press, 1977).

[15]John Hall Elliott, "The Image of Mary: A Lutheran View," *America* 146 (1982) 226-29, p. 227.

[16]*Decree on Ecumenism*, no. 11 in *The Documents of Vatican II*, ed. Walter M. Abbott (New York: America Press, 1966), p. 354.

that Mary was born "without the stain of original sin." But the concept of original sin itself needs to be more deeply understood. It is not a stain, still less a condition of guilt inherited like a bad gene. Original sin refers to the *condition* of each person born into a sinful world. Because each human person as a radically social being is born into a network of human relationships touched by sin (but also touched by grace), every human being is born affected by sin, "damaged" in the sense of being existentially inclined towards prejudice, self-centeredness, and a capacity for self-deception which leads eventually to actual sinfulness. The Genesis creation story teaches that we are made for intimacy with God. Yet what develops in our lives—without grace— is a state of alienation, and thus we need redemption. The dogma of the Immaculate Conception does not deny Mary's own need for grace and redemption; what it affirms is that because she was destined to be the mother of her redeemer she was united to God in a most intimate way from the beginning of her life. The grace God offers to all people was especially effective in her.

The second Marian dogma is less complex. Unpacking it can help demythologize Christian eschatology and provide some insight into the mystery of death. Popular eschatology, expressed in the Platonic symbols of a separate soul and body, teaches that at death the soul enters heaven or hell but must wait for the end of the world and the general resurrection of the dead to be reunited with the body. The dogma of the "bodily" assumption of Mary into heaven simply affirms that from the moment of her death Mary shares fully in the victory of the resurrection of Jesus. She too in her full humanity—that is bodily—has entered into glory. What about others who have died "in the state of grace?" Is Mary's case unique? The latter question has not been answered. Although the church believes firmly in the resurrection it has not defined just how and when it takes place for each person. A number of theologians today argue that what the church has affirmed about Mary's entry into glory in her full humanity in fact takes place in a similar way for all the just at the moment of their deaths. Thus the

Assumption of Mary becomes a powerful symbol of our own hope and destiny.

The Marian dogmas represent legitimate examples of doctrinal developments within the Roman Catholic Church. But it is not necessary for unity that all Christians be bound by such doctrinal developments. Recognizing this, Avery Dulles has suggested that the Roman Catholic Church remove the anathemas associated with the definitions of the Immaculate Conception and the Assumption as a gesture of ecumenical good will.[17] This is a reasonable suggestion. Christians today are becoming more tolerant of a considerable pluralism in theological expressions and devotional practice within their respective churches and increasingly they are coming to recognize the need for this kind of tolerance of diversity between churches as well. Unity in faith does not mean uniformity in theology and spirituality. Devotion to Mary is one of the great treasures of the Catholic tradition. But Catholics do not seek to impose the veneration of Mary on Protestants. But neither should Protestant Christians see Catholic veneration of Mary as an obstacle to Christian unity. This is a question of piety, not an issue that should divide the church.

Conclusion

From the earliest days of the Christian community the figure of the mother of Jesus has appealed to the imagination of Christians. In the New Testament Mary is often presented as an example of the true disciple. The frequent references to her in the apocryphal writings of the early centuries testify to the interest her story evoked. An early theological tradition saw in her a type of the church. The confession of Mary as "Mother of God" at Ephesus in 431 and Chalcedon in 451 helped to safeguard the church's christological faith. And as early as the fourth century

[17]Avery Dulles, "A Proposal to Lift Anathemas," *Origins* 4 (Dec. 26, 1974) 417-421.

Christians began turning to Mary as an intercessor.

By the Middle Ages devotion to Mary had developed into a cult. The reaction of the Reformers to Catholic excesses meant that a defensive Catholic Church could not really restore the balance until the Second Vatican Council. Vatican II ultimately rejected a proposal to add a new Marian definition and properly situated Mary within its treatment of the church. Still Mary holds a place of honor in Catholicism, both in its doctrinal heritage and even more in the hearts of Catholic peoples.

10. SACRAMENTALITY

> "Philip," Jesus replied, "after I have been with you all this time, you still do not know me? Whoever has seen me has seen the Father."
>
> John 14:9

Catholicism has always appealed unabashedly to the imagination. Especially for those growing up in the church prior to Vatican II, being Catholic meant growing up in a church in which a whole world of meaning was mediated by symbols, sounds, smells, and stories. The church itself may have become frozen; it was very much in need of reform and renewal. There were too many rules, too many certainties, and not enough questions.

Yet the real experience of Catholicism was communicated on a deeper level. The Catholic world was a world which appealed richly to the senses. Churches were usually dark, yet warmed with glimmers of light and color filtering through stained glass windows or twinkling from banks of vigil lights along the communion rail, reds and blues and greens and ambers; they invited prayer and contemplation. There was much which left a lasting impression: the smell of incense and extinguished candles heavy in the air after a Friday Benediction; the plaintive tones of Gregorian chant or the sweeping crescendo of the great organ at Mass; the quiet cadence of the priest's Latin and the rhythmic responses of the servers... *Introibo ad altare Dei... ad Deum qui laetificat juventutem meam...* servers in special capes and sashes on feast days or kneeling in long lines, torches in hand, at Forty Hours; children dressed in white suits and dresses for First Communion; the smell of beeswax and the feel of candles cool against the throat on the feast of St. Blase; ashes on Ash Wednesday to remind one that death was a personal event; the statues draped in violet during Lent; palms on Palm Sunday; the Paschal Candle saluted in song at the Easter Vigil; rosaries and May crownings; little sacrifices during Advent to prepare for Christmas.

At school Catholic children learned stories of the saints: Catherine of Siena who did not shrink from admonishing kings and popes and was later named a Doctor of the Church; Sir Thomas More who defied the king and went to his death with a joke on his lips; Isaac Jogues, tortured by the Iroquois, freed, only to return to them and be tomahawked to death; Dominic Savio, a boy already a saint; Maria Goretti who died as a girl rather than give up her chastity. One popular story told of Monsignor Pacelli who later became Pope Pius XII facing down communist rioters in the living room of his residence in Munich. Some perhaps were legendary. But they appealed to the imagination, gave Catholic children ideals to strive for and a clear sense of their own identity as Catholics.

More importantly these symbols and stories gave concrete expression to the sense for the sacramental which has always characterized the Catholic tradition.[1] They are no less important today.

The Sacramental Principle

The New Testament does not use the word "sacrament," but it gives evidence that sacramental action was very much

---

[1]See Andrew Greeley's essay, "Sacramental Experience," in Andrew M. Greeley and Mary Greeley Durkin, *How to Save the Catholic Church* (New York: Elisabeth Sifton Books, 1984), pp. 33-50.

part of the experience of the early Christian communities just as it was part of the religion of Israel. Basic to the concept of sacrament is the sense that the infinite God is disclosed in finite reality, that God can be encountered through historical events, human gestures, and personal stories. Israel experienced God as being revealed in the words and actions of its prophets and in the retelling of the stories of its people. Thus history became the locus of God's action. But Israel also had a rich tradition of sacramental rituals, objects, places, and persons. The temple, the sanctuary or Holy of Holies, the ark, the sacred vessels, the rituals of sacrifice and purification, prophets, priests, and kings all could serve to mediate God's presence.

The early church shared the sacramental consciousness of the Jewish tradition from which the first Christians came. Yet in a sense within the Christian communities a "desacralization" gradually occurred, for the emphasis on where the disclosure of God took place shifted from temple and priesthood to the community itself.[2] Remembering (*anamnēsis*) the death and resurrection of Jesus, symbolic expression, and narrative became more important than the temple cult. But the early Christians had their own sacramental actions. For them God's presence was disclosed and mediated in the ritual washing of Christian initiation (Acts 2:38-41; 8:36-38), in gestures of healing (Acts 3:1-10) which sometimes included an anointing with oil accompanied by prayer (James 5:14), in the laying on of hands to communicate the Holy Spirit (Acts 8:17) or to confer a ministry (Acts 6:6; 1 Tim 5:22), and especially in breaking bread and sharing the cup of wine in memory of Jesus (1 Cor 10:16-17; 11:24-25).

When Paul discusses the role of God's ministers in 1 Corinthians he describes them as "servants of Christ and administrators of the mysteries of God" (1 Cor. 4:1). In secular Greek *mysterion* meant "secret" or "hidden." In the Greek mystery religions *mysterion* was used of a hidden reality made present symbolically through a ritual. Paul

[2]See David N. Power, *Unsearchable Riches: The Symbolic Nature of Liturgy* (New York: Pueblo, 1984), pp. 35-40.

used the word to refer to the mysterious wisdom of God (1 Cor 2:7), the salvation accomplished through the death of Jesus and now made manifest. The concept of mystery is more developed in Ephesians and Colossians. Colossians speaks of the mystery hidden from ages past but now revealed (1:26), "the mystery of Christ in you" (1:27). Ephesians describes the union of husband and wife in marriage as a "mystery" which points to the union of Christ and his church (Eph. 5:32).

In the post-New Testament period *mysterion* was used of Christian rites. Around the year 210 Tertullian first used the Latin *sacramentum* as a correlative term. *Sacramentum* was used in reference to the Roman religious rites. Tertullian compared the *sacramentum* or oath which initiated a soldier into the Roman army to the initiation of Christian baptism. In the writings of the church fathers both *mysterion* and *sacramentum* were used broadly to include not only the rites of the church but also a great number of symbols, ceremonies, blessings, liturgical objects, even feasts. Only in the Middle Ages was an effort made to restrict and number the sacraments. The traditional number seven comes from Peter Lombard (d. 1160). In his *Book of the Sentences*, a basic medieval theology text, Peter distinguished the seven sacraments as causes of grace from "sacramentals" such as statues, crucifixes, holy water and oils, and other church ceremonies which he described as signs of grace. The Council of Florence in 1439 made Lombard's enumeration official church teaching.

The actual number of the sacraments is not especially important. The Protestant Reformers, using a strict concept of institution by the historical Jesus (which today neither Protestants nor Catholics would insist on) recognized only two, baptism and the Lord's Supper. Holy Orders could be counted as one sacrament or if the diaconate, presbyterate, and episcopate is each considered a sacrament, as three. What is of primary importance is the conviction that God's grace is mediated through sacramental signs consisting of material realities, human gestures, and persons. Protestant theologian Langdon Gilkey points to this sense of the presence of God through symbols as a continuing Catholic experience "unequalled in other forms of Western Christianity."[3]

At the root of this sacramental experience is the incarnationalism so basic to the Catholic tradition, and thus, its sense of God's immanence in creation. It has often been observed that this stress on God's immanence is most characteristic of Catholicism, just as a strong sense of God's sovereign transcendence typifies Protestantism.[4] Though the two perspectives are not mutually exclusive, an incarnational orientation emphasizes that in the person of Jesus the invisible God has become visible, has entered into the mainstream of human history by his birth into a particular people and into what has become through his Spirit an historical community of believers, the church. The incarnation grounds the principle of sacramentality, the disclosure of the divine immanence through created realities and symbols. Because it grasped implicitly the power of symbolic expression the early church did not scruple over adapting and absorbing symbols, customs, feasts, and rituals popular in the pre-Christian traditions. In more contemporary terms, Christianity became "inculturated." Andrew Greeley points to the Celtic cross, originally an Indo-European fertility symbol, the Roman midwinter festival of Saturnalia which became Christmas, and the plunging of the Paschal Candle into the Easter baptismal waters to make them fruitful, a rite which he argues was once part of a pagan Spring fertility festival, as among those pagan symbols taken over by the early church. Similarly the efforts of the Jesuit missionaries to China in the 17th century to adapt Chinese customs such as ancestor veneration represent another instance of this Catholic sensibility for sacramentality.[5]

[3]Langdon Gilkey, *Catholicism Confronts Modernity* (New York: Seabury Press, 1975), p. 20.

[4]Cf. John O'Donnell, "Handing on the Catholic Tradition," *America* 135 (1976) 231-33, p. 232. Also Greeley, op. cit., pp. 38-39.

[5]Greeley, pp. 44-45.

The original terms *mysterion* and *sacramentum* suggest the idea of disclosure through symbol or ritual. Unfortunately in the Middle Ages the notion of sacramental causality developed under the influence of Aristotelianism into a model based on efficient causality. Augustine—himself a Platonist—had stressed God's work through the sacraments in a way that placed little importance on the subjective disposition of the minister. This hardened into the notion that sacraments conferred grace *ex opere operato* ("by the work having been worked") simply by the correct and valid performance of the rite. Even though the notion that the disposition of the recipient of the sacrament—*ex opere operantis* ("the work of the one working") —was also part of the tradition, this mechanistic explanation of sacramental causality led eventually to sterile discussions of the conditions for sacramental validity rather than to care for the symbolic and personal character of the sacramental action. Correct ritual rather than celebration was the determining idea.

Besides the legalism this led to, the efficient causality model tended to foster a magical concept of sacramentality; sacraments "give grace," have their effect regardless of the faith of the participants or the quality of the celebration. Varieties of this magical concept can be recognized in the attitude that good liturgical planning and celebration is not important, in the all too common practice of baptizing an infant when there is no real expression or practice of faith in the home in which the child will be raised, or celebrating a marriage in the church when such an event is not really an expression of the faith of the couple.

In the twentieth century the liturgical renewal as well as research into the function of symbol, myth, and ritual has led to a new understanding of sacramentality. Rather than stressing efficient causality, theologians today tend to speak of the sacraments in terms of a theory of symbolic causality.[6] Sacraments mediate grace by symbolizing. What is

[6]See Power, *Unsearchable Riches*, pp. 196-206.

operative here is the insight that a self-communication of God is mediated by certain symbols. When a symbol discloses something of that mysterious depth of goodness, life, love, compassion, and tenderness which ultimately we recognize as the presence of God, it becomes sacramental.

A concrete illustration of symbolic causality is the way that the human spirit is disclosed through the body. The body is a symbol of the human spirit which discloses itself through gestures more profoundly than through words. A handshake, a kiss, a hug, a caress, each is a symbolic action. The most powerful bodily symbol is sexual intercourse itself, with its profound drive for a union which embraces body and spirit. Intercourse which fails to respect this orientation towards integrated union becomes violent or exploitative. But intercourse can also express a love and commitment which discloses the tender and life-giving love of God.[7]

The two Roman Catholic theologians who have been most responsible for the shift in Catholic sacramental thinking have been Edward Schillebeeckx and Karl Rahner.[8] Both were concerned with the question of how the invisible grace of God can become visible and tangible for human beings.

Schillebeeckx chose as his basic model for sacramentality the existential encounter of two persons. Just as any genuine human encounter is mediated through the body, so also the humanity of Jesus is the primordial sacrament of the encounter with God; for in the person of Jesus the invisible God is actually present. Those who truly encountered the historical Jesus encountered the living God; those who were scandalized by him did not recognize or experience the salvation present in him. After the resurrection the com-

[7]Cf. Mary Greeley Durkin, "Sex as Sacramental Experience," in *How to Save the Catholic Church*, pp. 105-129.

[8]Edward Schillebeeckx, *Christ the Sacrament of the Encounter with God*, trans. Cornelius Ernst (New York: Sheed and Ward, 1963); Karl Rahner, *The Church and the Sacraments*, trans. W. J. O'Hara (New York: Herder and Herder, 1963); "The Theology of the Symbol," *Theological Investigations* 4 (New York: Seabury Press, 1964), pp. 221-52.

munity of disciples, the church, becomes a sacrament of the risen Christ; it is through the church that the grace of the risen Christ remains present and visible in human history. The continuing presence of Christ himself becomes visible through the sacramental actions of the Christian community, sharing new life in the Spirit of Jesus, proclaiming the forgiveness of sins, healing the sick, celebrating that presence in the Eucharist.

Working independently Karl Rahner developed a sacramental theology in many ways similar to that of Schillebeeckx. Rahner begins from the standpoint of a theological anthropology, stressing that human existence as spirit in the world is an example of symbolic activity, constantly transcending itself. For Rahner Jesus in all his actions constantly transcended the limits of ordinary human existence in such a way that he must be seen as totally united with God and so the perfect incarnation of God's grace. The church as the continuation in history of God's grace present in Jesus becomes then the basic and fundamental sacrament, while the traditional seven sacraments are acts of the church, different ways in which God's offer of salvation becomes manifest in the concrete life of an individual. The sacraments are thus a realization of the church's own essence as a visible sign of the saving grace of God.

Grace is not limited to the sacraments of the church. The Catholic tradition has always recognized a broader sacramentality rooted in its incarnational emphasis. Rahner has argued that even the particular graces of baptism, penance, and the Eucharist can be realized apart from these sacraments.[9] Yet the Catholic imagination recognizes the seven sacraments as privileged moments of encounter with the risen Lord who remains present in history in a special way in the spirit-filled community of disciples which is the church.

[9]Rahner, "Theological Reflections on the Priestly Image of Today and Tomorrow," *Theological Investigations 12* (New York: Seabury Press, 1974), 39-60, p. 48.

The Seven Sacraments

Baptism. In the early church baptism and confirmation were different moments in a single rite of Christian initiation which was completed by the sharing for the first time fully in the Eucharist. The fundamental model for understanding baptism should always be the initiation of an adult into the church; baptism is an adult sacrament. Those who chose to become Christians underwent a long period of preparation and instruction, *catechesis,* from which came the term catechumenate.[10] This process was not simply academic; it presumed a conversion to Christ and had a number of important elements. Each candidate had a sponsor, a member of the community who helped to guide the candidate through prayer, faith sharing, and instruction. The candidates were introduced to the bishop and community and had their names entered into the baptismal register. They were expected to test out their desire to lead a Christian life, often over a period of several years. During this period they would be present on the Lord's Day for the liturgy of the word but would be dismissed by the deacon from the assembly before the liturgy of the Eucharist. After the candidate was ready to formally request baptism, the final weeks prior to the great celebration of Easter were given to an intensive preparation consisting of prayer, fasting,and interrogations called scrutinies. This time of formal preparation for the celebration of Easter survives in the church as the liturgical season of Lent.

Finally the initiation of the candidates was completed as part of the celebration of Holy Saturday. The candidates, accompanied by their sponsors, would make a dramatic renunciation of Satan; then they undressed and were

---

[10]William J. Bausch recreates the whole process of the catechumenate and Easter initiation in *A New Look at the Sacraments* (Mystic, Connecticut: Twenty-third Publications, 1983), pp. 49-60. For the historical development of the individual sacraments see Bausch, also Joseph Martos, *Doors to the Sacred* (Garden City, New York: Doubleday & Co., 1981) and Thomas Bokenkotter, *Essential Catholicism* (Garden City, New York: Doubleday & Co., 1985).

anointed with oil several times, taken down into the waters of the baptistry to be immersed three times; after this baptism they were anointed again with oil, dressed in white linen robes symbolizing newness of life, and finally led into the assembly to join for the first time in the Eucharist.

Thus baptism incorporates an individual into Christ and his body, the church. In this way the person comes to a new life in Christ, is cleansed of all sin, and acknowledges the presence of the Spirit which has brought him or her to this profession of faith. The catechumenate as a process of prayer, discernment, and instruction was restored to the church in 1972 in the text called *The Rite of Christian Initiation of Adults* (RCIA) and already has done much to renew the experience of initiation within the Catholic Church.

Confirmation. The New Testament does not show a separate rite which can be identified with confirmation but by the year 200 the rite of Christian initiation included baptism itself and another rite, usually involving a laying on of hands and anointing with oil, associated with the reception of the Holy Spirit. In the Eastern church confirmation never emerged as a separate sacrament; Christian initiation even of infants was and is celebrated with baptism, an anointing with oil (chrismation) and Eucharist—in the case of infants usually by means of a spoon dipped in the consecrated wine. The ordinary minister is still the presbyter. In this way the East preserved the proper sequence of Christian initiation.

In the West the post-baptismal anointing and laying on of hands ultimately became a separate sacrament, and though the process of its emergence is complex, the liturgical practice of Rome seems to have finally become the norm. Christian initiation at Rome had two post-baptismal anointings, the second of which was reserved to the bishop. The West seems to have regarded this completion or sealing of baptism—often called consignation—through the ministry of the bishop as the ideal; the French council of Orange in 441 allowed priests to do the final anointing as long as the chrism used was blessed by the bishop. However the rite differed considerably from church to church and a number of factors made it difficult for the bishop to preside over every baptism. As Christianity became the official religion of the Roman empire the number of candidates for baptism increased dramatically. Augustine's teaching on the necessity of baptism for the remission of original sin made even infant baptism more urgent and thus led to more frequent celebrations with the result that the bishop could not always be present. Finally the missionary expansion of the church meant that baptisms were frequently celebrated in rural areas far from the bishop. Sometimes, in an attempt to follow the Roman practice, the second anointing or completion of baptism was delayed until it could be performed by the bishop when he made his rounds. Often local presbyters performed the second anointing or "confirmation" as it was called by the French council at Riez in 439. In 784 Charlemagne mandated that the Roman practice be followed throughout his domain and in spite of some resistance from churches accustomed to different usages, the Roman tradition gradually came to prevail in the West. Confirmation had become a separate sacrament.

In the Middle Ages a theology of confirmation was developed, emphasizing the role of the bishop. Today priests frequently administer the sacrament when baptising or receiving adults into the church as part of the renewed rite of Christian initiation.

Eucharist. Christian initiation is completed by the reception of the Eucharist. As we saw earlier, the roots of this sacrament are to be found in the table-fellowship practiced by Jesus during his ministry and in the new meaning he gave to this tradition at the Last Supper. In celebrating the Eucharist the church gives thanks for the death and resurrection of Jesus recalled through narrative and recognizes his presence in the breaking of the bread. The Eucharist is the most basic sacrament of reconciliation for it celebrates the oneness of the community in the body of Christ and calls each Christian to be a sign of reconciliation in a divided world; thus sharing in the eucharist should deepen within each Christian the conversion and new life in Christ symbolized by baptism.

Penance. In the early church the forgiveness of sins was associated primarily with baptism and the Eucharist. However, even from the beginning it was evident that not all the baptized were able to live out the holiness of life to which they were called. Just as in the Jewish community, serious sin was seen as something that was social in nature; it affected the entire community. At Corinth Paul demanded that the community cast out a member guilty of living in an incestuous relationship with his stepmother (1 Cor. 5:1-13). Later he urged forgiveness of an individual disciplined for some offense (2 Cor. 2:5-11). This breaking of communion with an offender and later reconciliation was known in the Jewish tradition as "binding and loosing." In Matthew's gospel Jesus gives this authority to the church (Matt. 18:15-18).

The second century work *Shepherd of Hermas* presumes post-baptismal forgiveness and reconciliation, but emphasizes that it should be practiced "not repeatedly" (Mandate 4,1). From the New Testament practice a clear pattern for penance and reconciliation began to emergy in the third century. Those guilty of serious sin—apostasy, murder, adultery—were excluded from the community and could only be readmitted after a period of prayer and penance. Like the catechumens they had to leave the assembly after the liturgy of the word and were only readmitted by the bishop when their penance and conversion were judged complete. Sometimes this took several years.

This process, described as a "second and more laborious baptism," was a rigorous one. It was public and because a person could seek reconciliation this way only once, there was a tendency to postpone it until the person was close to death. Gradually this "canonical penance" fell into disuse or was celebrated only as a ministry to the dying despite various efforts of councils and popes to revitalize it.

The renewal of penance came largely from a new practice rooted in the monastic tradition and introduced onto the continent in the sixth and seventh centuries by the Irish missionaries. In the monasteries monks seeking spiritual guidance and direction would often confess their sins to an older member of the community—not necessarily a priest—and would receive an assurance of God's forgiveness. In the Celtic churches of Ireland, Scotland, and England where most of the priests were monks, this practice of private confession which could be celebrated repeatedly spread to people living in rural areas and towns served by the monks. In place of the long period of public penance the Irish practice was to assign a particular penance appropriate to the offense. Lists of these penances were collected and published to assist confessors in books known as *penitentials*. Penances might range from abstinence from certain foods and drink for lesser sins to refraining from marital intercourse or the use of weapons for sins involving adultery or the shedding of blood. The duration of these penances also varied according to the gravity of the sins and the particular penitential followed, from a specified number of days (one, seven, twenty, forty) to a certain number of years.[11]

The Irish missionaries brought this practice of private confession to the continent and in spite of the efforts of various councils and synods to root out this innovation, it obviously met a real pastoral need and became the universal practice. In 1215 the Fourth Lateran Council decreed that every Christian who had committed a serious sin should confess it within the year. Private confession remained the norm until the Second Vatican Council revised the rite in such a way as to call for more frequent communal celebrations and for the possibility of general absolution under certain conditions. The new rite, usually referred to as the sacrament of reconciliation, places much more emphasis on healing and reconciliation than on a juridical remission of sins.

The Anointing of the Sick. The New Testament letter of James mentions a ritual for ministering to the sick: "Is there

---

[11]See Bernhard Poschmann, *Penance and the Anointing of the Sick*, trans. Francis Courtney (New York: Herder and Herder, 1964), pp. 126-27.

anyone sick among you? He should ask for the presbyters of the church. They in turn are to pray over him, anointing him with oil in the Name [of the Lord]. This prayer uttered in faith will reclaim the one who is ill, and the Lord will restore him to health. If he has committed any sins, forgiveness will be his" (James 5:14-15). This text shows an awareness that sickness is a sign of a greater evil which touches human beings, and that the grace of Christ mediated through the anointing brings about a forgiveness of sin. Thus ministering to a sick person through prayer and anointing represents a proclamation of God's salvation, calling him or her to conversion and hope.

Reference to this ritual in succeeding centuries is sparse. Hippolytus of Rome speaks of the bishop blessing oil with a prayer that it might "give strength to all that taste of it and health to all that use it" (*Apostolic Tradition* 10). In the first eight centuries the blessing by the bishops seems to have been more important than the question of who applied it. There is evidence that lay people used it to anoint the sick.

After the eighth century anointing was reserved to the priest and it began to be associated not with sickness but with preparation for death. In the twelfth century Peter Lombard included it in his list of the seven sacraments, calling it the last anointing (*extrema unctio*), from which came the unfortunate name Extreme Unction by which the sacrament was known by Catholics until the revision of the rite after Vatican II. Today anointing is situated within the much broader context of a communal celebration of a prayer for the restoration of health and healing; it is used for the seriously sick, the aged, for those preparing for major surgery and sometimes for those suffering from psychological trauma.

Matrimony. It was only in the eleventh century that an official ritual for Christian marriage began to develop in the church and marriage was not considered a sacrament in the strict sense until Lombard treated it among the seven sacraments in his *Sentences*. Yet a broad sacramental dimension to marriage had been recognized since very early times.

Paul's remarks on marriage in 1 Corinthians seem rather negative, for the letter still reflects the anticipation of the Lord's imminent return. Yet Paul is aware of Jesus' absolute prohibition of divorce and remarriage (1 Cor. 7:10-11), argues that an unbelieving partner in a marriage can be consecrated by the believing one (7:14), and identifies both marriage and celibacy (for the sake of the kingdom) as among the charisms, manifestations of the Spirit and spiritual gifts for the service of the community. The author of Ephesians, stressing the mutual love of husband and wife, describes marriage as a great *mysterion* or mystery which suggests the union of Christ and the church (Eph. 5:32).

In the early centuries marriage was regulated by civil law and though the bishops did not approve of divorce, it was frequently allowed in the case of adultery, though all too often a double standard prevailed which allowed remarriage to men but not to women.[12] Ambrose of Milan (d. 397) was one of the first to argue against divorce for any reason but the prohibition did not become absolute until the twelfth century; after that a marriage could be dissolved only on the basis of some lack or impediment at the time of the marriage itself.

About this same time the bishops began to insist on each marriage being blessed by a priest. This was frequently done in the past as an optional addition to the marriage ceremony, often in the church itself. In the East the Greek church held that marriage was not valid if not performed and blessed by a priest. By the twelfth century a church wedding was becoming the widespread practice in Europe as well. The Council of Trent reaffirmed against the teaching of the Protestant Reformers that marriage was a sacrament as well as the church's right to regulate it. To regularize Catholic practice it made valid marriage contingent on the requirement of canonical form, marriage in the presence of a priest and two witnesses.

[12]Martos, pp. 409-12.

Augustine was the first to speak of marriage as a sacrament; even though his approach to sex in marriage was rather narrow—he argued that sexual desire itself was evil—he used Ephesians 5:32 to describe marriage as an image of the union of Christ and his church. Today the sacramental meaning of marriage can best be seen, not in what a couple receive but in what they become. In loving each other with an unconditional, forgiving, and life-giving love each becomes a sacramental embodiment of the unconditional, forgiving, and life-giving love of God, for each other, for any children they may have, and for all who come to know them. In this way Christian marriage becomes a sacrament that is lived rather than received; it is a living and efficacious sign of God's love and faithfulness.

A pastoral problem yet to be resolved is the great number of divorces today and the dilemma of couples in second marriages who are unable to obtain an annulment and thus cannot receive the Eucharist. Two values are in conflict here, on the one hand, the indissolubility of marriage and on the other, the need to recognize the reality of second marriages, many of which in time show a profound level of love and commitment. Perhaps the best solution is one increasingly advocated by canonists and moral theologians: to allow a couple whose union gives evidence of a deeply committed love access to the Eucharist without formally celebrating the second marriage sacramentally.

Orders. Ordination means that one has been authorized to minister in the name of the church. The sacramental sign of this appointment to the church's official ministry of leadership is the laying on of hands. When this rite emerged in the church is not certain; though there is no evidence that it was practiced from the very beginning it is clearly present in the later New Testament books (Acts 6:6; 13:3; 1 Tim. 4:14; 5:22). The roots of the laying on of hands lie in the Old Testament. Many scholars argue that it was a practice inherited from Palestinian Judaism.[13]

[13]Eduard Lohse, *Die Ordination im spät Judentum und im Neuen Testament* (Göttingen: Evangelische Verlagsanstalt, 1951).

Tertullian (c. 210) was the first to apply the Latin word *ordo*, order, to the church's official ministry. In Latin *ordo* referred to a group or class such as the order of senators into which a person would be "instituted"(*ordinari*). Some see in the adoption of this term the beginning of the clericalization of the ministry.[14] The *Apostolic Tradition* of Hippolytus is evidence of how ordination was practiced at Rome early in the third century. A bishop was elected by the people and received the laying on of hands from other bishops. A presbyter was ordained by the bishop with the other presbyters present also imposing hands. Deacons as assistants to the bishop received the imposition of hands from him alone. The prayer for the ordination of a bishop asks that he might "exercise high priesthood" (3.5). By the fourth century the word priest (*hiereus/sacerdos*) was being used for presbyters as well (though the English word priest is derived from the Greek word *presbyteros*).

Gradually a number of traditions became attached to the ordained ministry which were to contribute to its becoming a special and often privileged class. They have no intrinsic connection with the sacrament. With Constantine's Edict of Tolerance in 313 the higher clergy began to receive special recognition. They began to take on many of the honors and trappings of the Roman magistrates and were exempted from military service and from having to pay taxes on their personal property. Towards the middle of the fourth century bishops began to wear the insignia of their office during the liturgy. In the fifth century other clergy took to wearing distinctive dress.

The requirement of clerical celibacy was established only gradually. Celibacy itself is a gospel value (Matt. 19:12) and there were some unmarried ministers from the beginning, not the least among them St. Paul. The first legislation requiring sexual abstinence for married priests appeared at

---

[14]See Edward Schillebeeckx, *Ministry: Leadership in the Community of Jesus Christ*, trans. John Bowden (New York: Crossroad, 1981), p. 39.

Rome toward the end of the fourth century.[15] However the law of celibacy was not made mandatory for the entire western church until the Second Lateran Council in 1139.

The question of how the ordained ministry is to be defined has long been a source of division among the different churches. In Roman Catholicism the emphasis has traditionally been on the concept of priesthood (*sacerdotium*).[16] The Reformation churches rejected the idea of a special priesthood on the basis of the fact that the New Testament does not call any church minister a priest (*hiereus*). Luther and the subsequent Lutheran tradition characterized the ordained ministry as a preaching office [*Predigtamt*], while the Reformed tradition used almost exclusively the concept of ministry. Today the focus is on ordained ministry as a particular ministry of leadership, presiding, and coordination within a multiplicity of ministries. As John Coleman has pointed out, the contemporary emphasis on ministry as the basic category has effected a shift of priorities: "To speak of ministry is to evoke this whole gestalt of the priority of baptism, charism, competence and collegiality over ordination, office, status and hierarchy."[17] In the past an overemphasis on the ordained minister as priest has led to an overly cultic and clerical concept of ordained ministry. This is changing rapidly today. Still for the Catholic tradition calling presbyters and bishops priests has served to safeguard the unique nature of the church's ministry of leadership as well as the nature of the church itself as a eucharistic community.

---

[15]Schillebeeckx, has argued that the dominant reason behind the legislation was a concern for ritual purity, that is, with the belief that intercourse prior to the celebration of the Eucharist rendered one ritually impure. See his *Ministry*, pp. 86-88. A recent article by Daniel Callam argues that the issue was more one of asceticism, in "Clerical Continence in the Fourth Century: Three Papal Decretals," *Theological Studies* 41 (1980) 3-50.

[16]Schillebeeckx, "The Catholic Understanding of Office in the Church," *Theological Studies* 30 (1969) 567-587.

[17]John A. Coleman, "The Future of Ministry," *America* 144 (1981) 243-49, p. 245.

Conclusion

A review of the history of the sacraments illustrates several things. First, the forms of different sacraments have changed over the centuries and therefore the church has considerable freedom in respect to how the sacraments are to be celebrated. Second, an emphasis on sacramental causality which ignores the character of sacraments as signs easily leads to a sterile legalism and even to a magical concept of sacramentality. Third, the theory of symbolic causality calls attention to the importance of careful liturgical planning and faith-filled celebration. Sacraments are mysteries entered into, not rites dispensed.

The principle of sacramentality is rooted in the incarnation; the Word became flesh and therefore creation itself can reveal the presence of the Creator. The divine presence is disclosed through signs. Any story, symbol, or human gesture which embodies the graciousness and compassion of God is sacramental. Catholicism finds this symbolic causality operative everywhere, but it is particularly in the church that it encounters its risen Lord. It recognizes his presence through narrative, prayer, and celebration. When new members are welcomed through the waters of regeneration, when hands reach out to bless or heal or reconcile, when love is made visible in the lives of men and women or the bread and cup of wine are shared in memory of the death and resurrection of Jesus, the community recognizes Christ himself as present in its midst. And when the members of the community seek to live out the mystery of his life in their own they become themselves sacraments to the world.

11. THE CHURCH TOMORROW

> I do not pray for them alone. I pray also for those who
> will believe in me through their word, that all may be one
> as you, Father, are in me, and I in you.

John 17:20-21

As we come to the end of our study it is time to shift our
focus from the roots of the Catholic tradition to the contribution that tradition might be able to make to the church of
the future. That future church is already in the process of
being formed. Karl Rahner pointed this out a few years ago
when he observed that the church today is undergoing a
transition of a magnitude it has experienced only once
before, very early in its history. Then the brief period of
Jewish Christianity gave way to the long period in which the
culture and character of the church was transformed by
Hellenism and ultimately became European. That transition was the subject of the apostolic "council" of Jerusalem
described in Acts 15. For Rahner the Second Vatican Council marked the beginning of a second great transformation
in the cultural and theological situation of the church; what
is already underway is the transformation of western
Christianity—a church largely of Europe and North
America—into a world church.[1]

---

[1]Karl Rahner, "Towards a Fundamental Theological Interpretation of Vatican
Council II," *Theological Studies* 40 (1979) 716-27.

What will such a church be like? First, it will be pluralistic. A church which will be inculturated in Africa and Asia, in South America and in Islamic regions will of necessity develop different expressions of its worship and theology, even of its proclamation. Thus it will have to be able to combine a Catholic fullness and universality with an ecumenical inclusiveness of particular churches and traditions which are confessionally or culturally distinct.

Second, the church of tomorrow will have to be truly universal, catholic in the original sense. It will have to represent a true community of peoples in a deeply divided world. The divisions between Christians today are not simply confessional. Many of them are related to issues such as wealth and poverty, power, racism, political oppression, and human rights. The alienation stemming from the great and ever increasing division between the rich and the poor is an expression of the lack of unity of the church. Christians are called to a unity that transcends human divisions (cf. Gal. 3:8) and the violence such divisions result in. Therefore the struggle for justice is intrinsically related to the search for Christian unity and the emergence of a world church. It may complicate the ecumenical agenda, but a common concern for justice has also helped many Christians to discover a new oneness in the Spirit which crosses the boundaries of confession and church.

In this study we have tried to trace the roots of the Catholic tradition and to single out certain elements of ritual, piety, and church structure which have helped to articulate the experience of Catholic Christianity. Elements such as the ordained ministry, apostolic succession, the Eucharist, the Petrine ministry, mariology, and sacramentality do not exhaust the Catholic tradition. Nor with the exception of the Petrine ministry are they exclusive to it. But in a special way they have shaped the Catholic imagination and experience.

Furthermore, because of the particular way they have been understood within the Catholic tradition, the questions they raise have presented special obstacles to the reconciliation of churches which must still take place.

Therefore in bringing this work to a close I would like to call attention to some new understandings and developments which may place these disputed questions in a new context.

One of the most momentous changes at Vatican II was effected by the mere change of verbs in a sentence in paragraph 8 of the *Dogmatic Constitution on the Church* (*Lumen Gentium*). In the original draft submitted to the bishops by the Theological Commission, "the unique Church of Christ" was identified as follows: "This Church, constituted and organized in the world as a society, is the Catholic Church..." But the bishops rejected this draft. In the text ultimately approved by the Council the sentence reads as follows: "This Church, constituted and organized in the world as a society, subsists in the Catholic Church..." In this substitution of "subsists in" for "is" a whole new ecclesiology had appeared. First of all, the Council made a distinction between the Church of Christ and the Roman Catholic Church. The relation between the two is not one of simple identity, even though the Council sees the Church of Christ as present in its essential completeness in the Roman Catholic Church (cf. LG 14). Second, this distinction implies that the Roman Catholic Church can become the Church of Christ in a more complete way; that is it can become even more one, holy, catholic, and apostolic.[2] Finally, there is the implication that the Church of Christ can also be present to some degree in other churches.

The shift in Roman Catholic ecclesiology evident in the *Dogmatic Constitution in the Church* together with the Council's *Decree on Ecumenism* brought about a change in the way Roman Catholics understood their church. No longer could they hold on to a "one true church" mentality or envision the goal of ecumenism as a simplistic "return to Rome." In a sense Vatican II represented for Catholics a rediscovery of the plurality of church orders and communities visible in the New Testament. If the Christians of the Johannine communities could maintain communion with

[2]Avery Dulles, *Models of the Church* (Garden City, New York: Doubleday & Co., 1974), p. 118.

those of the "apostolic churches" identified with Peter and the other apostles, then certainly there is room for a plurality of churches today. At the same time an urgency exists today for the separate churches to reestablish ecclesial communion, a communion which is both symbolized and effected in the Eucharist.

Eucharist

The concept of communion (*koinōnia*), whether it refers to the relation of the individual to the church or to the relation between churches, describes a real, social relationship, and therefore, a relationship which has a visible, public character. In the early church, the communion between the churches was expressed in the Eucharist by a practice known as the *fermentum*. It involved the transmission of a particle of consecrated bread from the bishop to the bishop or priests in the vicinity; each recipient would then consume the particle at his own liturgy as an expression of communion. Archdale King states that this practice at Rome dates from at least the second century, but he notes that Irenaeus recalled the fermentum being sent from the Eucharist at Rome uninterruptedly for over thirty years, hence from about the year 120.[3] A vestige of this rite remains in the Roman Catholic liturgy to this day; the rubrics call for the celebrant to drop a particle of the consecrated bread into the cup during the fraction rite, the moment before communion marked by the breaking of the bread. Unfortunately this gesture no longer communicates the importance attached to communion between churches. And today, when Christians from different churches come together, the Eucharist is a sign not of unity but of division, for their inability to join together at the same table makes the lack of communion most evident.

The question of intercommunion or mutual eucharistic

[3]Archdale A. King, *Eucharistic Reservation in the Western Church* (London: A. R. Mowbray Co., 1965), pp. 8-9.

hospitality is a very difficult and frequently painful one. For many Protestants intercommunion is a sign of a growing unity and a means to its fulfillment. They emphasize that it is the Lord who invites baptized believers to his one table and stress that no church has the right to restrict it. Rome and the Orthodox churches, stressing that intercommunion is a sign of an already existing unity in faith, apostolic tradition, and ecclesial life, do not permit it.

In addition the Roman Catholic Church has questioned the sacramental "validity" of Protestant Eucharists. Vatican II's *Decree on Ecumenism* said that because of the lack ("*defectum*") of the sacrament of orders, Protestant churches have not preserved "the genuine and total reality of the Eucharistic mystery."[4] Discussions since the Council have made clear that the Council's concern in regard to ordination and thus ministry was the loss of the apostolic succession through episcopal ordination. But the Council was not specific as to the precise way in which the Eucharist celebrated in Protestant churches was to be considered defective, nor is there any agreement among Catholic theologians on this point.

Few if any Catholic theologians would go so far as to say that a Protestant Eucharist has no eucharistic reality. The *Decree on Ecumenism* itself implies that the eucharistic mystery is in some way present. Similarly, just as the Roman Catholic Church recognizes that Protestant ordained ministries have ecclesial and spiritual qualities that cannot be ignored, so also many Catholic theologians would argue that a Protestant church realizes a eucharistic sacramentality that is commensurate with its eucharistic faith and ecclesial life. Others go even further. According to Karl Rahner Protestant ministries are legitimate and "in many cases . . . are sacramental both in their conferal (ordination) and in exercise of these ministries (the celebration of the Eucharist.)"[5] Certainly as Protestant churches continue to restore

[4] *Decree on Ecumenism*, no 22 in *The Documents of Vatican II*, ed. Walter M. Abbott (New York: America Press, 1966), p. 364.

[5] Karl Rahner, "Open Questions in Dogma Considered by the Institutional Church as Definitively Answered." *Journal of Ecumenical Studies* 15 (1978) 211-26, p. 217.

the Eucharist to its central place in the church's worship it will become increasingly difficult for the Roman Catholic Church to continue to question the sacramental validity of their eucharistic celebrations or to refuse even occasional intercommunion.

A second obstacle to the restoration of communion between the different churches is the lack of consensus on the theological and ecclesiological differences which have kept the churches divided. In this area great progress has been achieved through the bilateral dialogues and agreed statements. Perhaps no document holds greater promise for bringing about theological consensus on these issues than the text of the World Council of Churches entitled *Baptism, Eucharist and Ministry* (BEM) formulated by the WCC Faith and Order Commission and unanimously accepted at its meeting at Lima, Peru, in 1982.[6] BEM represents the theological convergence resulting from some fifty years of study and discussion on the part of the Faith and Order Commission. As the Commission includes both Orthodox and Catholic scholars, BEM is remarkably compatible with Catholic theological concerns. It speaks of the Eucharist as "the sacrament of the unique sacrifice of Christ" which cannot be repeated (E no. 8). Noting the traditional Roman Catholic references to the Eucharist as a "propitiatory sacrifice," BEM points out that this term should be understood as meaning "that there is only one expiation, that of the unique sacrifice of the cross, made actual in the Eucharist and presented before the Father in the intercession of Christ and of the church for all humanity" (E Com. no. 8).

In respect to the question of the eucharistic presence of Christ, BEM speaks of the variety of ways in which Christ fulfills his promise to be with his own. Then it adds: "But Christ's mode of presence in the Eucharist is unique. Jesus said over the bread and wine of the Eucharist: 'This is my body ... this is my blood ...' What Christ declared is true,

[6] *Baptism, Eucharist and Ministry*, (Geneva: World Council of Churches, 1982). For the history of this document and commentary see *Ecumenical Perspectives on Baptism, Eucharist and Ministry*, ed. Max Thurian (Geneva: WCC, 1983).

and this truth is fulfilled everytime the Eucharist is celebrated" (E no. 13). BEM clearly identifies the Eucharist as "the central act of the church's worship" (E no. 1) and states that "it should take place at least every Sunday" (E no. 31). Noting that some churches stress "that Christ's presence in the consecrated elements continues after the celebration," it points out that "the way in which the elements are treated requires special attention" (E no. 32). Thus the BEM statement on Eucharist shows a remarkable convergence, one which the Roman Catholic Church should be able to recognize as compatible with its own eucharistic faith.

Ministry

We saw earlier that there seems to have been more than one form of church order within the different New Testament communities. The multiplicity of charisms and ministries visible within the Pauline churches makes it evident that ministry belongs to the whole people of God. Within this fullness of gifts, the various ministries of local church leadership gradually coalesced into the threefold ministry of bishops, presbyters, and deacons which became universal in the Catholic tradition. Yet the process was not uniform and it seems clear that in the early period there were ways into the presbyteral office other than by ordination at the hands of a bishop.[7]

Today reconciliation between the churches cannot come about without a mutual recognition of ministries. The Roman Catholic Church finds the lack of episcopal ordination in the churches of the Reformation an obstacle to the recognition of their ministries while those churches frequently show a bias against the episcopal office rooted in their own historical experience.[8] Here the convergence on the ordained ministry expressed in BEM represents a chal

[7]See above pp. 136-37

[8]Cf. Joseph F. Eagan, "Ordained Ministry in BEM," *The Ecumenical Review* 36 (1984) 263-77, p. 263.

lenge to the internal renewal of all the churches. Churches of the Reformation will have to consider its argument for the recovery of the episcopal succession (M no. 23b) and thus the adoption of the historic episcopate. BEM recognizes the episcopal succession "as a sign, though not a guarantee, of the continuity and unity of the Church" (M no. 38). But it will be needed in the church of tomorrow to express the link between that church and the church of the apostles.

At the same time it would be very difficult to argue that a Protestant church would have to adopt the traditional threefold structure for the ordained ministry which presently exists in the Catholic tradition. What will be necessary is an office exercising the episcopal function, that is to say a ministry of unity over local congregations capable of representing regional or particular churches within the communion of the world church.

On the Catholic side, the Roman Catholic Church needs to consider carefully the case BEM makes for recognizing non-episcopal ministry as a real ministry of word and sacrament having "apostolic content" (M no. 32a), its call for a reform of the threefold ministry to make it more personal, collegial, and communal (M nos. 24-27), and its openness to the ordination of women. Here much can be learned from the ecumenical encounter with other churches. Certainly the increasing number of ordained women and their ever greater involvement in the direction of their churches makes it clear that the ministry of ordained women in the church of tomorrow is to be taken for granted. Similarly it is already evident that the church today is becoming more and more dependent on a new variety of ministries ordained and non-ordained. This will be even more the case in the church of tomorrow.

Related to ministry is the question of authority. On the Catholic side, as the Roman Catholic Church continues to draw closer to Protestant churches on local and institutional levels it will have to develop structures for a less clerical, more participatory style of governance and decision-making. This became particularly obvious to me in June, 1984, when I was present for Pope John Paul II's visit to the WCC Ecumenical Center in Geneva. Awaiting him and his party on the dais were members of the WCC's top leadership, a group of men and women, ordained and lay. When Pope John Paul arrived he was accompanied by about ten men, all clerics. What flashed in my mind was the unwelcome recognition that yes, as far as decision-making is concerned, the Roman Catholic Church is a patriarchy.

On the other hand if Roman Catholic decision-making authority is too centralized, that of the Protestant churches may be too diffuse. A frequent question of Catholics in dialogue with Protestants is who speaks for a particular Protestant church? In the U.S. Lutheran-Catholic dialogue statement *Teaching Authority and Infallibility* (1977), the Lutheran participants acknowledged the need to develop "an effective magisterium" (III, 19), a magisterial authority capable of making doctrinal decisions for the Lutheran churches.[9] Similarly the question of common decision-making has been raised in the context of the WCC's vision of a conciliar fellowship of local churches.

Petrine Ministry

Authority brings us again to the question of the papacy. At the beginning of his address at the WCC Ecumenical Center in June 1984 Pope John Paul II emphasized that the Catholic Church believes that the bishop of Rome has received his mission of witnessing to the apostolic faith from the Lord; he stressed that "to be in communion with the bishop of Rome is to give visible evidence that one is in communion with all who confess that same faith ... since Pentecost ... until the Day of the Lord shall come."[10]

The office of the bishop of Rome as a ministry of unity is

[9] *Teaching Authority and Infallibility; Lutherans and Catholics in Dialogue VI*, ed. Paul C. Empie, T. Austin Murphy, and Joseph A. Burgess (Minneapolis: Augsburg Publishing House, 1980).

[10] John Paul II, "Ecumenism and the Role of the Bishop of Rome," *Origins* 14 (1984) 97-102, p. 97.

becoming increasingly appreciated. Dr. Eugene Brand, secretary for interconfessional dialogue and ecumenical research at the Lutheran World Federation, acknowledged this in commenting on Pope John Paul II's visit to Geneva. But he also observed that "the pope remains for many the symbol of clerical authoritarianism and reactionary ethics, and they make constructive consideration of the papacy within the variegated fellowship of the WCC impossible."[11] Therefore if the papacy is to play its role as a ministry of unity in the church of the future the Roman Catholic Church itself must develop a new style for the exercise of that office.

It is certainly true that not every prerogative which has accrued to the papal office historically belongs necessarily to its essence. Historical factors in the last several hundred years have led to the development of a highly centralized, juridical form of administration, one which sometimes seems to stress the primacy of the pope at the expense of the collegial rights and responsibilities of his brother bishops. Some years ago Karl Rahner suggested that Rome might undertake a self-limitation of the primacy. Since many of the historically acquired powers and rights of the Roman See "do not in fact pertain dogmatically to the inalienable essence of the primacy," Rome could begin, Rahner suggests, by listing those elements that in principle it could not renounce.[12] This could be an important step on the road to unity.

As far as infallibility is concerned, Rahner raises the question as to "whether in the foreseeable future we are able to expect papal *ex cathedra* definitions at all, or whether for a variety of reasons these are improbable."[13] However one answers this question, it is becoming clear that any exercise of magisterial authority in the church of the future will be

[11]Eugene Brand, "The Pope at the WCC—Ecclesial Implications," *Ecumenical Press Service* (26-30 June 1984) 128.

[12]Rahner, "Open Questions," p. 219.

[13]Ibid, p. 225.

both a collegial and a communal undertaking, for infallibility is a charism belonging to the whole church.

Mariology

The Roman Catholic dogmas of the Immaculate Conception and the Assumption raise the same question for the church of tomorrow as does Vatican I's teaching on papal primacy and infallibility: are Christians of other traditions bound by them? Specifically, can the Roman Catholic Church require Christian communities which separated from Rome in the 16th century to accept Roman Catholic dogmatic developments of the 19th and 20th centuries? The answer may appear from Rome's relationship with the Orthodox. For Roman Catholics eucharistic fellowship is possible in principle with the Orthodox churches who do not acknowledge the papal dogma of the First Vatican Council. In respect to the future Joseph (now Cardinal) Ratzinger has argued:

> One who stands on the ground of Catholic theology cannot consider the forms of the 19th and 20th century papacy as the only possible and necessary forms for all Christians. One cannot say that what was possible for a thousand years is not possible today. Rome should not demand from the East more on the doctrine of the primacy than was formulated and taught in the first thousand years. On this basis recognition is possible. The East should not describe the Western development as heretical.[14]

For today's church, what Ratzinger argues in relation to the Orthodox could also be argued for the churches of the

---

[14]Joseph Ratzinger, cited by Heinrich Fries, "Katholische Anerkennung des Augsburger Bekenntnisses?" *Stimmen der Zeit* 7 (1978) 467-78, p. 476. Ratzinger's statement appears in his "Prognosen für die Zukunft des Ökumenismus" in *Bausteine für die Einheit der Christen* 17 (1977) 10.

Reformation as far as the more recent papal and mariological dogmas are concerned. On the other hand, those churches should be able to recognize these dogmas as legitimate examples of Roman Catholic doctrinal development, not to be considered as heretical, even if they themselves are not bound by them. In the same way they should be able to recognize that the Catholic practice of venerating Mary and asking her intercession is deeply rooted in the Catholic tradition and should not be disparaged as superstitious or as contrary to the Gospel. Devotion to Mary has its own legitimation in the experience of generations of Christian people.

Conclusion

As the word Catholic itself suggests, there is a comprehensiveness and universality to Catholicism as a tradition. It is not founded on a particular doctrine, confession, or spirituality and it transcends movements, nations, and cultures. Throughout its history Catholicism has been able to embrace many diverse reformers, spiritualities, and traditions. At its heart is a shared experience, a living faith community gathered in the name of Jesus, renewing that faith in sacramental rituals, seeing it mediated in earthly realities, human experience, and institutional structures, celebrating it in art, and deepening it by means of both spirituality and critical reflection.

We have studied some of those elements of ritual, structure and piety which have made concrete the Catholic experience of church. In this concluding chapter we have raised the question of the church of tomorrow and tried to suggest what the Catholic tradition might contribute. Why could not a Catholic fullness—more framework than particular confession—in the hopefully not too distant future embrace the churches of the Reformation as distinctive particular churches, each with its own tradition, spirituality, liturgy, and government, and yet integrated into a universal communion.

A model for this already exists. With its genius for embracing diversity Catholicism over the centuries has been able to include within itself various religious orders and families, many of which are themselves presbyteral communities integrated with the episcopal structure of the church.[15] In this way the Catholic tradition has found room within its comprehensiveness for expressions of the Christian life quite diverse in charism, spirituality, and mission. A reconciliation with the Reformation churches could come about by means of a similar association. As particular churches they would have to be able to maintain their own identities and independence. Substantial agreement in faith can coexist with different theological traditions, for unity does not mean uniformity. But if a basic consensus in faith emerges through ecumenical documents such as the WCC *Baptism, Eucharist and Ministry* text, the churches of the Reformation could find a home within the fullness of the Catholic tradition.

---

[15]This point is made by Pierre Duprey in "The Unity We Seek," *Mid-Stream* 17 (1978) 374-84, p. 381.

GLOSSARY

APOCALYPTIC — from the Greek *apocalypsis,* "uncovering," "revelation." The word is used of a type of literature which claims to be a revelation, granted to a seer or visionary, expressed in highly symbolic or allegorical language, of what is soon to take place at the end of the world. Chapters 7-12 of the book of Daniel in the Old Testament and the book of Revelations or the Apocalypse in the New Testament are examples of apocalyptic writings.

APOCRYPHA — from the Greek *apokryphos,* "hidden," apocryphal books are Jewish or Christian writings for which divine authority is claimed but which are not recognized as having such authority by the community. There are false or pseudo prophetic books, apocalypses, gospels, and epistles. The expression "the Apocrypha" is also used by Protestants to refer to those six books (the Deuterocanonical books) in the Catholic Old Testament canon which were included in the Greek translation of the Old Testament known as the Septuagint.

APOSTLE — from the Greek *apostellein,* "to send," an apostle is literally one who has been sent. There are a number of apostle-concepts in the New Testament. The word is used of the early Christian missionaries; for Paul an apostle is one who has seen the risen Lord and been sent on a mission to preach the Gospel, even to suffer for it; Luke-Acts tends to restrict the term to "the Twelve," the original group within the broader circle of Jesus' disciples who were witnesses to his earthly ministry as well as to his resurrection. Paul lists apostles as first among the charisms (1 Cor 12:28). The church is built upon the apostles and prophets (Eph. 2:20).

CANON — from the Greek word for "reed," hence a standard for measuring. The word is used of authoritative statements or lists, thus of the decrees of church councils, for church laws (canon law), and for the collection of books accepted as having divine authority, the canon of Scripture. To canonize can also mean to add a person's name to the calendar of the saints.

CATECHESIS — instruction, derived from the Greek verb meaning "to teach by word of mouth." The catechumenate was the process of preparation and instruction of those candidates (catechumens) preparing for baptism.

CATHOLIC — from the Greek *kath holou,* "referring to the whole," "universal."

CHARISM — Greek *charisma,* a "gift" or manifestation of the spirit to perform some service for the building up of the church. Among the charisms Paul lists prophecy, teaching, administration, tongues, marriage, and celibacy.

CHRISTOLOGY — that area of theology concerned with the study of Jesus. Christology seeks to understand the relationship between the historical Jesus (the Jesus of history) and Jesus as he is confessed by the Church (the Christ of faith) as well as the meaning of his life, work, death, and resurrection.

CHURCH — see ekklesia.

CHURCH ORDER — refers to the way a particular church is structured in respect to ministry and authority (e.g., episcopal, presbyterial, congregational, etc.).

DEUTEROCANONICAL BOOKS — term referring to six Jewish books (1,2 Maccabees, Tobit, Judith, Sirach, Wisdom of Solomon and Baruch, plus some additional parts of Daniel and Esther) which were included in the

Greek translation (Septuagint) of the Hebrew Scriptures used by the early church. Thus they are included in the Catholic Old Testament canon though they were not included in the Jewish canon established at Jamnia after the fall of Jerusalem (70 A.D.) by the Pharisees who excluded works not available in Hebrew or Aramaic. Because they are not found in the Jewish Bible the Deuterocanonical books were rejected by the Protestant Reformers in the 16th century. Protestants refer to these books as "the Apocrypha."

DIAKONOS — Greek for "servant," specifically one who serves at table. *Diakonos* (Latin *minister*), is used for persons exercising roles of service or ministry (*diakonia*) in the church. The specific office of the deacon seems to have developed later.

DOCTRINE — an official teaching of the church.

DOGMA — a doctrine proclaimed with the church's highest authority and solemnity.

ECUMENISM — movement seeking to bring the different Christian churches together into unity.

EKKLĒSIA — the New Testament word for church, from the Greek *ex* "out" and *kaleō* "to call," thus "those who have been called out," "assembly." Originally a secular Greek word for an assembly of the citizens, the word is used in the Septuagint for the religious assembly of Israel. In the New Testament the word is used for the local Christian community, also, especially in the later books, for the entire church.

EPISKOPE — the function of supervision or oversight in the pastoral, doctrinal, and sacramental life of the church.

EPISKOPOS — literally "overseer." The Greek word from which the English word bishop is ultimately derived.

ESCHATOLOGY — from the Greek *eschatos*, "last," "furthest," refers to teaching about what comes at the end of history, "the last things." Among Christian eschatological images and concepts are the last judgment, heaven, hell, the resurrection of the dead, and the second coming of Christ.

ESSENES — a group of Jewish sectarians who lived a quasi-monastic life in the desert near the Dead Sea. Originally members of the Hasidim, the "Pious Ones" who joined in the revolt of the Maccabees, the Essenes withdrew from the mainline Jewish community under a leader called "the Teacher of Righteousness" in the second half of the 2nd century B.C. in protest of the assumption of the office of high priest by the Hasmoneans. They lived a communal life, shared a communal meal, and studied the Scriptures which they interpreted in an apocalyptic context. They produced the Dead Sea Scrolls, found at the Wadi Qumran in 1947, important because of the information they give us about Jewish religious thought in the time of Jesus and because they include the oldest texts of the Old Testament extant.

EXEGESIS — the critical interpretation and exposition of a text.

FORM CRITICISM — from the German *Formgeschichte,* literally "form history," a literary science which seeks to identify the various literary forms in the Bible and to trace particular forms through the various levels of the tradition.

FUNDAMENTALISM — a literalist approach to Scripture which identifies the meaning of a text with the literal meaning of the words, e.g., that God created the world in six days or destroyed it in a flood.

GNOSTICISM — a sectarian movement, partly philosophical, partly religious, which promised its adherents salvation through the secret knowledge (*gnosis*) possessed only by those initiated into the sect. The Gnostics found in Christian symbols and concepts an apt vehicle for expressing their doctrines and produced in the 2nd and 3rd centuries a number of gnostic epistles and gospels modeled on authentic Christian works. The Gospel of Thomas is a typical gnostic work.

GOSPEL — from the Anglo-Saxon *godspell* "good tidings," itself a literal translation of the Greek *euangelion,* "good news." In its primary sense the Gospel is the good news of what God has done in Jesus.

HERMENEUTICS — the science of interpretation.

HISTORICAL CRITICAL METHOD — an approach to Scripture which seeks to discover the literal sense or historical meaning of a text by using historical and literary methods of investigation.

KOINŌNIA — generally translated as "communion" or "fellowship," hence community, *koinōnia* refers to a relationship which exists among believers based on sharing in a common life and the same Spirit. Paul grounds the unity of the community in the communion (*koinōnia*) of its members in the Eucharist (1 Cor 10:16-17). "Excommunication" was the exclusion of one whose conduct was injurious to the *koinōnia.* The term *koinōnia* is also used to describe the relationship between churches: the universal church is a communion of local churches while each local church needs to be in communion with the universal church.

LITERAL SENSE — the meaning intended by the author or historical meaning of a text, as opposed to literalism (see below).

LITERALISM — identifying the meaning of a text with the literal meaning of the words.

LITERARY FORM — a type or species of literature (e.g. myth, legend, court history, prophetic oracle, law code, apocalyptic vision, miracle story, parable).

LITURGY — from the Greek words *laos,* "people" and *ergon* "work," "a work of the people," the official public prayer and worship of the Church. Thus the Eucharist, the sacraments, also the Liturgy of the Hours or Divine Office.

MAGISTERIUM — the teaching office of the Church, exercised by the bishops in council or by the pope as head of the college of bishops.

MESSIAH — Hebrew word meaning "anointed," Greek *christos*, English Christ. In the Old Testament kings and priests were anointed with oil as a sign of appointment to sacred office. Generally the word is used in the Old Testament to designate the king of Israel.

MESSIANISM — that complex of ideas concerned with Israel's future salvation; the figure of the Messiah was only one image expressing Jewish messianic hope.

MINISTRY — from the Greek *diakonia*, "service," specifically service at table. Ministry is any service done for the building up of the church.

ORTHODOXY — literally "right praise," the adjective orthodox is used of teaching which is in agreement with the faith of the church, as opposed to heterodox or heretical teaching. Also used of the Orthodox or Eastern churches which lost communion with Rome and the Latin West in 1054.

PETRINE MINISTRY — a ministry which serves and expresses the unity of the entire church based on the image of Peter. Historically this ministry has been exercised by the Bishop of Rome.

PRESBYTER — from the Greek *presbyteros*, literally "elder." The institution of local leaders called presbyters in the early church was borrowed from the synagogues of Pharisaic Judaism, each of which had a governing council of elders. In the New Testament period the terms *presbyteroi* and *episkopoi* were generally interchangeable, hence the term presbyter-bishop. The English word priest is derived from the Latin *presbyter*.

Q — abbreviation for the German *Quelle*, "source," the collection, possibly written, of the sayings and parables of Jesus used as a source by both Matthew and Luke.

QUMRAN — the site of the Essene community on the western shore of the Dead Sea where the Dead Sea Scrolls were discovered.

REDACTION CRITICISM — a literary science which seeks to discover the particular theology and point of view of an author by analyzing how the author modifies the received tradition, structures a work or story, or stresses a particular theme.

SACRAMENT — a visible sign disclosing the invisible grace of God, specifically the seven sacraments of the church.

SEPTUAGINT (LXX) — Greek translation of the Hebrew Scriptures done at Alexandria in Egypt, probably in the first half of the 2nd century B.C. According to an ancient legend, it was the work of 72 scholars who accomplished the work in 70 days, hence the name from the Latin word for 70 (*septuaginta*). Most of the early Christians whose language was Greek used the Septuagint.

SITZ IM LEBEN — German expression meaning "situation in life," refers to the time, place, and circumstances affecting the community when a work was written.

SYNOPTIC — from the Greek *synoptikos,* "seeing together," used for the gospel of Matthew, Mark, and Luke because of their similar structure and content.

THEOLOGY — the scientific and systematic reflection of the church upon its faith; according to St. Anselm, theology is "faith seeking understanding."

TRADITION — from the Greek *paradosis* and Latin *traditio,* "that which has been handed over" or "passed on," the living faith experience of a community, and in a secondary sense, the handing on of that faith experience in various ways, official and unofficial.

VULGATE — the name given to the Latin translation of the Bible produced by St. Jerome between the years 383-405.

SELECTED BIBLIOGRAPHY

Basic Reference Works

Abbott, Walter M. (ed.). *The Documents of Vatican Council II.* New York: America Press, 1966.

Brown, Raymond E., Joseph A. Fitzmyer, and Roland Murphy, eds. *The Jerome Biblical Commentary.* Englewood Cliffs, New Jersey: Prentice-Hall, 1968. The best and most comprehensive Catholic commentary available, it covers all the books of the Bible and includes many useful articles on biblical topics.

McBrien, Richard P. *Catholicism* Study Edition. Minneapolis: Winston Press, 1981. A compendium of Catholic teaching which provides a well-organized synthesis of biblical foundations, historical development, and contemporary interpretations, plus an excellent glossary of terms.

McKenzie, John L. *Dictionary of the Bible.* Milwaukee: Bruce Publishing House, 1965. Excellent resource for looking up a biblical person, place, term, concept, or book; a goldmine of information in one reasonably priced volume.

Rahner, Karl (ed.). *Sacramentum Mundi: an Encyclopedia of Theology.* Vol. 1-6. New York: Herder and Herder, 1968-70. A modern summa of Catholic theology, European in orientation.

_____. (ed.). *The Teaching of the Catholic Church.*
Originally prepared by Joseph Neuner and Heinrich
Roos. Staten Island, New York: Alba House, 1967.
Lists the official teachings of the Councils topically,
drawing heavily on Denzinger's *Enchiridion Symbo-
lorum.*

Throckmorton, Burton H., Jr. *Gospel Parallels: A Synopsis
of the First Three Gospels.* Toronto: Thomas Nelson
& Sons, 1949. Gives the texts of Matthew, Mark, and
Luke in parallel columns.

Scripture, Tradition, and
Interpretation (Hermeneutics)

Brown, Raymond E. *Biblical Reflections on Crises Facing
the Church.* New York: Paulist Press, 1975.

Paulist Press, 1975.

_____. *The Critical Meaning of the Bible.* New York:
Paulist Press, 1981.

_____. "Hermeneutics," in *The Jerome Biblical
Commentary*, pp. 605-23.

Childs, Brevard. *Biblical Theology in Crisis.* Philadelphia:
Westminster Press, 1970.

Dulles, Avery. *Models of Revelation.* Garden City, New
York: Doubleday & Company, 1983.

Harrington, Daniel J. *Interpreting the New Testament:
A Practical Guide.* Wilmington, Delaware: Michael
Glazier, 1979.

Hasel, Gerhard. *Old Testament Theology: Basic Issues in
the Current Debate.* Grand Rapids, Michigan: William
B. Eerdmans, 1972.

Pannenberg, Wolfhart. "The Crisis of the Scripture Principle," in *Basic Questions in Theology*, Vol. I. Philadelphia: Fortress Press, 1970, pp. 1-14.

Rahner, Karl. "Scripture and Theology," pp. 89-97 and "Scripture and Tradition," pp. 98-112 in *Theological Investigations*, Vol. 6. New York: Seabury Press, 1969.

Ratzinger, Joseph. "Revelation and Tradition," in Karl Rahner and Joseph Ratzinger, *Revelation and Tradition (Questiones Disputatae* 17). New York: Herder and Herder, 1966, pp. 26-49.

Robinson, James M. "Hermeneutic Since Barth," in James M. Robinson and John B. Cobb (eds.). *New Frontiers in Theology: The New Hermeneutic*, Vol. II. New York: Harper and Row, 1964, pp. 1-77.

Schneiders, Sandra M. "Faith, Hermeneutics, and the Literal Sense of Scripture," *Theological Studies* 39 (1978) 719-36.

_____. "The Paschal Imagination: Objectivity and Subjectivity in New Testament Interpretation,"*Theological Studies* 43 (1982) 52-68.

Vatican Council II, *Dogmatic Constitution on Divine Revelation.*

Old Testament

Anderson, Bernard W.   *Understanding the Old Testament.* Englewood Cliffs, New Jersey: Prentice Hall, 1975.

Boadt, Lawrence.   *Reading the Old Testament.* New York: Paulist Press, 1984.

Bright, John.   *A History of Israel.* Philadelphia: Westminster Press, 1959.

Childs, Brevard.   *Introduction to the Old Testament as Scripture.* Philadelphia: Fortress Press, 1979.

Collins, John J.   *The Apocalyptic Imagination: An Introduction to the Jewish Matrix of Christianity.* New York: Crossroad, 1984.

Jacob, Edmond. *Theology of the Old Testament.* New York: Harper and Row, 1958.

Jagersma, Henk. *A History of Israel in the Old Testament Period.* Philadelphia: Fortress Press, 1983.

Laurin, Robert B. *Contemporary Old Testament Theologians.* Valley Forge, Pennsylvania: Judson Press, 1970.

McKenzie, John L. *Dictionary of the Bible.* Milwaukee: Bruce Publishing House, 1965.

_____. *A Theology of the Old Testament.* Garden City, New York: Doubleday & Company, 1976.

Murphy, Roland. "The Relation Between the Testaments," *Catholic Biblical Quarterly* 26 (1964), pp. 349-359.

von Rad, Gerhard. *The Message of the Prophets.* London: SCM Press, 1968.

_____. *Old Testament Theology,* Vol. I & II. New York: Harper and Row, 1962/65.

Vermes, Geza. *The Dead Sea Scrolls: Qumran in Perspective.* Philadelphia: Fortress Press, 1981.

Westermann, Claus. *Praise and Lament in the Psalms.* Atlanta, Georgia: John Knox Press, 1981.

New Testament

Barrett, Charles K. *A Commentary on the First Epistle to the Corinthians.* New York: Harper and Row, 1968.

Brown, Raymond E. *The Gospel According to John.* Anchor Bible 29 & 29A. Garden City, New York: Doubleday & Company, 1966/70.

Bultmann, Rudolf. *The History of the Synoptic Tradition.* Oxford: Basil Blackwell, 1963.

Conzelmann, Hans. *An Outline of the Theology of the New Testament.* New York: Harper & Row, 1969.

Crowe, Jerome. *The Acts.* Wilmington, Delaware: Michael Glazier, 1980.

Fitzmyer, Joseph A. "A Life of Paul," pp. 215-222; "New Testament Epistles," pp. 223-226; and "Pauline Theology," pp. 800-827 in *The Jerome Biblical Commentary.*

Fuller, Reginald. *Interpreting the Miracles.* Philadelphia: Westminster Press, 1963.

Harrington, Wilfrid J. *Mark.* Wilmington, Delaware: Michael Glazier, 1979.

Jeremias, Joachim. *Rediscovering the Parable.* New York: Scribners, 1966.

Käsemann, Ernst. *Perspectives on Paul.* Philadelphia: Fortress Press, 1971.

Kugelman, Richard. "The First Letter to the Corinthians." *The Jerome Biblical Commentary*, pp. 254-275.

McEleney, Neil J. *The Growth of the Gospels.* New York: Paulist Press, 1979.

Meier, John P. *The Vision of St. Matthew: Christ, Church, and Morality in the First Gospel.* New York: Paulist Press, 1979.

Perkins, Pheme. *Hearing the Parables of Jesus.* New York: Paulist Press, 1981.

_____. *Reading the New Testament: An Introduction.* New York: Paulist Press, 1978.

Perrin, Norman and Dennis C. Duling. *The New Testament: An Introduction.* New York: Harcourt Brace Jovanovich, Inc., 1982.

Spivey, Robert A. and D. Moody Smith, Jr. *Anatomy of the New Testament.* New York: Macmillan, 1969.

La Verdiere, Eugene. *Luke.* Wilmington, Delaware: Michael Glazier, 1980.

Christology

Boff, Leonardo. *Jesus Christ Liberator*. Maryknoll, New York: Orbis Books, 1978.

Brown, Raymond E. "'Who Do Men Say That I Am?'— A Survey of Modern Scholarship on Gospel Christology," in *Biblical Reflections on Crises Facing the Church*. New York: Paulist Press, 1975, pp. 20-37.

Cook, Michael. *The Jesus of Faith*. New York: Paulist Press, 1981.

Fuller, Reginald. *The Foundations of New Testament Christology*. London: Collins, 1969.

Hellwig, Monika K. *Jesus: the Compassion of God*. Wilmington, Delaware: Michael Glazier, 1983.

Jeremias, Joachim. *New Testament Theology: Part I— The Proclamation of Jesus*. London: SCM Press, 1971.

_____. *The Prayers of Jesus*. Naperville: A. R. Allenson, 1967.

Kasper, Walter. *Jesus the Christ*. New York: Paulist Press, 1976.

Lane, Dermot A. *The Reality of Jesus*. New York: Paulist Press, 1975.

Nolan, Albert. *Jesus Before Christianity*. Maryknoll, New York: Orbis Books, 1978.

O'Collins, Gerald. *What Are They Saying About Jesus?* New York: Paulist Press, 1977.

O'Grady, John. *Models of Jesus*. Garden City, New York: Doubleday & Company, 1981.

Perrin, Norman. *Rediscovering the Parables of Jesus*. London: SCM Press, 1967.

Schillebeeckx, Edward. *Jesus: An Experiment in Christology*. New York: Crossroad, 1981.

_____. *Christ: The Experience of Jesus as Lord.* New York: Seabury Press, 1980.

Sobrino, Jon.   *Christology at the Crossroads.* Maryknoll, New York: Orbis Books, 1978.

The New Testament Church

Brown, Raymond E.   *The Churches the Apostles Left Behind.* New York: Paulist Press, 1984.

_____. *The Community of the Beloved Disciple.* New York: Paulist Press, 1982.

_____. *Priest and Bishop.* New York: Paulist Press, 1970.

Brown, Raymond E. and John P. Meier.   *Antioch and Rome.* New York: Paulist Press, 1982.

Conzelmann, Hans.   *History of Primitive Christianity.* London: Darton, Longman & Todd, 1973.

Fiorenza, Elisabeth Schüssler.   *In Memory of Her.* New York: Crossroad, 1983.

Fuller, Reginald.   "The Ministry in the New Testament," in *Episcopalians and Roman Catholics: Can They Ever Get Together?* ed. Herbert J. Ryan and J. Robert Wright. Denville, New Jersey: Dimension Books, 1972, pp. 88-103.

Harrington, Daniel J.   *God's People in Christ.* Philadelphia: Fortress Press, 1980.

Hengel, Martin.   *Acts and the History of Earliest Christianity.* Philadelphia: Fortress Press, 1980.

Küng, Hans.   *The Church.* New York: Sheed and Ward, 1967.

Lohse, Eduard.   *The First Christians: Their Beginnings, Writings, and Beliefs.* Philadelphia: Fortress Press, 1983.

Meier, John P. And Raymond E. Brown. *Antioch and Rome.* New York: Paulist Press, 1982, pp. 11-86.

Perkins, Pheme. *The Gnostic Dialogue: the Early Church and the Crisis of Gnosticism.* New York: Paulist Press, 1980.

Schillebeeckx, Edward. *The Church with A Human Face.* New York: Crossroad, 1985.

_____. *Ministry: Leadership in the Community of Jesus Christ.* New York: Crossroad, 1981.

The Eucharist

Bouley, Allan. *From Freedom to Formula: the Evolution of the Eucharistic Prayer.* Washington, D.C.: Catholic University of America Press, 1981.

Delling, Gerhard. *Worship in the New Testament.* Philadelphia: Westminster Press, 1962.

Emminghaus, Johannes H. *The Eucharist: Essence, Form, Celebration.* Collegeville, Minnesota: the Liturgical Press, 1978.

Guzie, Tad. *Jesus and the Eucharist.* New York: Paulist Press, 1974.

Jeremias, Joachim. *The Eucharistic Words of Jesus.* New York: Scribners, 1966.

Jungmann, Joseph A. *The Mass of the Roman Rite*, Vol. I-II. New York: Benzinger Brothers, 1951/55.

Keifer, Ralph A. *Blessed and Broken: An Exploration of the Contemporary Experience of God in Eucharistic Celebrations.* Wilmington, Delaware: Michael Glazier, 1982.

Kilmartin, Edward J. *The Eucharist in the Primitive Church.* Englewood Cliffs, New Jersey: Prentice Hall, 1964.

Power, David.   *Unsearchable Riches: the Symbolic Nature of Liturgy.* New York: Pueblo, 1984.

Powers, Joseph M.   *Eucharistic Theology.* New York: Herder and Herder, 1967.

Prayers of the Eucharist: Early and Reformed Texts. trans. and ed. by R. C. D. Jasper and G. J. Cuming. New York: Oxford University Press, 1980.

Roles in the Liturgical Assembly: the Twenty-third Liturgical Conference Saint Serge. New York: Pueblo, 1981.

Rordorf, Willy et. al.   *The Eucharist of the Early Christians.* New York: Pueblo, 1978.

Rouillard, Philippe.   "From Human Meal to Christian Eucharist," *Worship* 52 (1978) 425-439; 53 (1979) 40-56.

Schillebeeckx, Edward.   *The Eucharist.* New York: Sheed and Ward, 1968.

Talley, Thomas J.   "From *Berakah* to *Eucharistia*: A Reopening Question," *Worship* 50 (1976) 115-37; 120-24.

Thurian, Max.   *The One Bread.* New York: Sheed and Ward, 1969.

The Petrine Ministry

Brown, Raymond E., Karl P. Donfried, and John Reumann. *Peter in the New Testament.* Minneapolis: Augsburg Publishing House, and New York: Paulist Press, 1973.

Dulles, Avery.   "Towards a Renewed Papacy," in *The Resilient Church.* Garden City, New York: Doubleday & Company, 1977, pp. 113-131.

Empie, Paul C., and T. Austin Murphy (eds.). *Papal Primacy and the Universal Church: Lutherans and Catholics in Dialogue V.* Minneapolis: Augsburg Publishing House, 1980.

Empie, Paul C., T. Austin Murphy, and Joseph A. Burgess (eds). *Teaching Authority and Infallibility: Lutherans and Catholics in Dialogue VI.* Minneapolis: Augsburg Publishing House, 1980.

Granfield, Patrick. *The Papacy in Transition.* New York: Doubleday & Company, 1980.

Küng, Hans (ed.). *Papal Ministry in the Church* (Concilium vol. 64). New York: Herder and Herder, 1971.

Küng, Hans. "The Petrine Office in the Church and in Council," pp. 201-304 and "What Does Infallibility Mean?" pp. 305-351 in his *Structues of the Church.* Notre Dame: University of Notre Dame Press, 1968.

McCord, Peter J. (ed.). *A Pope for All Christians? An Inquiry into the Role of Peter in the Modern Church.* New York: Paulist Press, 1976.

Tillard, J. M. R. *The Bishop of Rome.* Wilmington, Delaware: Michael Glazier, 1983.

Mariology

Brown, Raymond E., Karl P. Donfried, Joseph A. Fitzmyer, and John Reumann (eds.). *Mary in the New Testament.* Philadelphia: Fortress Press, and New York: Paulist Press, 1978.

Graef, Hilda. *Mary: A History of Doctrine and Devotion,* Vol. I. New York: Sheed and Ward, 1963.

Greeley, Andrew. *The Mary Myth. On the Femininity of God.* New York: Seabury Press, 1977.

Küng, Hans and Jürgen Moltmann (eds.). *Mary in the Churches* (Concilium Vol. 168). New York: Seabury Press, 1983.

Mary in the Christian Tradition: Papers of the 1984 International Congress of the Ecumenical Society of the Blessed Virgin Mary. London: The Way, 1984.

O'Carroll, Michael. *Theotokos: A Theological Encyclopedia of the Blessed Virgin Mary.* Wilmington, Delaware: Michael Glazier, 1983.

Sacraments and Sacramentality

Bausch, William J. *A New Look at the Sacraments.* Mystic, Connecticut: Twenty-third Publications, 1983.

Cooke, Bernard. *Ministry to Word and Sacrament.* Philadelphia: Fortress Press, 1980.

_____. *Sacraments and Sacramentality.* Mystic, Connecticut: Twenty-third Publications, 1983.

Gelpi, Donald L. *Charism and Sacrament.* New York: Paulist Press, 1976.

Greeley, Andrew. "Sacramental Experience," in Andrew M. Greeley and Mary Greeley Durkin, *How to Save the Catholic Church.* New York: Elisabeth Sifton Books, 1984, pp. 33-50.

Guzie, Tad. *The Book of Sacramental Basics.* New York: Paulist Press, 1981.

Hellwig, Monika K. *The Meaning of the Sacraments.* Dayton, Ohio: Pflaum/Standard, 1972.

Mackin, Theodore. *What Is Marriage? Marriage in the Catholic Church.* New York: Paulist Press, 1982.

Martos, Joseph. *Doors to the Sacred.* Garden City, New York: Doubleday & Company, 1981.

Power, David. *Unsearchable Riches. The Symbolic Nature of Liturgy.* New York: Pueblo, 1984.

Powers, Joseph M. *Spirit and Sacrament.* New York: Seabury Press, 1973.

Rahner, Karl, *The Church and the Sacraments.* New York: Herder and Herder, 1963.

Schillebeeckx, Edward. *Christ the Sacrament of the Encounter with God.* New York: Sheed and Ward, 1963.

Segundo, Juan L. *The Sacraments Today.* Maryknoll, New York: Orbis Books, 1974.

Catholicism

Bokenkotter, Thomas. *Essential Catholicism.* Garden City, New York: Doubleday & Company, 1985.

Chilson, Richard. *An Introduction to the Faith of Catholics.* New York: Paulist Press, 1975.

Dulles, Avery. *Models of the Church.* Garden City, New York: Doubleday & Company, 1974.

Gilkey, Langdon. *Catholicism Confronts Modernity: A Protestant View.* New York: Seabury Press, 1975.

Haughton, Rosemary. *The Catholic Thing.* Springfield, Illinois: Templegate Publishers, 1979.

Hellwig, Monika K. *Understanding Catholicism.* New York: Paulist Press, 1981.

McBrien, Richard P. *Catholicism* (Study Edition). Minneapolis: Winston Press, 1981. esp. Ch. XXX "Catholicism: A Synthesis," pp. 1169-1186.

The Church Tomorrow

Anglican Roman Catholic International Commission. *The Final Report.* Washington, D.C.: United States Catholic Conference, 1982.

Baptism, Eucharist and Ministry. Geneva: World Council of Churches, 1982.

Bühlmann, Walbert. *The Coming of the Third Church.* Maryknoll, New York: Orbis Books, 1978.

Desseaux, Jacques. *Twenty Centuries of Ecumenism.* New York: Paulist Press, 1984.

Fries, Heinrich and Karl Rahner.   *Unity of the Churches: A Real Possibility.* Philadelphia: Fortress Press, and New York: Paulist Press, 1985.

Küng, Hans (ed.).   *Post-ecumenical Christianity* (Concilium Vol. 54). New York: Herder and Herder, 1970.

Rahner, Karl.   "Open Questions in Dogma Considered by the Institutional Church as Definitively Answered," *Journal of Ecumenical Studies* 15 (1978) 211-226.

_____.   "Towards a Fundamental Theological Interpretation of Vatican Council II," *Theological Studies* 40 (1979) 716-727.

_____.   *The Shape of the Church to Come.* New York: Seabury Press, 1974.

Thurian, Max (ed.).   *Ecumenical Perspectives on Baptism, Eucharist and Ministry.* Geneva: World Council of Churches, 1983.

INDEX OF AUTHORS

209

INDEX OF SUBJECTS

INDEX OF BIBLICAL REFERENCES

OLD TESTAMENT

NEW TESTAMENT